Dummies 101: Windows NT®

S0-BLM-296

Using the CD

With Windows NT up and running, follow these steps:

1. **Insert the Dummies 101 CD (label side up) into your computer's CD drive and wait about 30 seconds to see whether AutoPlay starts the CD for you.**

   If your computer has the Windows CD AutoPlay feature, the CD installer should begin automatically.

   If nothing seems to happen after a minute or so, continue to Step 2.

2. **If the installation program doesn't start automatically, click the Start button and click Run.**

3. **In the dialog box that appears, type d:\seticon.exe (if your CD drive is not drive D, substitute the appropriate letter for D) and click OK.**

   A message informs you that the program is about to install the icons.

4. **Click OK in the message window.**

   After a moment, a program group called Dummies 101 appears on the Start menu, with a set of icons. Then another message appears, asking whether you want to use the CD now.

5. **Click Yes to use the CD now or click No if you want to use the CD later.**

   If you click No, you can start the CD later simply by clicking the Dummies 101 – Windows NT CD icon in the Dummies 101 program group (on the Start button).

CHEAT SHEET

Start Menu Tips

The Start menu contains the following items in these menu groups. When you install additional programs, they usually create their own, new menu groups.

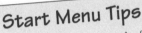

Menu Window	Items	Description
Programs	Accessories	Windows NT programs like Calculator, HyperTerminal, Notepad, Paint, Phone Dialer, WordPad and others.
	Applications	Larger Windows NT programs that you've paid for, as well as old programs that Windows NT found on your com-puter when it installed itself.
	Administrative tools (common)	Computer tools for your network administrator to play with.
	Startup	Any icon living in here automatically starts up its program when Windows NT loads itself.
Documents	Filenames	Lists the last ten files you opened. Click on a filename to load the file.
Settings	Control Panel,	Use for changing your computer's Printers, Taskbar settings, adjusting printer settings, and changing the settings of your taskbar.
Find	Files, folders, or	Can search your entire computer or other networked network for other computers, a computers particular filename, or for filenames containing certain words.
Help	Help program	Click here for general help with Windows NT.
Run	Program	Runs a program when you type that program's filename and location into the box.

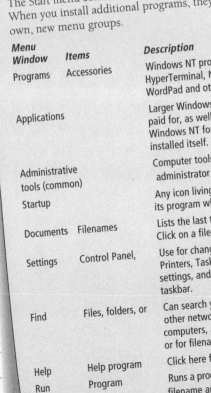

Dummies 101:® Windows NT®

CHEAT SHEET

Organizing Your Desktop

To Do This	Press These Keys
See a list of all open programs	Hold Alt while pressing Tab
Tile the windows across the screen	Right-click on the taskbar and choose Tile
Cascade the windows across the screen	Right-click on the taskbar and choose Cascade
Shrink a window into an icon	Alt, spacebar, N
Make a window fill the screen	Alt, spacebar, X

Popular Keystrokes in Windows NT

To Do This	Press These Keys
Log on to Windows NT	Press Ctrl+Alt+Del simultaneously
Call up the Help menu	F1
Undo the mistake you just made	Ctrl+Z or Alt+Backspace
Close a window	Alt+F4
View the Start menu	Ctrl+Esc
Switch windows	Alt+Tab

To press a key combination such as Ctrl+Esc, press and hold down the first key (Ctrl), press the second key (Esc), and then release both keys.

Handling Files within a Program

To Do This	Press These Keys
Start a new file	Alt, F, N
Open an existing file	Alt, F, O
Save a file	Alt, F, S
Save a file under a new name	Alt, F, A
Print a file	Alt, F, P

To press a key combination such as Alt, F, N, press and release the Alt key, press and release the F key, and then press and release the N key (you don't have to worry about typing uppercase letters).

Working in My Computer or Explorer

To Do This	Do This
Copy a file to another location on the *same* disk drive	Hold down Ctrl and drag the file there
Copy a file to a *different* disk drive or move a file to another location on the *same* disk drive	Drag the file there
Move a file to a *different* disk drive	Hold down Alt and drag the file there
Select several files	Hold down Ctrl and click on the files' names
Load a program as an icon	Hold down Ctrl while double-clicking on the program name

DUMMIES 101®: WINDOWS NT®

DUMMIES 101:®
WINDOWS NT®

by Andy Rathbone

and Rich Grace

IDG Books Worldwide, Inc.
An International Data Group Company

Foster City, CA ✦ Chicago, IL ✦ Indianapolis, IN ✦ Southlake, TX

Dummies 101:® Windows NT®

Published by
IDG Books Worldwide, Inc.
An International Data Group Company
919 E. Hillsdale Blvd.
Suite 400
Foster City, CA 94404
http://www.idgbooks.com (IDG Books Worldwide Web site)
http://www.dummies.com (Dummies Press Web site)

Library of Congress Catalog Card No.: 97-70739

ISBN: 0-7645-0167-4

Printed in the United States of America

10 9 8 7 6 5 4 3 2 1

1M/RV/QV/ZX/IN

Distributed in the United States by IDG Books Worldwide, Inc.

Distributed by Macmillan Canada for Canada; by Transworld Publishers Limited in the United Kingdom and Europe; by WoodsLane Pty. Ltd. for Australia; by WoodsLane Enterprises Ltd. for New Zealand; by Longman Singapore Publishers Ltd. for Singapore, Malaysia, Thailand, and Indonesia; by Simron Pty. Ltd. for South Africa; by Toppan Company Ltd. for Japan; by Distribuidora Cuspide for Argentina; by Livraria Cultura for Brazil; by Ediciencia S.A. for Ecuador; by Addison-Wesley Publishing Company for Korea; by Ediciones ZETA S.C.R. Ltda. for Peru; by WS Computer Publishing Company, Inc., for the Philippines; by Unalis Corporation for Taiwan; by Contemporanea de Ediciones for Venezuela. Authorized Sales Agent: Anthony Rudkin Associates for the Middle East and North Africa.

For general information on IDG Books Worldwide's books in the U.S., please call our Consumer Customer Service department at 800-762-2974. For reseller information, including discounts and premium sales, please call our Reseller Customer Service department at 800-434-3422.

For information on where to purchase IDG Books Worldwide's books outside the U.S., please contact our International Sales department at 415-655-3023 or fax 415-655-3299.

For information on foreign language translations, please contact our Foreign & Subsidiary Rights department at 415-655-3021 or fax 415-655-3281.

For sales inquiries and special prices for bulk quantities, please contact our Sales department at 415-655-3200 or write to the address above.

For information on using IDG Books Worldwide's books in the classroom or for ordering examination copies, please contact our Educational Sales department at 800-434-2086 or fax 817-251-8174.

For press review copies, author interviews, or other publicity information, please contact our Public Relations department at 415-655-3000 or fax 415-655-3299.

For authorization to photocopy items for corporate, personal, or educational use, please contact Copyright Clearance Center, 222 Rosewood Drive, Danvers, MA 01923, or fax 508-750-4470.

 is a trademark under exclusive license to IDG Books Worldwide, Inc., from International Data Group, Inc.

About the Author

Andy Rathbone started geeking around with computers in 1985 when he bought a boxy CP/ M Kaypro 2X with lime-green letters. Like other budding nerds, he soon began playing with null-modem adaptors, dialing up computer bulletin boards, and working part-time at Radio Shack.

In between playing computer games, he served as editor of the *Daily Aztec* newspaper at San Diego State University. After graduating with a comparative literature degree, he went to work for a bizarre underground coffee-table magazine that sort of disappeared.

Andy began combining his two interests, words and computers, by selling articles to a local computer magazine. During the next few years, Andy started ghostwriting computer books for more famous computer authors, as well as writing several hundred articles about computers for technoid publications like Supercomputing Review, CompuServe Magazine, ID Systems, DataPro, and Shareware.

In 1992, Andy and *DOS For Dummies* author/legend Dan Gookin teamed up to write *PCs For Dummies*, which was runner-up in the Computer Press Association's 1993 awards. Andy subsequently wrote the first edition of *Windows For Dummies* plus *OS/2 For Dummies, Upgrading & Fixing PCs For Dummies, Multimedia & CD-ROMs For Dummies, MORE Windows For Dummies,* and *Windows 95 For Dummies.* He also cowrote *VCRs and Camcorders For Dummies* with Gordon McComb and *Windows NT 4 For Dummies* with Sharon Crawford.

Andy lives with his most-excellent wife, Tina, and their cat in San Diego, California. When not writing, he fiddles with his MIDI synthesizer and tries to keep the cat off both keyboards.

ABOUT IDG BOOKS WORLDWIDE

Welcome to the world of IDG Books Worldwide.

IDG Books Worldwide, Inc., is a subsidiary of International Data Group, the world's largest publisher of computer-related information and the leading global provider of information services on information technology. IDG was founded more than 25 years ago and now employs more than 8,500 people worldwide. IDG publishes more than 275 computer publications in over 75 countries (see listing below). More than 60 million people read one or more IDG publications each month.

Launched in 1990, IDG Books Worldwide is today the #1 publisher of best-selling computer books in the United States. We are proud to have received eight awards from the Computer Press Association in recognition of editorial excellence and three from *Computer Currents'* First Annual Readers' Choice Awards. Our best-selling *...For Dummies®* series has more than 30 million copies in print with translations in 30 languages. IDG Books Worldwide, through a joint venture with IDG's Hi-Tech Beijing, became the first U.S. publisher to publish a computer book in the People's Republic of China. In record time, IDG Books Worldwide has become the first choice for millions of readers around the world who want to learn how to better manage their businesses.

Our mission is simple: Every one of our books is designed to bring extra value and skill-building instructions to the reader. Our books are written by experts who understand and care about our readers. The knowledge base of our editorial staff comes from years of experience in publishing, education, and journalism — experience we use to produce books for the '90s. In short, we care about books, so we attract the best people. We devote special attention to details such as audience, interior design, use of icons, and illustrations. And because we use an efficient process of authoring, editing, and desktop publishing our books electronically, we can spend more time ensuring superior content and spend less time on the technicalities of making books.

You can count on our commitment to deliver high-quality books at competitive prices on topics you want to read about. At IDG Books Worldwide, we continue in the IDG tradition of delivering quality for more than 25 years. You'll find no better book on a subject than one from IDG Books Worldwide.

John Kilcullen
CEO
IDG Books Worldwide, Inc.

Steven Berkowitz
President and Publisher
IDG Books Worldwide, Inc.

Eighth Annual Computer Press Awards ≥1992

Ninth Annual Computer Press Awards ≥1993

Tenth Annual Computer Press Awards ≥1994

Eleventh Annual Computer Press Awards ≥1995

Dedication

To my wife, parents, sister, and cat. — Andy

To my fiancée, Elisabeth Parker, with whom I have far too many computers in our house
for our own good. — Rich

Author's Acknowledgments

Andy Rathbone: Thanks to Dan Gookin and his wife Sandy, Matt Wagner, Gareth Hancock, Colleen
Rainsberger, Michael Bolinger, Joyce Pepple, Heather Dismore, Kevin Spencer, Tim Stanley, Valery Bourke,
and all the Production folks at IDG Books Worldwide, Inc. Thanks also to Access Technology for designing
the *Dummies 101* series disks.

Rich Grace: First, I'd like to thank Andy for the chance to do this book with him.

I'd also like to thank Microsoft's press agency, Waggener Edstrom, for the review copies of Windows NT 4
Workstation and NT 4 Server that I used during this project.

And thanks to David Fugate and Matt Wagner at Waterside Productions for their assistance and
representation during this project.

Finally, thanks to David Rogelberg and the various contributors to the Studio B computer authors' list,
which helps me feed my e-mail addiction.

Publisher's Acknowledgments

We're proud of this book; please send us your comments about it by using the IDG Books Worldwide Registration Card at the back of the book or by e-mailing us at feedback/dummies@idgbooks.com. Some of the people who helped bring this book to market include the following:

Acquisitions, Development, and Editorial

Senior Project Editor: Colleen Rainsberger

Acquisitions Editor: Gareth Hancock

Product Development Director: Mary Bednarek

Media Development Manager: Joyce Pepple

Associate Permissions Editor: Heather H. Dismore

Copy Editors: Michael Bolinger, Diana Conover

Technical Editor: Tim Stanley

Editorial Manager: Seta K. Frantz

Production

Project Coordinator: Valery Bourke

Layout and Graphics: Lou Boudreau, Dominique DeFelice, Maridee Ennis, Jane E. Martin, Brent Savage, Michael A. Sullivan

Proofreaders: Nancy L. Reinhardt, Nancy Price, Rob Springer, Karen York

Indexer: Sherry Massey

Special Help

Stephanie Koutek, Proof Editor; Kevin Spencer, Associate Technical Editor, Access Technology, CD Developer

General and Administrative

IDG Books Worldwide, Inc.: John Kilcullen, CEO; Steven Berkowitz, President and Publisher

IDG Books Technology Publishing: Brenda McLaughlin, Senior Vice President and Group Publisher

Dummies Technology Press and Dummies Editorial: Diane Graves Steele, Vice President and Associate Publisher; Judith A. Taylor, Brand Manager; Kristin A. Cocks, Editorial Director

Dummies Trade Press: Kathleen A. Welton, Vice President and Publisher; Stacy S. Collins, Brand Manager

IDG Books Production for Dummies Press: Beth Jenkins, Production Director; Cindy L. Phipps, Supervisor of Project Coordination, Production Proofreading, and Indexing; Kathie S. Schutte, Supervisor of Page Layout; Shelley Lea, Supervisor of Graphics and Design; Debbie J. Gates, Production Systems Specialist; Tony Augsburger, Supervisor of Reprints and Bluelines; Leslie Popplewell, Media Archive Coordinator

Dummies Packaging and Book Design: Patti Sandez, Packaging Specialist; Lance Kayser, Packaging Assistant; Kavish + Kavish, Cover Design

◆

The publisher would like to give special thanks to Patrick J. McGovern, without whom this book would not have been possible.

◆

Files at a Glance

Contents
🖐 🌀 at a Glance

Table of Contents

Introduction

Welcome to *Dummies 101: Windows NT,* the textbook for people who want to learn Windows NT as quickly as possible so that they can move on to the truly important things in their lives.

Of course, you're no dummy; it's just that the awkwardness of Windows sometimes makes you *feel* like a dummy. And no, you're not alone, either: Almost everyone feels like a dummy when he or she first sits in front of a computer. (Some people are a little better at hiding their grimaces, that's all.)

Don't think of this book as another boring school course, where you learn something snoozable like computer theory. Instead, it's more of a hands-on wood shop — a place where you can come to build your own Windows knowledge at your own pace.

Learning How to Use Windows NT

Learning how to control a computer with Windows NT is a little like moving into a new house. A house is just a big, empty room. Sure, the house probably has basics like paint or wallpaper and a stove and refrigerator. But it doesn't have anything that you've added or rearranged.

The same holds true with Windows NT. Your computer probably came with a couple of Windows programs already on it. But until you begin arranging Windows so that it meets your personal needs, working with it is like living in an empty house — and that's not very fun or relaxing.

In fact, computers often seem so frustrating for that very reason: They seem sterile, rigid, and uncontrollable. But when you know how to push *them* around a little bit, things change for the better. And that's where this book comes in.

This book teaches you how to push the right buttons so that the right things happen, which makes Windows NT much less intimidating and much easier to use. (And you won't have to rely so much on the person sitting next to you at work.)

Why You're Reading This Book

Notes:

You could be peering through these pages for any of the following reasons:

▶ The manual that came in the Windows NT box is too hard to read.

▶ Someone is making you learn Windows NT at work. (If so, consider yourself lucky — at least you're getting paid to learn it.)

▶ You already know how to use earlier versions of Windows, but this new version — Windows NT — leaves you feeling a little sketchy.

▶ You're tired of looking through *Windows NT For Dummies* (IDG Books Worldwide, Inc.) whenever you need instructions for installing a program. Or worse yet, your office copy disappeared — Fred from Receiving never returned it after he promised to borrow it "just over the weekend."

▶ You want to become a little more serious about computing because you know that the beasts aren't going away. In fact, they're so trendy that *Vogue* magazine listed Iomega's Zip drives as #2 on its "Ten most wanted objects of desire" list (right between the Charles David boot and S-Papa tote bag).

▶ You don't have time for one of those evening-college computing courses, and you sure aren't giving up a weekend for one, either.

▶ You don't want to be a know-it-all computer guru, but you want to gain some basic knowledge of Windows NT so that you can hold your own when the guru's nowhere to be found.

That's where this book comes in handy. It won't make you a Windows NT expert, but it will teach you how to use Windows NT in a day-to-day setting. And when your coworkers find out that you know how to "drag and drop" a fast form letter, you'll start to be pretty popular around the office, too. When people start asking you Windows NT-related questions, toss the book at them. Let them do their own homework.

How to Use This Book

This book's a textbook, plain and simple. Very plain and simple, hopefully. It starts by teaching you how to turn on your computer and bring Windows NT to the screen. From there, it shows you how to maneuver a mouse and move windows around on-screen. Step by step, this book teaches you how to load programs. And eventually, as you progress through the units, you'll learn how to write letters, create drawings, dial other computers with a modem, and copy files to and from your computer's assortment of disks.

You're free to move at your own pace, starting on page 1 and finishing the course with the last unit. Or if you want to learn only the exact steps required to save a file, for example, head straight to Unit 9.

If you're determined to learn — and *remember* — the information, feel free to take the quiz at the end of each unit. That shows you which areas you've mastered and which (if any) you may need to brush up on. (You can find the correct answers to the quizzes in the Appendix.) Then practice what you learned by completing the Unit Exercise.

To make things easier for you, this book follows certain conventions. For example, if you have to type something into the computer, you'll see easy-to-follow text that looks like this:

In the dialog box, type **these letters**.

That's your cue to type the words *these letters* in the box on-screen and then press the Enter key.

Whenever I describe a message or information that you'll see on-screen, I present it as follows:

```
This is a message on-screen.
```

(And don't worry, you'll see plenty of pictures along the tops of the pages, too.)

Don't know whether you can handle a unit? The first page of the unit contains a Prerequisites section that lists the skills you need to complete that unit's lessons.

Right below the Prerequisites, you'll find a list of files that you'll need for the unit; the files are found on the disk that comes in the back of this book.

Have a question? Q/A Sessions pop up throughout the text to answer particularly nagging questions.

Finally, people who prefer traditional course work will enjoy the review and test at the end of each part, as well as a Lab Assignment, which lets you bring together the skills that you learned in that part's units.

How about the Technical Stuff?

You don't need to know the mechanics of internal combustion to drive a car. And you don't need to know technical programming information to use Windows NT. So this book filters out the technical stuff that just gets in the way anyway.

Of course, I'll have to slip a few of the "whys" in there so that you know why the heck Windows NT is making you go through so many convoluted steps to do such a simple task. (Otherwise, you'd never believe me.)

Also, all the really nasty computer words are set in italic type and humanely defined in the text.

How This Book Is Organized

The information in this book is arranged like a long line of bread crumbs, along which you can move at your own pace. If you're ravenous for information about Windows NT, start at the beginning and scoop 'em up as fast as you can. Or if you just have time for a snack, pick up the book, start where you left off, and spend a few minutes with some exercises. Either way, you'll eventually reach the end of the trail and have all that Windows knowledge under your belt.

The parts

The book's divided into 5 parts and 16 units, but that's really not as much work as it sounds. Here's the breakdown.

Part I: Bare Bones Basics

First-time Windows users should definitely start here, learning how to start your computer and load Windows. You'll learn how to use that mouse by "clicking" in certain places on-screen in order to get some work done. Finally, you'll learn the best part: exiting Windows and getting away from the computer.

Part II: Working with Your Desktop

Windows NT turns your computer screen into a computerized desktop, complete with folders, stick-on notes, and random office tools. This part of the book shows you how Windows NT handles *programs* — computerized tools for getting your work done. You'll learn how to put little "push-buttons" on your desk that automatically find your favorite programs and put them to work.

Programs make you store your work in *files* — computerized collections of information such as your letters, spreadsheets, and other important things you don't want to lose. Unit 5 in this book teaches you what to do with your files: copy them, delete them, move them to and from floppy disks, store them in folders, and perform other often-complicated tasks.

Oh, yeah — you'll learn how to find the files you thought you'd lost, too. Unit 6 shows you how to find, lose, and find again files that are on *other* people's computers — a common practice in offices that link computers with network cables.

Part III: Getting into Windows NT

The bulk of the mechanics of Windows NT is in here. You'll learn how to load a program like a word processor or spreadsheet. Then you'll learn how to load information — a *file* — into that program. Changed the information? Then you'd better save it — a process that's explained fully, of course. Finally, you'll learn how to send a copy of your work to the printer so that you can do something with it.

You'll also learn about that "cut and paste" stuff for moving information to and from different programs. (That's how most of those computer owners get maps into their spiffy party flyers.)

Part IV: The Free Programs

You've probably seen some of those little on-screen push-buttons — *icons* — with names like Internet Explorer, Exchange, and other oddities. This part teaches you how to do something with these programs, from start to finish: connect to one of those "Web sites" you've been hearing about or send and receive electronic-mail (e-mail).

You'll also learn how to get your toes wet on the Internet; yep, you learn how to use Internet Explorer to surf the World Wide Web.

Part V: Fixing Problems

Windows NT stuck by the roadside? No help in sight? You'll find information about the Windows equivalent of changing a flat tire here. You'll learn how to organize your Windows desktop. Plus, if Windows NT is still giving you trouble, you'll learn how to wring the most help out of its built-in Help program.

The icons

Because Windows uses *icons* — little symbols — to stand for things, this book does the same. The icons in the book's margins mean the following:

If you spot this icon, look for filenames sitting next to it; you'll need those files for any exercises coming up in the unit.

Better remember this snippet of information so that you can spit it back out for the quiz at the unit's end or the test at the end of the part.

Like what you learned? Then delve a little deeper by reading the extra credit section. This section is entirely optional, however.

heads up

Watch out — this icon points to tasks or steps that may trip you up. Some of these tasks may be a little tricky or not work as you expect them to.

Notes: Nothing sneaky here. The word *Notes:* just means that you can write your own notes in the margins. (Highly paid psychologists say that simple action often transforms hard-to-remember stuff into easy-to-find stuff.)

Think you're ready to move on to the next lesson? Then take the simple "quiz" that follows this Progress Check icon. If you can do all the things listed there, check them off to show that you've mastered that lesson. You may even be able to skip a lesson and move ahead, you lucky dog.

The tests (Well, you wanted a tutorial, didn't you?)

To make sure that you've absorbed the information in each unit, you'll find a quiz at the end of each unit. Hold on, though — that can be good news as well as bad. If you can pass the quiz without reading the unit, you've passed. You don't have to read the unit!

If some of the questions catch you off guard, you'd better budget some time for a little review.

Finally, if you want to really jump ahead of the game, you'll find a full-fledged exam at the end of each of the book's five parts. By looking at these exams, you can start reading the book and taking its lessons at your own level of knowledge.

(And if you *do* need to read the book from the beginning, don't worry — the tests aren't too hard. A distinctive "on the test" icon appears in the margin next to nearly every snippet of information that you'll need to know.)

You'll find the answers to all the unit quizzes and part tests in Appendix A. If you miss a question, this appendix will tell you which lesson or unit to go back and review.

About the CD

You can use the files on the CD that comes with this book to work through the practice exercises. But first you need to install those files on your computer. The CD includes a handy installation program that makes the installation process a cinch for you to complete; you just stick the CD in the computer, click on a few things, and then follow the instructions on-screen. If you're brand-new at this Windows stuff, though, you may want to complete Part I of this book before you try to install the CD — but make sure to put the CD in a *very* safe place so that you'll have it when you're ready for it.

With Windows NT running, follow these steps:

1 Insert the Dummies 101 CD (label side up) into your computer's CD drive and wait about 30 seconds to see whether AutoPlay starts the CD for you.

Be careful to touch only the edges of the CD. The CD drive is the one that pops out with a circular drawer.

If your computer has the Windows CD AutoPlay feature, the CD installer should begin automatically, so just click the OK button that appears. If you see the CD installer window (it looks like a piece of notebook paper with the book's title), go to the section, "Installing the exercise files."

If nothing seems to happen after a minute or so, continue to Step 2.

2 If the installation program doesn't start automatically, click the Start button and click Run.

3 In the dialog box that appears, type d:\seticon.exe **(if your CD drive is not drive D, substitute the appropriate letter for D) and click OK.**

A message informs you that the program is about to install the icons.

4 Click OK in the message window.

After a moment, a program group called Dummies 101 appears on the Start menu, with a set of icons. Then another message appears, asking whether you want to use the CD now.

5 Click Yes to use the CD now or click No if you want to use the CD later.

If you click No, you can start the CD later simply by clicking the Dummies 101 - Windows NT CD icon in the Dummies 101 program group (on the Start button).

After you complete the installation process, all the files you'll need for this book will be ready and waiting for you in the C:\Dummies 101\Windows NT folder. Store the CD where it will be free from harm so that you can reinstall a file in case the one that's installed on your computer gets messed up.

If you have problems with the installation process, you can call the IDG Books Worldwide Customer Support number: 800-762-2974.

Where to Go from Here

Never used Windows NT before? Then flip ahead to Unit 1 and start reading. If you've already used Windows a little bit, skim Part I to make sure that you've caught all the basics, and then jump ahead to Part II for a little more advanced information.

Notes:

Although this book is a full-fledged tutorial course, you don't *have* to learn how Windows works. Because the book contains step-by-step instructions for most of the tasks that you'll do in Windows NT, you can simply turn back to those pages when you want. Later, if you tire of looking stuff up and want to memorize the steps, master the quiz at the end of the unit.

Either way, this book teaches you how to make Windows NT work the way you want it to with as little pain as possible. Good luck!

Bare Bones Basics

Part 1

In this part . . .

Windows works like those expensive picture-in-picture TV sets, where viewers can watch the Raiders yet still keep an eye on the Chargers game playing in the corner window.

Windows software, too, lets you put more than one program on the computer screen, each visible in its own little window. Or if your fancy multimedia computer has a TV card for presentation, you can put the Chargers game in a corner window while typing business reports in the foreground.

To introduce you to this world of Windows, this book starts at the most elementary level: how to turn your computer (and Windows) on and off. The procedure is only a little more complicated than turning on your TV set and less complicated than anything involving recording on your VCR.

When windows start filling your screen, you'll have to learn ways to manipulate them. A unit in this part of the book shows you how to shuffle programs around, pushing their windows aside when you don't need them and bringing them to the forefront when desired. You'll learn how to make the important windows bigger and shrink or delete the unnecessary ones.

Finally, you'll learn to make a Windows program do your bidding, which is usually as simple as ordering food from a restaurant's menu.

Note: When Windows is capitalized, it refers to the software that's sold on little floppy disks or CD-ROMs in computer stores. When windows is lowercase, the word refers to the little square box on-screen containing a program. Also, don't confuse Windows NT with earlier versions of Windows, like Windows 95 or Windows 3.11. Windows NT will run most programs written for other versions of Windows, but most earlier versions of Windows won't run programs written for Windows NT.

Windows software sells like hamburgers at Jack-in-the-Box: Several different versions are currently for sale, all with their own pros and cons. Home and small office users usually use a version called *Windows 95;* bigger offices often use Windows NT — the subject of this book. (People who can't afford to buy the newest software make do with their tried, true, and tired versions of Windows 3.1.)

Although each version of Windows has its own flavor, they all have the same basic structure. After you learn the basics of one version, you know enough to get by with the next.

Windows NT software actually comes in two different versions: Windows NT Workstation and Windows NT Server. The Server version costs more, and includes complicated controls for stringing together bunches of other computers. The less-expensive Workstation version — the subject of this book — runs on the desktops of less-demanding users.

Unit 1

• • • • • • • • • • •

Starting and Exiting Windows NT

Prerequisites

◗ A computer

◗ Windows NT installed on
the computer

Objectives for This Unit

✓ Turning on your computer

✓ Loading and exiting Windows NT

✓ Turning off the computer and monitor

Right after firing up the office coffee machine, turning on your computer
and starting Windows NT are probably your first steps of the day. So this
unit starts with the absolute basics: finding the computer's On switch, flipping
it in the right direction, and watching Windows NT jump to life.

Or if Windows doesn't jump onto your screen automatically, you'll learn the
easiest ways to drag it up there yourself.

Finally, this unit explains how to shut down Windows and your computer at
day's end. Plus, it explores the topic that's been plaguing computer users for
years: Should computers *really* be turned off at night?

Lesson 1-1

Turning On Your Computer

Notes:

If your computer isn't making any noise, it's either turned off, unplugged, or broken. The good news is that turning the computer on usually brings it to life.

The bad news is that computer designers didn't hang out at the same bar when designing the On/Off switch. Sometimes a big red lever on the side controls the power; other times the switch is a little nub along the front. However, it's almost always the biggest switch on the computer.

Found the switch? Then here's how to turn on the computer:

1 Turn on the monitor.

Most monitors make a "click" sound when you turn them on, just like a TV set. They usually don't display anything until you turn on the computer, though.

2 Flip the computer's On/Off switch in the opposite direction.

Some On/Off switches have little symbols on them; the side with the little line means On, and the side with the little circle means Off. Your computer should gently whir itself to life and make high-tech clicking noises.

Doesn't work? Try this: If the computer still doesn't start making noise, turn the On/Off switch back to off. Then check to make sure that the computer's power cord is plugged securely into the computer's rear. Check to see where the cord plugs into the wall or power strip, too. Are the connections tight? Try flipping the switch again.

Still doesn't work? Check the *power strip* — a collection of outlets that powers some computers. Power strips have their own On/Off switches that control *everything* plugged into them.

If all works normally, the Windows NT log-on screen eventually appears on your monitor. The log-on screen is a cartoon of a little hand reaching eagerly for the keyboard. No cartoon hand? Then read the "Q/A session" sidebar a few paragraphs ahead. Your program will need a hand from your system administrator to get your computer on the run.

The next lesson takes you through the log-on process so that you can actually use Windows NT for something.

Got Windows NT on-screen? Skip ahead to Lesson 1-2.

Either way, congratulations! You've taken the first step toward computer literacy.

Q/A session

Question: When I turn on the computer, I see a weird blue screen covered with numbers and a confusing message. What happened?

Answer: You've run into the bane of Windows NT users: the "Blue Screen of Death." When Windows NT collapses, the computer screen turns blue, displays a bunch of incomprehensible numbers, and sends an extraordinarily cryptic message describing the nature of the problem.

Fortunately, Windows NT is a hardy soul — you may never see this eerie blue screen. But if the screen shows itself to you, don't try to fix anything yourself. Save this for your office's least exasperated computer person.

Don't confuse the Blue Screen of Death for the normal starting-up process of Windows NT. When you first turn on your computer, a blue screen also appears on the monitor, showing a few lines of text along the very top. That blue screen only lasts a few minutes, though, before Windows NT arrives to do your bidding.

☑ **Progress Check**

If you can do the following, you've mastered this lesson:

❑ Turn on your monitor.

❑ Turn on your computer.

❑ Recognize the Windows NT startup screen with its log-on box.

Logging On to and Exiting Windows NT   Lesson 1-2

After you turn on the computer, it loads Windows NT automatically. Then it simply sits there, waiting for somebody to sit down at the keyboard and introduce themselves. This is the process of logging on, and you'll learn how to do that in this lesson. Plus, you'll learn how to exit Windows when you're through working. Whew!

Logging on to Windows NT

Windows NT grants different access to different people, so it needs to know who's sitting in front of the computer. The following steps tell you how to remove the little cartoon hand log-on screen and log on to Windows NT.

1 **Press the Ctrl, Alt, and Delete keys at the same time.**

Pressing these keys simultaneously "wakes up" Window NT, and a new box appears on the screen.

2 **Type your name in the box marked User name and press the Tab key.**

The User name tells Windows NT who you are. Different people have access to different levels of office secrets buried inside the computers. Your office computer manager will probably already have given you a user name to type into the computer; if not, use your own name. Common ways to enter a name are using the first name and last initial or the first initial plus the last name.

Notes:

3 Type your password into the box marked P̲assword and press Enter.

Nobody but you should ever know your password. Because your computer can't see you, your password is its way of making sure that you're really you. That way coworkers can't type in your user name, steal all your work on the McCormick ad campaign, and tell the boss it was all their idea.

on the test

Don't share your password with anybody, and don't write it down on a little yellow note that you stick to your monitor. If you forget your password, head to your office manager with a mournful, repentant look. (This trick doesn't work very often, though.)

Note: See the little welcome note that Windows NT tosses your way as a greeting? To get the note off the screen, click on the button marked Close. Or if you're getting sick of seeing those notes whenever you turn on your computer, first click in the little check box where it says Show this Welcome Screen next time you start Windows; Windows NT will then stop trying to be so helpful. Don't know how to click your mouse? Jump ahead a few pages to Lesson 2-1 for a quick tutorial.

Q/A session

Question: Where can I get my password? I don't have it!

Answer: When you get a Windows NT computer at your desk, you also get some important information from your company's computer guru. (Company computer gurus are usually called "system administrators" or the "the IS department" or even worse terms.) The most important pieces of information are your assigned user name and a password that allows you access to the system. Sometimes, the office will let you define those things yourself, but if you happen to lose them or somehow never receive them, start by talking to your boss. (Sometimes, the administrator will assign the name but leave the password blank. Then the first time the user logs on, Windows NT requires the user to assign a password.)

---

never turn off
computer when
Windows is running

Exiting Windows

heads up

Never simply turn off your computer while Windows NT is on-screen. First, that doesn't give it a chance to save your work. Second, Windows often stores information in the background, and it subsequently loses it if it doesn't have a chance to pack up. You can lose your data if you simply turn off its power without going through the normal shutdown process. Always exit Windows NT by using the following steps:

1 Find the Start button and click on it.

If you can spot the Start button, shown in the bottom-left corner of Figure 1-1, head for Step 2. If you don't see it, you can hold down the Ctrl key and the Esc key at the same time to bring the Start button to the forefront.

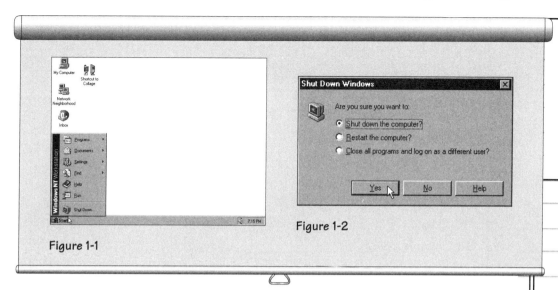

Figure 1-1

Figure 1-2

Figure 1-1: Click on the Start button, in the screen's bottom-left corner, to begin shutting down Windows NT.

Figure 1-2: Click on the Yes button if you're sure that you want to shut down your computer.

on the test

The Start button contains the buttons that let you start other programs and get some work done.

2 Click on the words Sh<u>u</u>t Down from the Start menu and choose the Shut down the computer? option

Sh<u>u</u>t Down is the official Off switch, and clicking on it tells Windows NT to shut itself down. First, however, Windows sends out the warning shown in Figure 1-2.

Although the Start button is labeled Start, you also use it for stopping Windows NT when you're ready to stop working.

on the test

3 Click on the <u>Y</u>es button.

After being convinced that you really want to exit, Windows shuts itself down, making sure that you've saved all your work in your Windows programs. (Just in case, make a habit of saving your work whenever you think of it; you'll find more information about saving files in Unit 9.)

heads up

Running any of those old DOS programs? (Yes, this can be done under Windows NT.) Then you'd better shut them down before trying to shut down Windows. Windows refuses to close DOS programs, leaving that chore to you.

extra credit

Hey, what's a double-click?

See that mouse attached to the computer by its tail? See the little buttons on the mouse? Rest your right hand on the mouse and look at the button that your index finger touches. When you click the button once, you've *clicked* the mouse. Click the button twice in rapid succession, and you've *double-clicked*. (Chapter 2 shows how left-handers can reverse their mouse buttons.)

See how the arrow on-screen moves when you move the mouse with your hand? That's how you control things in Windows: by pointing the mouse's arrow at buttons on-screen and pushing the mouse's buttons with strategic clicks. (Mice — and their subsequent double-clicks — get their own section in Unit 2.)

✓ **Progress Check**

If you can do the following, you've mastered this lesson:

❑ Load Windows NT.

❑ Find the Start button.

❑ Exit Windows NT by choosing the Start menu's Shut Down command.

Notes:

What are those other Sh<u>u</u>t Down options?

Windows NT gives you a few other options under the Sh<u>u</u>t Down command, as shown in Figure 1-2. Although computers differ, you'll probably encounter these options:

▶ **Shut down the computer?**

If you want to turn off your computer, choose this option in order to close down Windows NT first.

▶ **Restart the computer?**

Some newly-installed programs want you to restart your computer by choosing this option. An office computer repair person may also use it to resuscitate ailing computers.

▶ **Close all programs and log on as a different user?**

Some people set up Windows NT so that different people can work on the same computer but still keep their work separate. If your computer is set up this way, this option appears in the Shut Down box, ready for different users to play with Windows at different times.

Lesson 1-3

Turning Off Your Computer

Both sides of the "Should I turn off my computer at night?" debate are covered at the end of this lesson; I'm not going to tackle that issue here. In the meantime, *everybody* agrees that you should follow these basic steps before leaving your computer at the day's end (Step 5 is optional):

1 Save your work and exit your Windows and DOS programs.

Make sure that you save all your work before turning off your computer — that's the most important step of all. (Not sure how to save a file? Here are the basic steps, but Unit 9 has the full details: Click on the word <u>F</u>ile along the program's top edge; when a menu drops down, click on the word <u>S</u>ave. If you haven't saved the file before, type a short, descriptive name and press Enter.)

DOS programs aren't always shut down in the same way, unfortunately, but you need to shut them down, too.

2 Back up your computer's information.

If you have a backup system — a tape system, Zip drive, or some other device that your company has given you — now's the time to use it. A backup system is a must, particularly in the office environment. If you accidentally delete something really important, you can grab an earlier version out of the backup system. Ask your office computer person about your office backup system, and whether it can back everything up automatically. Respond with a worried look if the answer is "no."

3 Exit Windows.

You already learned this trick — you choose <u>S</u>hut down the computer from the Start menu's Sh<u>u</u>t Down command — in Lesson 1-2.

4 Turn off the monitor.

Flip that same switch that you flipped in Lesson 1-1. *Everybody* turns off their monitors at night except the security guy in the lobby.

5 Turn off the computer (optional).

Again, flip that same On switch that you flipped in Lesson 1-1. Or if you prefer to leave your computer on, just make sure that nobody puts a cover over it so that it won't heat up at night.

extra credit

Debating the merits of leaving the computer on at night

Some people don't turn their computers off. Ever. See, when you turn off the computer, its sensitive internal components cool down. When you turn it back on, they heat up again. Because most of the components sit on a big fiberglass plate called a *motherboard,* all that flexing can cause them to loosen. Keeping the temperature constant keeps the fluctuation down, which keeps everything more comfortable inside.

Other people turn their computers off at night, saying that 24-hour wear and tear can't be good for the fans and hard drives. Plus, the computer will catch any power surge that comes down the wire.

Which method works best? There's no cut-and-dried answer; you'll have to decide that one yourself or ask your boss about the company policy. (Some of my computers are on constantly, and the others are on for only a few hours a day.)

☑ Progress Check

If you can do the following, you've mastered this lesson:

❏ Safely exit Windows NT.

❏ Turn off your monitor.

❏ Turn off your computer (if desired).

Unit 1 Quiz

For each question, circle the letter of the correct answer or answers. Some questions may have more than one right answer.

1. **When trying to fix a broken computer, you should try this:**

   A. Make sure that its power switch is turned on.

   B. Make sure that it's plugged in.

   C. If it's plugged into a power strip, make sure that the power strip is turned on.

   D. Raise your hand and slowly wave it back and forth.

2. **To shut down Windows NT, you do this:**

   A. Choose Shut Down from the Start menu.

   B. Click on the Close button.

   C. Just flip the computer's Off switch.

   D. Just turn off the monitor.

3. **Should you leave your computer turned on at night?**

   A. Yes

   B. No

   C. Maybe

   D. There are more important things to worry about.

4. **What does "backing up" your data mean?**

   A. Putting the computer into reverse and hitting the gas.

   B. Copying important files onto floppy disks, tape drives, or other storage devices.

   C. Storing your programs and boxes in a safe place.

   D. Making sure that you have two copies of your most important files.

5. **Should you write down your password?**

   A. Yes

   B. No

   C. Maybe

   D. Perhaps in my next life.

Unit 1 Exercise

1. Turn on the monitor and computer.

2. If Windows NT doesn't load itself automatically, load it yourself.

3. Find the Start button.

4. Close down Windows by choosing Shut Down from the Start menu and clicking on the Yes button.

5. Turn off your monitor and your computer, if you choose to.

Using a Mouse
and Keyboard

Prerequisites

▶ Turning on your computer
(Lesson 1-1)

▶ Loading Windows NT
(Lesson 1-2)

Objectives for This Unit

✓ Clicking the mouse

✓ Double-clicking the mouse

✓ Dragging and dropping

✓ Using the function keys

✓ Using the Alt and Ctrl keys

✓ Using the Esc key

✓ Using the arrow keys

Just as you control a car by moving the steering wheel, you control Windows by moving the mouse and pressing keys on the keyboard. (Talking at computers — or even yelling at them — doesn't control them nearly as well, as most people have discovered.)

This unit shows you how to use the mouse to press buttons and make choices from on-screen menus. You'll learn how to drag and drop bits of important information from one program window to another. Plus, you'll learn about some of those extra keys that computers have on their keyboards: Alt, Ctrl, Esc, the function keys, and the four little arrows.

This unit also shows you how to get into Solitaire, the most oft-used computer program in an office setting.

Finally, here's some good news: If you've used any version of Windows software, you'll find Windows NT to be very similar. Mouse clicks, dragging and dropping, and keyboard strokes are almost always the same. If you've used Windows 95, you'll have a definite advantage.

Lesson 2-1

Using the Mouse

Notes:

In the days of olde, people merely typed text into computers. To control the programs, they pushed little arrows on their keyboards.

Today's computer users don't get as much exercise because they rely on a mouse. Shown in Figure 2-1, the *mouse* is a palm-sized contraption with a wire that connects to the back of the computer.

Moving the mouse with your hand moves an arrow across the computer screen. By pointing at buttons on-screen — and pushing a button on the mouse — you can boss programs around.

You can manipulate your mouse in three basic ways, which are described in the following sections.

Making a click

Whenever you press and release a button on the mouse, the mouse makes a *click.* Computer programmers used that scientific phrase to describe pushing one of the mouse's buttons with your finger. To give a click a try, follow these steps:

1 Load Windows NT.

Don't have Windows NT on your screen? Unit 1 is waiting for you.

2 Move your mouse and watch the arrow or cursor move across the screen.

Moving the mouse means sliding it across the desktop with the clickable buttons facing upward. (The mouse doesn't slide against the face of the monitor, and yes, people have certainly tried.)

3 Aim the mouse's arrow at the Start button, shown in Figure 2-2, and click the left mouse button.

See how the mouse's arrow is pointing to the Start button in the lower-left corner of your screen? When you click the left mouse button, a menu shoots up, just as it does in Figure 2-2.

Click the mouse by quickly pressing and releasing its left mouse button with your right index finger.

The menu reveals a bunch more options to choose from, but you don't have to play with any of those now; menus are covered in Unit 3. But you've mastered clicking, and that's a *big* part of using Windows. (To get the menu back down, click on the Start button again. Or you can press the Esc key, but that trick is covered in Lesson 2-2.)

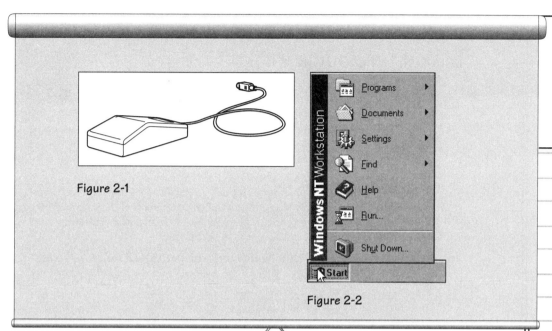

Figure 2-1

Figure 2-2

Figure 2-1: The mouse.

Figure 2-2: Press and release the mouse button with the mouse arrow over the Start button to "click" the mouse on that spot.

on the test

Windows NT — and all earlier versions of Windows — normally prefers that you use the *left* mouse button (unless, of course, some wiseguy switched the functions of your left and right mouse buttons, in which case Windows prefers the *right* mouse button). Windows NT, however, also makes use of the right button. In fact, whenever you're curious about what an icon or window can do, click on it with your right mouse button. A menu appears, listing the things that you can do with that icon or window.

extra credit

Getting helpful hints from the mouse

Windows NT dumps a lot of information onto the screen at one time. How can you tell which button, box, or window does what? Luckily, your mouse can help you out.

First, if a button or icon in a Windows NT program has you confused, simply point at it and wait a few seconds. Sometimes that's enough to make the program send a little window to the screen, explaining that button's or icon's reason for existence.

Or if an icon, window, or menu item has you confused, click on it with your *right* mouse button. Windows NT usually brings up a menu listing the things that you can do with that icon or window.

on the test

For the most part, Windows NT doesn't care where the mouse pointer happens to be resting on-screen — *until you click the mouse.* So when you move the mouse pointer to where you want the action to happen, click the mouse button to make Windows notice your presence.

Making a double-click

Got the mouse click down pat? Then get ready for the double-click. The *double-click* is just like it sounds: pointing the mouse's arrow at someplace on-screen and clicking the mouse's left button with your index finger twice in rapid succession. In other words, you make two clicks, one right after the other. Follow these steps for some practice:

1 Load Windows NT.

By now, you probably have Windows NT on-screen most of the time, so I'll soon start leaving it off as the first step. (Feel free to keep loading Windows, though.)

2 Move your mouse and watch the arrow or the cursor move across the screen.

Most new computer owners get mouse pads for Christmas; a good mouse pad lets the mouse roll more smoothly.

3 Aim the mouse's arrow at the My Computer button in the screen's top-left corner (shown in Figure 2-3), and double-click the left mouse button.

Instead of just clicking the mouse button like you did in the last set of steps, double-click the mouse by quickly pressing and releasing the left mouse button twice with your right index finger.

The My Computer program, shown in Figure 2-4, opens to reveal even more buttons — called *icons.* By double-clicking on the icons in this My Computer contraption, you can view the files and programs stored inside your computer. (You'll find a lot more My Computer information in Part II.)

4 Click on the little X in the My Computer window's upper-right corner to close the window.

To close down any window in Windows NT, just click on the X in its upper-right corner. (Figure 2-4 shows the arrow pointing at the proper place.)

Although a double-click sounds easy — just two rapid clicks — getting the hang of it can be hard at first. However, double-clicking is the key to making just about anything happen in Windows.

Is all this clicking stuff too easy for you? Then jump ahead to the quiz at this unit's end. You may be able to flip ahead a few pages and save yourself some time.

extra credit

Q/A session

Question: My double-clicks don't work!

Answer: You're probably not keeping the mouse pointer steady enough while you press the mouse button. See, your mouse's arrow needs to hover over the object while you press *and* release the button twice. If you push too hard — or too quickly — you may slide the mouse arrow off of its destination before the last click release has a chance to register.

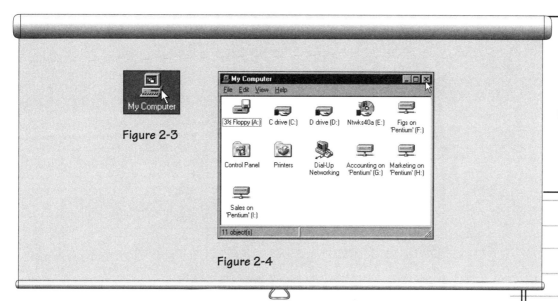

Figure 2-3

Figure 2-4

Figure 2-3: Double-click on the My Computer icon to see the folders and disk drives stored inside.

Figure 2-4: Click on the little X in any window's upper-right corner to close it down and get it off the screen.

Dragging and dropping

A *drag and drop* is really a slow, slow click, when you think about it. Basically, it's a slick trick for moving something across the screen, and it works like this:

Point the mouse's arrow at the object you want to move — a window or box on-screen, for example — and then *hold down* the mouse button. Now, while holding down the mouse button, move the mouse across your desktop. When the arrow hovers over the place you'd like to drop the object, let go of the mouse button, and you *drop* the object there.

extra credit

Q/A session

Question: Hey, I'm left-handed. Can I switch my mouse buttons?

Answer: Sure. The Windows Control Panel lets you switch the mouse button to work on either the left or right side, whichever feels best.

I'll use the Solitaire game to teach dragging and dropping, for two reasons. First, Solitaire is a game, so working with it is fun. Second, loading Solitaire teaches you how to load any program by using the Start button's menus, which is another task you need to know in Windows NT. Follow these steps:

1 Click on the Start button.

By now, you probably know that the Start button lives in the bottom-left corner of your screen. A menu pops up, as shown in Figure 2-5.

Figure 2-5: Click on the Start button, and a menu pops up.

Figure 2-6: Click on the word Programs, and another menu pops up.

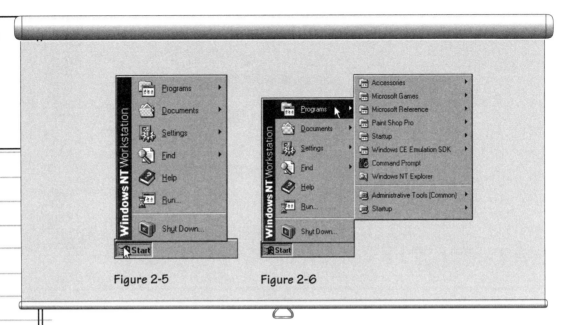

Figure 2-5   Figure 2-6

2 **Click on the word Programs.**

Yet another menu pops out, as shown in Figure 2-6.

3 **Click on the word Accessories.**

Yep — it's yet another menu, as shown in Figure 2-7.

4 **Click on the word Games.**

Yawn. *Another* menu pops out, as shown in Figure 2-8.

extra credit

Q/A session

Question: Is there some way for me to make scrolling through long documents a little easier?

Answer: Microsoft recently released an *IntelliMouse* that features a strange wheel along its top. Spinning the wheel back and forth with your finger affects your program in different ways. You can make portions of the screen larger or smaller, for example, or you can change font sizes in Microsoft Word. The Microsoft AutoMap Streets Plus program lets you spin the wheel to "zoom in or out" of the map, quickly changing the view from an entire county to individual streets. The catch? The IntelliMouse only works if a program specifically supports it, and so far, very few programs have rolled onto the IntelliMouse bandwagon. If it's not working with your favorite program, that program probably doesn't support the IntelliMouse.

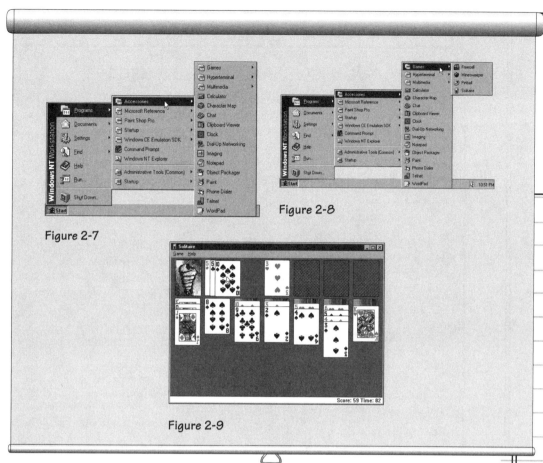

Figure 2-7

Figure 2-8

Figure 2-9

Figure 2-7: Click on the word Accessories, and another menu pops up.

Figure 2-8: Click on the word Games, and yet another menu pops up.

Figure 2-9: Windows comes with Solitaire, a great way to learn mouse mechanics.

Notes:

heads up

What? No listing for Games on your menu? That means that the person who installed Windows NT on your computer didn't install any games. Ask the person next to you where they got their copy; perhaps there's a secret access network. Or, ask the office network person to install Solitaire on your computer so that you can practice your point-and-click skills.

5 Click on the word Solitaire.

Shown in Figure 2-9, Solitaire is an officially endorsed method of learning how to use Windows. In fact, many people around the office never stop using this valuable tool.

6 Practice dragging and dropping cards with a game of Solitaire.

If you don't know how to play Solitaire, just point at a card, hold down the mouse button, and move the mouse across the desk. See how the card moves across the screen? Let go of the mouse button, and you drop the card. If you drop it in a spot approved by Hoyle, the card stays put; otherwise, Solitaire whisks the card back to its stack and you have to try dragging another card.

Notes:

☑ **Progress Check**

If you can do the following, you've mastered this lesson:

❑ Aim the mouse pointer.

❑ Click the mouse pointer on a button.

❑ Double-click the mouse pointer.

❑ Drag and drop an item on your desktop.

❑ Load a game of Solitaire and begin to play (you don't have to win).

extra credit

A first-time Solitaire user

Most people have a copy of Hoyle's around, so I'll stick with the mouse mechanics. Basically, you drag the face-up cards around from stack to stack, trying to sort them into the right order on-screen. For example, in Figure 2-9, the mouse pointer is dragging the nine of diamonds off of one stack and dropping it onto the ten of spades.

If you drag a card off of a stack, click on the face-down card that's left in its place on-screen; doing so flips the card over. If you drag the last remaining card off of a stack, then you can drag a king over and drop it on the blank stack.

One more basic rule exists: After you drop an ace onto any of the four card areas in the upper-right corner, you can start dropping other, similarly suited cards on top. (In numerical order, of course. And you can drop big chunks of cards, too.)

To start the game, look at the cards that Solitaire's stub-stogied dealer dumps on-screen. Can you immediately drag any aces to the piles along the top? Can you drop any cards from the seven bottom stacks onto those freshly dropped aces? Can you drag and drop any of the cards around on the seven stacks? The more

cards you're able to expose, the better you'll be able to plan your strategy.

Tip: If you have a card that can be dragged and dropped to the piles along the top, just double-click on the card. Windows moves the card to the pile automatically.

If you can't make any moves with what's currently showing, click on the deck of cards sitting in the upper-left corner to begin turning them over. Can you play that first exposed card anywhere? If so, go for it. If not, keep clicking on that stack of cards, turning them over until you find one that you can play.

When the deck's completely turned over, double-click the spot where the deck used to rest and it flips over. And over. And over.

Finally, if Solitaire still seems too complicated, give its Help system a whirl: Click on the word Help along its top edge. When the menu drops down, click on Help Topics. When the Help Topics window appears, click on the words How to play Solitaire. (A little icon with a question mark sits next to those words.) You'll find more information about the Windows Help system in Unit 18.

Although Unit 3 is packed with this stuff, Table 2-1 provides a preview of the kinds of things that Windows NT lets you drag and drop.

Table 2-1	Things That Windows NT Conveniently Lets You Drag and Drop
Accomplish This	*By Doing This*
Change a window's on-screen size	Dragging its corners or borders around on-screen
Move an entire window across the screen	Dragging the window's top-most edge, which usually contains the program's name
Change settings	Sliding levers back and forth

Accomplish This	By Doing This
Create organized batches of push buttons	Dragging and dropping *shortcut* icons to ease program launching on your desktop
"Scroll" your on-screen view of something contained in a window	Dragging the little "elevator" up or down the shaft on the window's right side and dropping it onto a new location
Customize your desktop	Dragging icons into new or different groups
Copy files from place to place	Dragging the file's names and dropping them in different locations in the My Computer folder or Explorer program
Move just about any item that's not nailed down	Pointing at the item, dragging it to a new place, and letting go of the mouse button

Using the Keyboard

Lesson 2-2

The keyboard's a little more familiar than a mouse to most new Windows users, but it's often just as awkward — especially because computers come with some sneaky extra keys that everyone's supposed to learn. And of course, those strange new keys are harder to reach than Q and Z. Plus, the keys are never in the same place on a friend's keyboard, either.

This lesson covers the four main types of sneaky keys that you'll find yourself using with Windows NT: function keys, arrow keys, the Alt key, and the Ctrl key.

Using a function key

Perched like spectators along a keyboard's top edge, function keys let you boss Windows NT around quickly and easily. Shown in Figure 2-10, for example, the function keys often appear listed next to the particular menu items they stand for. Pressing the function key works just like clicking the mouse on the menu item, and it's often a quick shortcut.

One function key almost always summons the Windows built-in Help program no matter what you happen to be doing. Here's how it works:

1 **Load Windows NT, and click anywhere on its background.**

Don't click on any programs, just aim for the background. (In fact, you may have to move some of the programs out of the way in order to see the background.) Although you won't see anything happen on the surface, that background click turns Windows' attention to its *desktop*, the platter that everything rests on.

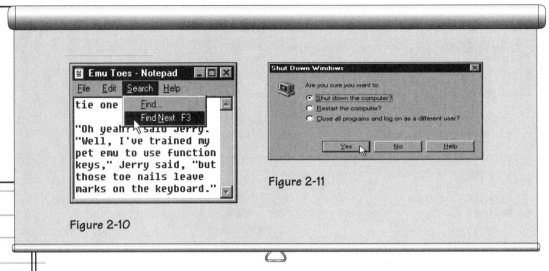

Figure 2-10: Some menus list their function key shortcuts; pressing F3 tells Notepad to perform the Find Next command.

Figure 2-11: Click on the No button if you don't want to exit Windows.

Figure 2-11

Figure 2-10

press the F1 key near the top-left corner of the keyboard, and Windows NT usually offers information that's helpful to the current situation

pressing Alt+F4 shuts down a window, just like double-clicking in the window's upper-left corner

2 Press F1.

The Help program pops up, ready to dish out information about the currently running window. In this case, the Help system explains basic Windows NT information, complete with tips and tricks, troubleshooting, and a short instructional tour.

The Windows Help system is covered completely in Unit 16; the desktop gets its due in Unit 4.

Whenever you see something in Windows NT, or in this book, like Ctrl+F1 or Alt+Backspace, that means that you press those two keys simultaneously. You don't have to be lightning fast; just press the first key listed, press the second key, and then let go of both of them.

Using the Alt and Ctrl keys

The Alt and Ctrl keys don't do anything by themselves. No, they almost always need another key as a buddy to make things happen on-screen. For example, here's how to close Windows NT — or any window, for that matter — without double-clicking on anything. (It's a handy trick to know if your mouse ever dies on you, heaven forbid.)

1 Click on your Windows NT desktop.

Don't click on any programs, just click on the desktop that all your programs run on.

2 Press F4 while holding down the Alt key.

Known as Alt+F4, this simultaneous combination of keys tells the currently running program to close itself down. Because shutting down the desktop also shuts down Windows NT, ever-cautious Windows NT sends you the message shown in Figure 2-11.

3 Click on the No button.

Doing so brings you back to Windows NT, but now you've got some function key know-how under your belt.

extra credit

Undeleting accidental deletions

Just erased a key paragraph with your word processor? Then hold down Alt and press the Backspace key. If you press Alt+Backspace before typing anything else, Windows NT may be able to spit your accidental deletion back onto the screen. (Some Windows NT programs may make you press Ctrl+Z to do the same thing.)

Notes:

press Alt+Backspace to undo deletion

Using the Esc (Escape) key

Although it sounds like a lifesaver from a bad computing situation, the Esc key is a pretty weak hero. But pressing Esc is worth a shot if nothing else is going right and things look weird.

For example, if you click on something and a menu shoots out, how do you make the menu pop back down without fuss? By pressing the Esc key, as shown in the following steps:

1 Click on the Start button.

A menu pops up, listing bunches of choices that you'll hear about in Unit 4.

2 Press the Esc key, usually found in the upper-left corner of most keyboards.

The menu goes away.

on the test

The Esc key doesn't do much by itself, but it's often a good first bet for clearing the screen of a popped-up menu.

Sometimes you may find it necessary to press Escape a couple times in succession to make sure that your system responds properly. This is rare, but keep it in mind.

Using the keyboard's arrow keys

No big surprises here. Pushing the keyboard's arrow keys simultaneously pushes your computer's cursor across the screen. In fact, the keyboard's arrow keys are often called *cursor keys*. The big thing to remember is that your *cursor* differs from your mouse *pointer*, and here's why.

When you move your *mouse,* you're moving your pointer. Doing so helps you choose among different options on-screen or move items to different on-screen locations. The mouse's little arrow can point just about anywhere on the monitor, and when you click on different spots, you're telling Windows NT where you want to work.

When you push your keyboard's *arrow keys,* you're only moving your cursor on-screen. The cursor stays stuck in the single window or program that you're currently working with; no big travels here. The following example shows a little of the difference between the two:

☑ **Progress Check**

If you can do the following, you've mastered this lesson:

❑ Use function keys as shortcuts.

❑ Uses the Alt, Ctrl, and Esc keys.

❑ Use a keyboard's arrow keys.

use mouse pointer
for switching
between programs
or moving cursor to
new location inside
programs

use arrow keys for
more subtle cursor
movements within
programs

1 Click on the Start button.

As always, a menu shoots up.

2 Press the keyboard's up arrow key.

See how the word Sh<u>u</u>t Down is now highlighted? Pushing the arrow lets you control the Start button's menu with the arrow keys instead of the mouse.

3 Press the up arrow again.

The word <u>R</u>un is highlighted now.

4 Press the up arrow until it highlights the word <u>P</u>rograms.

5 Press the right arrow key.

A menu pops out listing the available programs. Notice how pressing the arrow keys lets you explore — but not leave — the Start menu.

6 Click on the desktop's My Computer icon in the upper-left corner of your desktop, and watch the Start menu disappear.

See how the mouse's arrow lets you leave the confines of the Start menu and head to the desktop area instead? Although the keyboard cursor and mouse arrow both perform similar functions, the mouse arrow has much more get-up-and-go.

The mouse pointer and the arrow-key cursor are two separate things on-screen, but they often look and act alike. Here's a big clue, though: If it blinks, it's probably an arrow-key cursor, because a mouse pointer never blinks.

Unit 2 Quiz

For each question, circle the letter of the correct answer or answers. Remember, each question may have more than one right answer, so don't be afraid to chew that pencil stub a little.

1. **Windows NT programs use only the left mouse button.**

   A. True

   B. False

2. **Double-clicking a mouse is an easy task.**

   A. True, because it's simply like knocking twice on a door.

   B. False, because everything's so darn small.

   C. False, because you're sunk if you accidentally jostle the mouse pointer off the target while clicking.

   D. Performance depends on mood.

Notes:

3. **Windows lets you adjust your mouse's double-click speed to match your finger speed.**

   A. Impossible.

   B. You speak the truth.

4. **To make Windows shift its attention to another place on-screen, do the following:**

   A. Move the mouse until the little on-screen arrow points at that spot.

   B. Move the mouse until the little on-screen arrow points at that spot, and then click the left mouse button.

   C. Move the mouse until the little on-screen arrow points at that spot, and then click the right mouse button.

   D. Push the keyboard's little arrow keys.

5. **You use the Esc key for the following tasks:**

   A. Fixing any computer mistakes you've made.

   B. Avoiding bad situations.

   C. Leaving work early.

   D. Making pop-up menus go back down.

6. **The expression "Press Ctrl+Esc" means the following:**

   A. Everybody should escape other people's control.

   B. You should press the Ctrl key, release it, and then press the Esc key.

   C. You should press the Esc key, followed by the Ctrl key.

   D. You should press the Esc key *while holding down* the Ctrl key.

Unit 2 Exercise

1. Click on the Start button.

2. Choose Programs from the Start menu.

3. Choose Accessories from the Programs menu.

4. Click on Notepad from the Accessories menu.

5. While pointing at the words Untitled - Notepad in the Notepad window's top edge, drag and drop the window a quarter of an inch in any direction.

6. Click on the word File located near Notepad's upper-left corner.

7. Press the Esc key to make the File menu disappear.

8. Press Alt+F4 to close down Notepad.

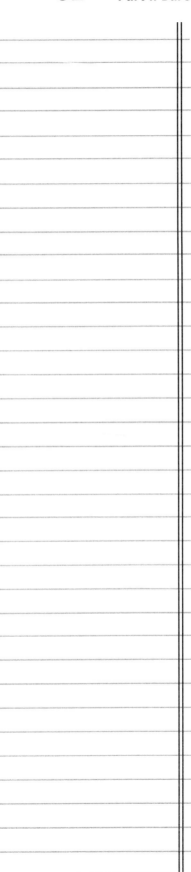

Understanding Windows and Menus

Objectives for This Unit

✓ Understanding window basics

✓ Finding and moving windows around on-screen

✓ Changing a window's size

✓ Minimizing and closing windows

✓ Choosing options from menus and buttons

✓ Filling out forms in Windows NT

Prerequisites

▶ Turning on your computer and loading Windows (Lessons 1-1 and 1-2)

▶ Pointing and clicking the mouse (Lesson 2-1)

▶ Double-clicking the mouse (Lesson 2-1)

▶ Dragging and dropping with the mouse (Lesson 2-1)

▶ Using the keyboard (Lesson 2-2)

In the old days, people worked on a plain-old desktop, grabbing and sliding around pieces of paper until it was time to go home. The newfangled software known as Windows NT creates a new type of desktop on your computer monitor. Instead of making you work with pieces of paper, however, Windows NT makes you work with *windows* — boxes of information that light up your computerized desktop.

Embedded along the edges of these windows are little buttons and menus for controlling the work inside. (Yeah, all this stuff sounds weird at first, but you'll get used to it.)

In fact, you *have* to get used to it; this window/button/menu concept appears in every Windows program.

You have to get used to a few other oddities as well. For starters, your computerized desktop is probably just a little over one square foot in size, meaning that the windows constantly overlap each other. Adding to the clumsiness, the windows don't let you reach over and grab them. Instead, you manipulate them with the computer's mouse and keyboard, which can be as awkward as grabbing logs with fireplace tongs.

This unit teaches you how to open and close the windows and programs on your new, computerized desktop. You'll learn how to move the unwanted windows out of the way and bring the desired ones to the forefront. You'll learn the locations of a window's most sensitive spots so that you'll know where to point and click. Finally, Unit 3 teaches you some shortcuts for scurrying past one of the most frequent and least entertaining Windows NT activities: filling out on-screen forms. Yaaaaawwwwnnnn.

Lesson 3-1	# Maximizing and Minimizing Windows

When installed in a house, windows come with two basic options: open or shut. Anything else requires a contractor, a fancy decorator, or a big rock.

Microsoft Windows NT jazzes things up in a few other ways. Its programs can run inside little windows on-screen, as you saw in Unit 1. Or a program can fill the entire screen for easier access. If other windows get in the way, you have yet another option: You can shrink currently unused windows into tiny icons that rest along the bottom of the screen.

By combining these skills, you can simultaneously juggle several programs on the desktop without dropping them all.

Opening and closing a window

Whenever you want Windows NT to do something, you load a *program:* a bunch of computerized instructions that tell the computer to get off its duff and do something. Some programs balance checkbooks, for example; others process words or communicate with other computers.

To make a program appear on-screen, double-click on the program's *icon,* located on the Start menu. Windows NT finds the program's instructions and loads them into your computer's memory, and the program appears on-screen, ready for action. (Don't worry if this sounds confusing at first; the Start menu gets complete coverage in Unit 4.)

Opening a window works like this:

1 Click on the Start button.

Unit 1 teaches this step; the Start button appears along the bottom-left corner of your screen whenever you turn on your computer and start Windows. Start button not visible? Press Ctrl+Esc to bring the Start menu to life.

2 Click on <u>P</u>rograms from the Start menu.

A list of programs shoots out from the side of the word Programs.

3 **Click on Windows Explorer in the Programs menu.**

When you click on an item on the Start menu, that item comes to life, either revealing another menu or loading itself and appearing as a program on your screen. In this case, the Windows Explorer program pops onto the screen in its own window. (Explorer, a complicated-looking little beast, lets you move files around on your computer, but you don't have to worry about using it until Unit 5.)

4 **Close Windows Explorer.**

As you learned in Lesson 2-1, close any program by clicking on the little X in the window's upper-right corner. Doing so always makes Windows NT shut down the program, whether the program is taking up the whole screen or living inside a window.

Or if a program happens to be a little icon at the bottom of the screen, click on the icon once with the right mouse button and choose Close from the menu that pops out of its head.

Some programs take up the entire screen when they're loaded; others automatically jump into a window, and still others load themselves as little icons along the bottom of the screen. The rest of this lesson teaches you how to toggle a program among all three varieties.

A window's borders enable programs to overlap on-screen without their contents getting mixed up. The borders also let you change the window's size and shape, a simple task described in the next lesson.

After you load some programs, you can move their windows around on-screen until they're easy to see and work with. The lessons later in this unit teach you all the ways to move windows, but be sure to check out the unit's last lesson; it teaches you some quick window-positioning tricks that everybody else spent three months learning through trial and error.

You can load Windows NT programs a few other ways, but the Start button (covered in Unit 4) is by far the easiest and most common way.

Making a window fill the screen (Maximizing)

Running programs in little on-screen windows often makes your work easier. You can glance back and forth between windows, grabbing information from one program and "pasting" it into another.

But sometimes you want a window to fill the entire screen. When writing a letter, for example, you don't want the sentences running off the edges.

To satisfy people who want their programs running at maximum size, Windows lets you *maximize* its windows. For example, here's how to maximize the Windows Explorer window:

Notes:

Figure 3-1: Double-click on the bar along the Windows Explorer window's top edge to maximize the window and make it completely fill the screen.

Figure 3-2: A click on the restore button in the upper-right corner shrinks a full-sized program back into a window.

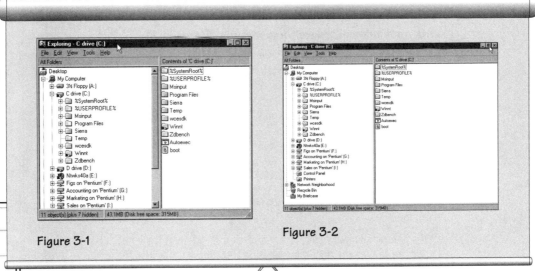

Figure 3-1   Figure 3-2

Notes:

1 **Click on the Start button and load Windows Explorer.**

You learned how to do this in the preceding lesson.

2 **Double-click on the bar along Explorer's top.**

In Figure 3-1, see that bar along the top that starts with the word Exploring? A double-click on that bar toggles the window's size between two positions, making it either fill the entire screen or fit inside a window.

Also in Figure 3-1, see the three little icons in the window's top-right corner? Clicking on the middle icon — the one with the square inside it — maximizes a window as well.

If double-clicking on your window's *title bar* — that little bar along the window's top edge — shrinks the window into a *smaller* window, then the window was maximized to begin with. (Why? Because double-clicking on the title bar toggles the program between full-screen to window-sized.)

on the test

The little bar along a window's top that lists a program's name is called the *title bar*.

on the test

You can tell that a window's been maximized because much of its window paraphernalia disappears; the borders drop off and the corners vanish.

Changing a full-screen program back into a window

If a program's been maximized — the window is borderless and filling the screen — you can push it back into a window with a single click, as described in the steps that follow.

1 **Maximize a window.**

Follow the instructions in the preceding section; they give you a maximized window to practice on.

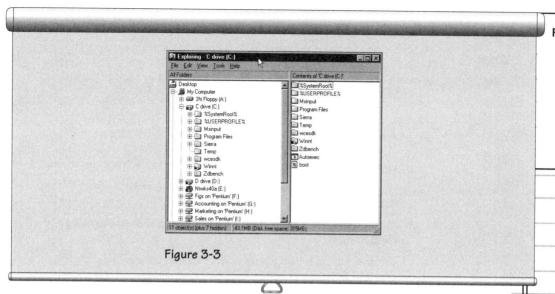

Figure 3-3

2 **Click on the icon containing the two little squares, located near the window's upper-right corner.**

Shown in Figure 3-2, the icon with the two little squares lets you toggle the window between filling the screen and living inside a window. The little button with the two squares is called a *restore button,* by the way. (More trivia: When the restore button lives in a window that fills the screen, the two little squares turn into one big square.)

Tip: You can also turn a full-screen program back into a window by double-clicking on the title bar along the top of the window. Because the title bar is bigger and easier to reach than the restore button, it's often the quickest way to toggle programs from big screen-fillers into more manageable window sizes.

Sometimes a window can be big — so big, in fact, that it fills the screen, just like the full-screen program did. That confuses things, because double-clicking on the title bar doesn't appear to do anything: Simply too little of a difference exists between that huge window and a full-screen program! Look carefully, however, at the screen-filling Windows Explorer window in Figure 3-3; you'll still be able to see the windows' borders around its edge as well as two little overlapping squares in one of the icons on its upper-right side. So to change the program's size, you can drag and drop the borders, a trick that Lesson 3-2 teaches.

Turning a window into an icon (Minimizing)

Even if you can afford enough memory to have bunches of programs running simultaneously on your computer, you still have a problem: Your computerized desktop is simply too small for spreading everything out. Sooner or later, you're going to have to move some of those windows out of the way.

Luckily, Windows offers a way to keep programs loaded in your computer's memory — and ready for quick action — yet away from view.

double-click on
title bar to toggle
between window-
size and full
screen

Notes:

Windows simply hides the program in its memory and then puts a little push button called an *icon* on a strip that runs across the bottom of your screen. Click on that little icon, and the hidden program comes back to the screen almost instantly.

If your screen's getting crowded, here's how to turn a currently running program into an icon along that strip at the bottom of your screen:

1 Load Windows Explorer from the Start button's Programs menu.

You learned how to do so earlier in this lesson in the section "Opening and closing a window."

2 Click on the little box containing the line in the window's upper-right corner.

That third icon over from the top right — the one containing the tiny line — is known as the *minimize* button. Click on it, and the window immediately shrinks into a little icon and awaits further duty along the screen's bottom.

You'll find yourself toggling programs between icons and windows throughout the day. Sometimes you'll want a program in a big window for easy access; other times you'll want the same program minimized as an icon for later reference.

Minimized programs can still run in the background. For instance, telecommunications gurus can be *downloading* a file from the Internet while the telecommunications program sits as an icon at the bottom of the screen.

If you minimize one of your programs — turning it into an icon along the screen's bottom — and then load that program from the Start menu, that program comes to the screen. But it is a *second copy* of the program! The first version of your program is still waiting for you along the bottom of the screen.

heads up

Watch out for accidentally running second copies of Windows NT programs simultaneously. The second copy usually just causes confusion and takes up memory.

Tip: Don't know whether or not your program is currently running? Press Alt+Tab to make Windows NT display a list of all your currently running programs. Keep pressing Tab until your program's icon is highlighted and its name appears; then let go of the Alt key. The program rises to the surface.

on the test

An icon living along the bottom of the screen stands for a program that's already loaded. The icons on the Start menu are push-buttons that launch a program — even a second copy of a program that's already running.

press Alt + Tab to display currently running programs

Q/A session

Question: What's the difference between a program's icon on the Start menu, a program's shortcut on the desktop, and that same program's icon at the bottom of the screen?

Answer: Because all three stand for the same program — Windows Explorer, for example — the program's little icon *looks* the same whether it's lying along the screen's bottom or resting on the Start menu, or living on the desktop. However, the icons do two completely different things.

If a program's icon currently lives along the bottom of the screen, the program has already been loaded into the computer's memory. Clicking on its icon merely brings the program back to a visible location on your desktop.

Clicking on that program's icon from the Start menu, by contrast, makes Windows NT pull that program off your computer's hard disk, load it into your computer's memory, and place it on-screen.

Shortcut icons on the desktop are just like the ones you find on your start menu. Just double-click them to load the program.

To sum it up: Shortcut icons on the desktop and the icons on the Start menu stand for the program *stored* on the hard drive; the icon at the screen's bottom stands for the program that's already been *loaded* into your computer's memory.

The verdict? If your program's icon rests along the screen's bottom, then that program is already loaded and ready for action. Don't load it again by clicking on its icon on the Start menu.

Turning an icon back into a window

Programs that squat inside the bar along the bottom of your screen are still loaded in your computer's memory for quick reference, yet they're stashed away from that cramped, computerized desktop.

When it's time to bring a program back to life — to bring Windows Explorer back to the forefront for moving files around, for example — follow these instructions:

1 Find the Explorer icon on your desktop.

Although the icon is probably lined up inside the taskbar — that strip of icons that runs along the screen's bottom — it may be hard to spot, especially if the taskbar is hidden from view. If you can't spot the icon, try pointing the mouse at the bottom of the screen (or its outside edges); sometimes that brings the taskbar into view. If other windows still cover the taskbar, try pressing Ctrl+Esc. (On the rare occasion that you still can't find the taskbar or icon, you may need to jump ahead to the taskbar section in Unit 5.)

2 Click on the Explorer program's button.

The button immediately turns back into a program, and Windows Explorer jumps back onto the screen.

If you can't find the program even after you double-click on its icon, head for Lesson 3-3 for tricks on tracking down wanton Windows NT programs.

❑ Progress Check

If you can do the following, you've mastered this lesson:

❑ Open and close a window.

❑ Make a window fill the screen (maximize it).

❑ Turn a full-screen program into a window.

❑ Turn a running program into an icon (minimize it).

❑ Turn an icon back into a running program.

Lesson 3-2	Carefully Adjusting a Windows Size

Notes:

The preceding lesson showed you how to shovel windows around on-screen with a heavy hand, making them appear and disappear, for example. You learned how to make them fill the screen or turn them into tiny push-button-sized icons at the bottom of the screen.

But how can you handle windows with a more delicate touch, moving them around the desktop until they're just the right size? This lesson teaches you how to move windows without breaking them.

Dragging a window's edges

If your window's not the right size, then change it. Luckily, you can do so with the "drag and drop" trick that you learned in Lesson 2-1: Just point at the windows' edge, hold down your mouse button, slide the mouse until the window is the desired size, and then let go of the mouse button. Here's how to change a window's size, step-by-step:

1 **Double-click on the My Computer icon.**

The My Computer program, found in the upper-left corner of your screen, leaps into view, listing all your computer's disk drives. (My Computer is covered in Unit 4, by the way.) Make sure that My Computer appears in a window and doesn't fill the entire screen.

Can't tell whether it's in a window or not? As you learned in Lesson 3-1, windows have visible borders that disappear when the window runs at full-screen size. (Lesson 3-1 also shows you how to toggle between window and full-screen size.)

2 **Point at the window's border.**

Hit Lesson 2-1 for mouse maneuvering instructions. When you point at the window's edge, the mouse pointer turns into a two-headed arrow, pointing in the direction in which you can drag the window's border, as shown in the margin.

3 **Hold down the left mouse button.**

4 **Slide the mouse to maneuver the border.**

As you slide the mouse inward, the border moves inward as well. Slide the mouse back and forth until the border is sitting where you want it.

5 **Let go of the mouse button when the border is positioned correctly.**

When you release the mouse button, the window's border snaps to its new position and stays put.

By dragging and dropping your windows' borders, you can change their sizes until they're all easy to see and work with on-screen. Borders slide in two directions: inward and outward.

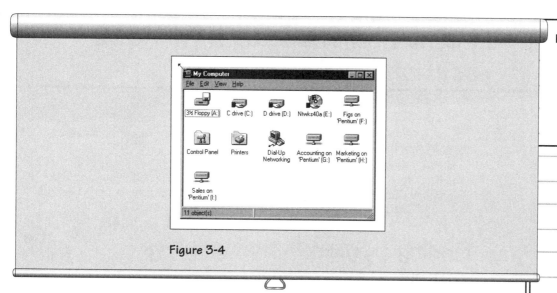

Figure 3-4

Figure 3-4: Pointing at a window's corner makes the mouse pointer grow two arrows, each showing a direction in which you can move the corner.

heads up

Started to move a border and then changed your mind? Press Esc before letting go of the mouse button, and Windows immediately puts the border back where it was, ignoring your faux pas.

Dragging and dropping a window's corners

There's nothing much new to learn here (unless you skipped the section immediately before this one).

You drag a window's *corners* in the exact same way you drag a window's borders; just point at the window's corner instead of its edge. Many people prefer to drag and drop corners because of the method's built-in speed; it lets you drag two borders simultaneously.

1 Double-click on the My Computer icon.

Or if you left the My Computer program running from the preceding example, move ahead to Step 2.

2 Point at the window's corner.

If you look really closely, as shown in Figure 3-4, you see that the mouse pointer grows two heads, each one pointing diagonally.

3 Hold down the mouse button.

4 Slide the mouse to reposition the corner's borders.

5 Let go of the mouse button when the corner is positioned correctly.

The window shrinks or expands to fill the newly placed borders. Quick and easy.

☑ **Progress Check**

If you can do the following, you've mastered this lesson:

❑ Change a window's shape and position by dragging its edges.

❑ Change a window's shape and position by dragging its corners.

Lesson 3-3

Finding and Changing a Window's Location On-Screen

Notes:

After you start running more than one Windows NT program on your desktop, you face a big problem: trying to keep track of all those programs on a desktop that's the size of your computer monitor.

The preceding lessons showed you how to change the window's shape; this lesson shows you how to find lost windows and move them around on-screen until they're easy to work with.

Finding a program that's hiding somewhere on-screen

As soon as you start loading more than one program, windows start covering each other up. Following are ways to find a lost window, ranging in order from least to most effort. (True to form, Windows NT provides about as many ways to *find* windows as to lose them.)

For this lesson, repeat the following steps until you locate every program currently running on your desktop. (Doing so won't take nearly as long as it sounds — maybe a minute or two.) If you don't have any programs running, load a few from the Start menu's Games or Accessories area, as described in Lesson 2-1, so that you have something to work with.

1 **If you spot any part of a window on your desktop, click on any portion of it.**

Windows NT turns its attention to that window, immediately bringing it to the forefront even if it was buried beneath a pile of other windows. From there, you can change the newly emerged window's size, as Lesson 3-2 describes.

2 **If you spot the window's button listed along the bottom of the screen, click on the button.**

I'm talking about a button that's living in the taskbar along the edge of your screen, not an icon that's sitting on the Start menu or living on your desk-top. Clicking on that button kicks the program back into visibility on the screen.

3 **Press Alt+Tab to bring up a list of all your currently running programs.**

The Alt+Tab window, shown in Figure 3-5, lists all the programs that Windows NT currently has loaded in its memory, ready to serve you. Do you spot your program on the list? Then move to Step 4 and retrieve it. (If your program isn't listed, then it's not currently running. You'll have to load the program from its place on the Start button, described more fully in Unit 4.)

4 **Find and click on your program's icon in the Alt+Tab window.**

Spot the name or icon of your missing program? Keep pressing Tab until you spot its name, and then let go of the Alt key — the program jumps to the top of the pile of windows on your desktop. From there, you can rearrange the windows by using the tricks that you learned earlier in this unit.

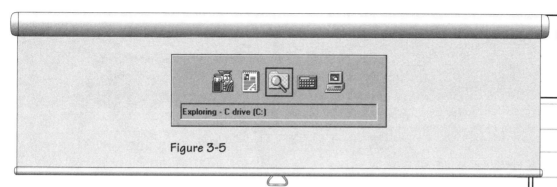

Figure 3-5

Figure 3-5: Pressing Alt+Tab lists all your currently running Windows NT programs.

Moving a window around on the desktop

Most people like to have more than one item on their "real-life" desktop: a paper-clip holder as well as a fast-food sandwich, for example. When something's in the wrong place, you simply pick it up and move it out of the way.

Moving windows around on the Windows NT "virtual" desktop is almost as simple, after you learn the following steps:

1 Find the window's title bar.

As explained in the preceding lesson, that's the top edge of the border where the program's name lives.

2 Point at the title bar and move the mouse while holding down the mouse button.

Yep, you're simply *dragging and dropping* the window's border. Let go of the border, and you move the window to its new location. Watch closely as you move the mouse, and you see a faint outline of the window's border.

on the test

By watching a window's outline move as you drag and drop its title bar, you can tell where you're repositioning the window.

Tiling and cascading windows on the desktop

Windows NT offers two quick ways to organize windows on your desktop. Both of them involve the taskbar, and these steps teach you how they work:

1 Bring up the taskbar.

The taskbar normally rests along the bottom of your screen, where it displays icons for your currently open programs. If it's not there, you can sometimes summon the taskbar by pressing Ctrl+Esc. Still not there? Try pointing at the bottom edge or sides of your screen. Sometimes the taskbar is configured to hide itself along an edge; if you can spot just a portion of it, try dragging it into view with your mouse. When the taskbar appears, it looks like the taskbar shown in Figure 3-6.

Ctrl+Esc displays taskbar

Figure 3-6: The taskbar lists your currently running programs.

Figure 3-7: Click on the taskbar's Cascade button, and Windows NT deals all your open windows across the screen like playing cards.

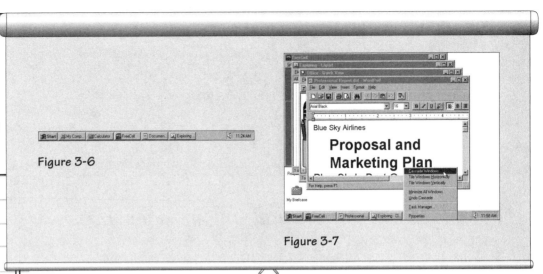

Figure 3-6

Figure 3-7

☑ Progress Check

If you can do the following, you've mastered this lesson:

❑ Find your Desktop's currently running windows and programs.

❑ Move windows around on the desktop.

❑ Tile and cascade windows across the desktop.

2 **Click on a blank area of the taskbar (usually near the clock) with your right mouse button, and choose Cascade from the menu that appears.**

Windows NT deals all the currently open windows across your desktop like playing cards, looking somewhat like Figure 3-7.

3 **Click on the taskbar with your right mouse button again.**

4 **Click on the taskbar's Tile Horizontally option.**

This time, Windows NT tiles the windows across the screen, giving each one equal space. They'll probably be a pretty awkward size, like the example in Figure 3-8. But hey, at least they're all out in front of you.

The taskbar's Tile and Cascade options work well for finding all your currently running programs and putting them on-screen in front of you. These commands work only on open *windows*, however; they don't affect programs that are minimized as icons along the bottom of the screen.

Lesson 3-4

Using a Window's Menus and Controls

The first few lessons in this unit show you how to move a window around the screen until you position it within easy reach. After the window is sitting comfortably in front of you, you boss it around through *menus*: little buttons, sliding levers, and check boxes that control a program's behavior.

By pointing and clicking on a window's various menus, you can handle just about any program's predicament.

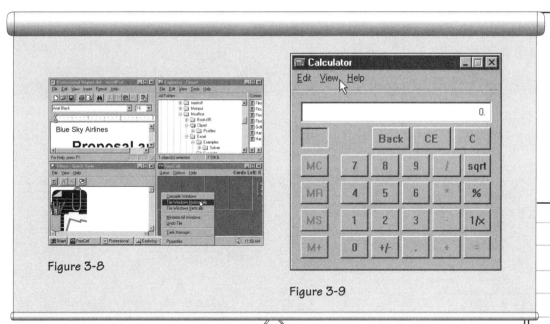

Figure 3-8

Figure 3-9

Figure 3-8: Click on either of the taskbar's Tile buttons, and Windows NT tiles all your open windows across the screen.

Figure 3-9: Click on the word Edit, View, or Help to see more options that have to do with those subjects.

Notes:

Choosing something from a drop-down menu

The most common menus live along a window's top, just beneath its title bar. In Figure 3-9, for example, notice that the words Edit, View, and Help appear beneath the Calculator program's title bar. The next few steps show you why they're there.

1 Load the Calculator program.

Load Calculator the same way you loaded Solitaire in Unit 2: Click on the Start button, and then choose Programs from the pop-up menu. Choose Accessories from the top of the Program's menu, and then click on Calculator from the Accessories menu. (Unit 4 covers loading programs in much more detail.)

2 Click on View on Calculator's menu bar.

A drop-down menu tumbles from the word View, as shown in Figure 3-10. The drop-down menu lists the two different ways in which you can view the Calculator program.

3 Click on the word Scientific.

The Calculator immediately turns into a scientific calculator, as shown in Figure 3-11.

4 Click on View and choose Standard.

The Calculator goes back to its normal mode, known as *standard*.

Most of the menus you encounter in Windows NT drop down from keywords along the program's top. Click on a keyword to see more options for that particular subject.

Figure 3-10: Click on the word View to see the different ways in which you can view the Calculator program's keypad.

Figure 3-11: Clicking on the Scientific option converts the calculator to scientific mode.

Notes:

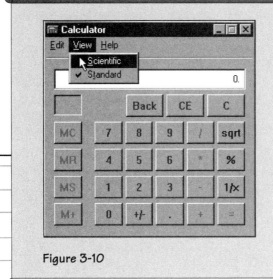

Figure 3-10

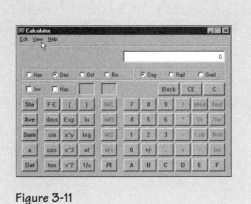

Figure 3-11

Sometimes choosing an option from a drop-down menu brings a box to the screen that's chock-full of more options. I cover those startling situations in Lesson 3-5.

Choosing something by clicking on a button

This task is one of the easiest: Windows NT puts two or more buttons on-screen and asks you to choose the one you want. The solution? Just click on the button you're after. Here's an example:

1 Click on the Start button.

Press Ctrl+Esc if you can't find the Start button.

2 Choose Sh<u>u</u>t Down from the menu that appears.

Worried, Windows NT sends a box to the screen, asking whether you're sure that you want to close it down.

3 Click on the <u>N</u>o button.

When you click on a button, Windows NT carries out the action written on the button's label. In this case, clicking on the No button tells Windows NT that no, you didn't *really* want to shut it down.

on the test

Holding down the Alt key and pressing the underlined letter in a menu does the same thing as clicking on the word containing the underlined letter.

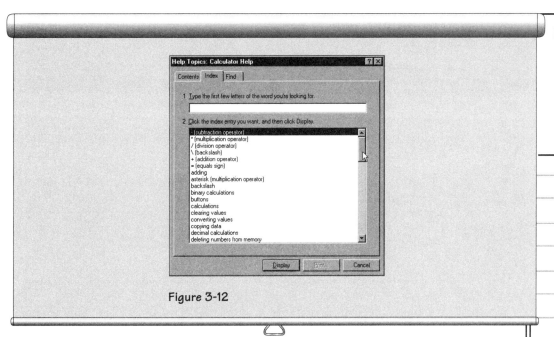

Figure 3-12

Figure 3-12: By dragging and dropping the little box (inside the scroll bar along the right side of the Help menu) to new positions, you can view different areas inside the window.

Sliding and dragging a box

Remember the drag and drop concept that you learned earlier? Windows NT brings it up again in its menus. By sliding certain objects around inside a window with the mouse, you can control various parts of a program.

For example, here's how to *scroll* up and down a list of topics in the Windows NT Help program:

1 Load the Calculator and press F1.

Load the Calculator from the Start menu, just as you did earlier in this unit. Then press F1, the function key near your keyboard's upper-left corner. Calculator's Help program rises to the forefront.

2 Click on Help from Calculator's top menu, and choose Help Topics from the menu that drops down.

3 Click on the tab marked Index along the Help program's top edge.

A window appears on-screen, as shown in Figure 3-12. Note the strange-looking edge along the window's right side.

4 Find the window's scroll bar and scroll box.

As shown in Figure 3-12, the *scroll bar* is that thick border along the window's right side; the *scroll box* is the box that lives inside the border.

5 Drag and drop the box about an inch down the bar.

Moving the box up or down the shaft is like moving an elevator to change floors. In this case, dragging and dropping the box changes your view of the window: Your new view is about an inch farther down.

☑ Progress Check

If you can do the following, you've mastered this lesson:

❑ Choose something from a drop-down menu.

❑ Click on a button.

❑ Drag and drop a box along a scroll bar.

When a program contains more information than it can pack into an on-screen window, the program puts scroll bars along the window's right side. By moving the scroll box up or down inside the bar, you can see different parts of the information.

Tip: To quickly scroll down through one screenful of information, click in the scroll bar *below* the scroll box. To quickly scroll upward one screen, click *above* the scroll box.

Sometimes Windows NT lets you adjust its settings by sliding a bar back and forth inside a box. Unit 16, for example, shows you how to change your mouse's double-click speed. (By sliding a little box along a bar, you can change how Windows NT tells the difference between a double-click and two single clicks.)

extra credit

Q/A session

Question: Why are some letters underlined in words like View and Standard?

Answer: Those underlined letters, which appear throughout Windows NT menus and forms, are for people who prefer using their keyboard to using their mouse.

Instead of clicking on the word, these people hold down their Alt key and press the underlined letter. To choose View, for example, they press Alt+V. Doing so makes Windows NT reveal the drop-down menu for View, just as if the person had clicked on View with the mouse.

Lesson 3-5   Filling Out Forms (Dialog Boxes)

In most people's offices, the administrative staff fills out the forms. If you're using Windows NT, however, you have to fill out a lot of forms yourself. Because Windows NT can't understand your voice, it requires you to fill out forms whenever you want it to do something relatively complicated.

Want to highlight a word in a letter? Fill out a form to choose between bold and italics. (And don't forget type size.) Try to change the options during a game of Solitaire, and you're hit with a form: Timed game? Single draw? Triple draw? Standard, Vegas, or no scoring?

You can't escape them, but the mouse makes the process of filling out forms faster than you may think. (You'll find a few keyboard shortcuts sprinkled in the lesson as well.) Forms come in several different parts, each discussed in the following sections.

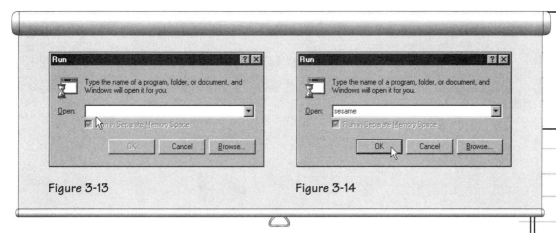

Figure 3-13: A text box lets you type text or numbers.

Figure 3-14: Type letters and numbers in text boxes for Windows NT to process.

Figure 3-13   Figure 3-14

Notes:

Filling in words and numbers

This type of form is probably the most familiar — it's the old fill-in-the-blank stuff that you learned in grade school. Whenever Windows NT needs some words or numbers, it usually tosses a box in your face and asks you to type the text.

Microsoft's Official Labelers refer to these types of forms as *text boxes,* and they work like this:

1 **Click on the Start button.**

2 **Click on Run from the Start menu.**

A box like the one shown in Figure 3-13 appears.

3 **Type the word sesame, as in Figure 3-14.**

4 **Click on the Cancel button.**

Normally, you click on the OK button after filling out a text box; doing so tells Windows NT to carry out its action by using the word or numbers that you typed in the box. But this is just an example, so click on Cancel. (The Open Sesame command rarely works in Windows NT, anyway.)

on the test

A text box can accept text, numbers, symbols, or blank spaces.

Choosing an item with a check box

Most people order more than one thing from a menu: an appetizer, a main course, and dessert, for example. When Windows NT offers you more than one choice on a menu, it often presents a check box. Here's how to change your game options in Solitaire by using a check box:

1 **Open the Solitaire program.**

You'll probably know how to load Solitaire by the end of Unit 3. (Hint: Start by clicking on the Start button and then move from Programs to Accessories to Games.)

2 **Click on Game.**

Notes:

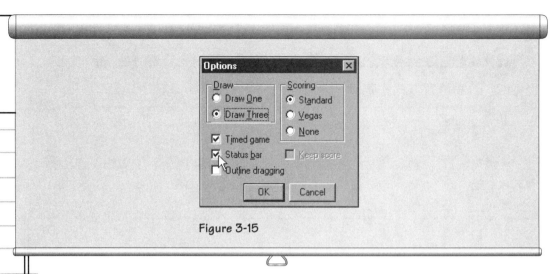

Figure 3-15

3 Click on Options.

A box with lots of options appears, as shown in Figure 3-15.

4 Click in the three boxes next to Timed game, Status bar, and Outline dragging.

As soon as you click in the box, you toggle its on or off position. If a check mark appears in the box, the option is activated. If no check mark is present, the option is turned off.

5 Press Esc.

Because you're here to learn about window mechanics, you're not supposed to be playing cards. Pressing Esc tells Windows NT to forget any changes you've made to the form and put the form away from harm.

Down the line, if you want to save changes that you make to a form, click on OK instead.

Tip: Keep the Timed game option turned on, or the little sun on the back of one of the decks of cards won't stick his tongue out every 60 seconds. (You won't see the flying bats, the energized robot, or the sneaky card dealer, either.)

Choosing an item from a list box

Lesson 3-4 showed you how some menus drop down from beneath words along the top of a window: Click on the word to see the menu, and then choose the option from the menu.

But Windows NT also packs menus into its forms. Known as a *list box,* it's a convenient way to stick a lot of options into a small box. The next few steps, for example, show you how to use a list box to see which programs you've loaded through the Start menu's Run box:

1 Click on the Start button.

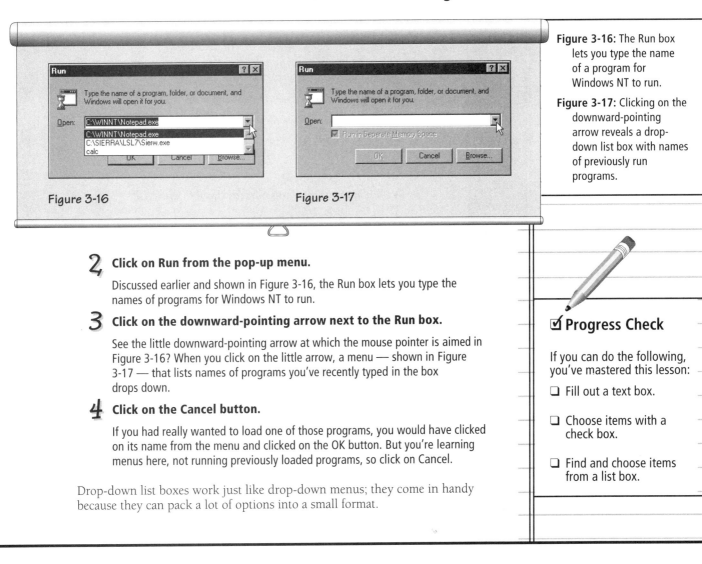

Figure 3-16: The Run box lets you type the name of a program for Windows NT to run.

Figure 3-17: Clicking on the downward-pointing arrow reveals a drop-down list box with names of previously run programs.

Figure 3-16

Figure 3-17

2 **Click on Run from the pop-up menu.**

Discussed earlier and shown in Figure 3-16, the Run box lets you type the names of programs for Windows NT to run.

3 **Click on the downward-pointing arrow next to the Run box.**

See the little downward-pointing arrow at which the mouse pointer is aimed in Figure 3-16? When you click on the little arrow, a menu — shown in Figure 3-17 — that lists names of programs you've recently typed in the box drops down.

4 **Click on the Cancel button.**

If you had really wanted to load one of those programs, you would have clicked on its name from the menu and clicked on the OK button. But you're learning menus here, not running previously loaded programs, so click on Cancel.

Drop-down list boxes work just like drop-down menus; they come in handy because they can pack a lot of options into a small format.

☑ Progress Check

If you can do the following, you've mastered this lesson:

❑ Fill out a text box.

❑ Choose items with a check box.

❑ Find and choose items from a list box.

Unit 3 Quiz

Circle the letter of the correct answer or answers to each of the following questions. Some questions have more than one correct answer, so don't be too hasty.

1. **The little bar along a window's top that lists a program's name is called:**

   A. Little top bar.

   B. Name bar.

   C. Title bar.

   D. Joe's Bar.

Notes:

2. **Double-clicking on the bar along a window's top, where the program's name is printed, does the following:**

   A. Makes a window-sized program completely fill the screen.

   B. Makes a full-screen program shrink itself into a window.

   C. Closes a window.

   D. Minimizes a program into an icon.

3. **When a window is maximized, the following things happen:**

   A. The window fills the screen.

   B. The window's borders disappear.

   C. The window's corner borders disappear.

   D. The window stops working.

4. **You can type text, numbers, symbols, or spaces in a text box.**

   A. True

   B. False

5. **What happens when you click on an icon in the Start menu, even when that icon is currently listed in the taskbar along the bottom of the screen?**

   A. The icon explodes.

   B. Windows loads a second copy of the program that's currently running.

   C. Windows ignores your action and safely brings your currently running program to the forefront.

6. **How can you tell where you're moving a window as you drag and drop it on-screen?**

   A. The entire window moves with the mouse.

   B. A faint border of the window moves with the mouse.

7. **If you don't have a mouse, can you still use the Windows NT menus?**

   A. Not at all.

   B. Yes, by holding down the Alt key and pressing the underlined letter within a menu's options.

Unit 3 Exercise

1. Click on the Start button and move to the Program menu's Accessories area.
2. Load the Calculator program.
3. Close Calculator.
4. Load Solitaire.
5. Maximize the Solitaire window.
6. Turn the Solitaire program back into a window.
7. Minimize Solitaire.
8. Turn Solitaire back into a window.
9. Make the Solitaire window a few inches smaller.
10. Move the Solitaire window a few inches over on your desktop.
11. Tile your windows across the screen with the taskbar.
12. Cascade your windows across the screen with the taskbar.
13. Choose a new deck of cards in Solitaire.

Part I Review

Unit 1 Summary

▶ **The mouse:** Windows NT lets you control your computer by pushing around a mouse that maneuvers a little arrow on your computer screen. By pointing the arrow at different on-screen locations and pushing buttons on the mouse, you can make Windows perform various tasks.

DOS, by contrast — an older method of controlling computers — makes you direct your computer by typing code words with your keyboard. (Chances are, you won't have to deal with DOS anymore.)

▶ **Logging On:** After you turn on the computer and press Ctrl+Alt+Del, the system asks you for your name and password. This is called *logging on to the system.*

▶ **Start button:** Whenever Windows NT is running on your screen, so is a program called the taskbar, which contains the Start button. To close down Windows, click on the Start button and choose Shut Down from the menu.

▶ **Closing a Windows program:** To close down a Windows program, click with the left mouse button on the little X in the window's upper-right corner.

▶ **Turning off your computer:** Some people leave their computers turned on all the time; others turn them off at the day's end. (Both methods have their advantages, so ask the person in charge of your office computers.) Everybody turns off the monitor after they finish working, though.

Unit 2 Summary

▶ **Clicking:** To *click* on something in Windows, move your mouse across the desktop until its arrow points to the on-screen object. Then press and release your left mouse button.

▶ **Right-clicking:** Clicking on something with your left mouse button usually makes Windows NT select it. Clicking on something with your right mouse button usually makes Windows NT bring up a menu or more information about that item.

▶ **Double-clicking:** A *double-click* works the same as a click with one exception: You press and release your left mouse button *twice in rapid succession.* (If you're not quick enough, Windows thinks that you're making two single clicks.)

▶ **Dragging and dropping:** To *drag and drop* something in Windows, point the mouse's arrow at the object you want to move — a window or box on-screen, for example. Then *hold down* the mouse button while sliding the mouse across your desktop. When the arrow hovers over the place you'd like to drop the object, let go of the mouse button, and you've "dropped" the object there.

▶ **IntelliMouse:** Microsoft's new IntelliMouse comes with a wheel positioned between its two buttons. Spinning the wheel brings more control to the program: You can quickly see more pages in Microsoft Word, for example. The IntelliMouse only works with programs that specially support it, however, like Microsoft Office 97 and a few others.

▶ **The function keys:** A keyboard's function keys — usually located along the keyboard's top or side edge — quickly perform actions when pressed. Pressing F1 usually brings up the Windows Help program, for example.

Part I Review

▶ **The Alt and Ctrl keys:** The Alt and Ctrl keys work in tandem with other keys. For example, pressing Alt and the Backspace keys simultaneously (known as Alt+Backspace) undoes your recent keystrokes.

▶ **The Esc key:** Pressing the Esc (Escape) key tells Windows to cancel what it's doing: put away an unneeded form, for example, or make a menu disappear.

▶ **The arrow keys:** The keyboard's arrow keys move your cursor around, letting you type words and numbers in various places within a form or program.

Unit 3 Summary

▶ **Loading a program:** To load a program, click on its icon or name from the Start menu.

▶ **Closing a program:** To close a program, click on the little icon in the program's upper-right corner. (The icon contains a big X.)

▶ **Making a program fill the screen:** To toggle a program into filling the whole screen, click on the middle-most little icon in the window's upper-right corner. (The icon contains a big square.)

▶ **Shrinking a full-screen program:** To toggle a full-screen program back into a window, click on the middle-most icon in the window's upper-right corner. (The icon contains two little overlapping squares.)

▶ **Minimizing a program to an icon on the taskbar:** To minimize a currently running program into an icon along the taskbar, click on the left-most little icon in the program's upper-right corner. (The icon contains a little line inside a square.)

▶ **Restoring a minimized program:** Double-clicking on an icon on the taskbar turns it back into a program.

▶ **Adjusting a window's size:** By dragging and dropping a window's borders and edges, you can carefully adjust the window's size.

▶ **Finding a program's window:** To find misplaced windows, press Alt+Tab. Doing so summons a window listing all your currently running programs.

▶ **Moving a window:** Dragging and dropping a window by its title bar is the quickest way to move it across the screen.

▶ **The taskbar:** Click on the Windows taskbar with your right mouse button for a menu that lets you deal your open windows across the screen like cards or tile them across the screen like a shower floor.

▶ **Revealing more menu options:** Clicking on a word listed along a program's top edge usually reveals a drop-down menu with more options.

▶ **Choosing an item:** To choose an item from a menu, button, or checkbox, click on it.

▶ **Getting more information about an icon:** To find out more information about an icon, rest the mouse pointer over it or click on it with the right mouse button.

▶ **Using list boxes:** Windows NT and Windows software programs make frequent use of drop-down list boxes, which you click on and scroll down to reveal longer lists of options than would normally fit in a small form or dialog box.

Part I Test

The questions on this test cover all the material presented in Part I, Units 1 through 3.

True False

Each statement is either true or false.

T   F   1.   Windows always loads itself automatically when you turn on the computer.

T   F   2.   Windows always closes down automatically when you click on Shut Down from the Start menu.

T   F   3.   Computer monitors should never be turned off.

T   F   4.   You need a mouse to use Windows.

T   F   5.   An icon listed on the taskbar is the same as an icon listed on the Start menu.

T   F   6.   Open windows can't be moved to different positions on-screen.

T   F   7.   You can run only one program at a time.

T   F   8.   Windows NT uses both the left and right mouse buttons.

T   F   9.   The Windows taskbar serves as an executive's To Do List.

T   F   10.   All windows come with the same parts that work pretty much the same way.

T   F   11.   A list box only appears when you use the Run command from the Start menu.

T   F   12.   The Esc key is not used in Windows NT.

T   F   13.   The Alt and Ctrl keys can be used in combination with other keys to make Windows NT do things.

T   F   14.   Pressing F1 shuts down the computer.

Multiple Choice

For each of the following questions, circle the correct answer or answers. Remember, each question may have more than one right answer.

15. **Windows lets you use a mouse for the following tasks:**

   A.   Changing a window's size and location

   B.   Loading a program

   C.   Doing laboratory experiments

   D.   Telling Windows what to do

16. **The Windows Start menu performs the following function:**

   A.   Loads your programs

   B.   Mangles your programs

   C.   Hides your programs

   D.   Shuts down Windows

17. **Save your work at these times:**

   A.   Before exiting a program

   B.   Before exiting Windows

   C.   Whenever you finish writing a paragraph

   D.   Whenever you think about it

Part I Test

18. **Windows lets you drag and drop the following items:**

    A. Icons across the desktop

    B. On-screen windows

    C. The edges and bordervîof windows

    D. Cards in Solitaire

19. **What is a Windows dialog box?**

    A. A way for people to communicate on the Information Superhighway

    B. A fancy form for giving information to Windows programs

    C. Software that comes free with a mail-in card

    D. The psychologist program that's built into Windows NT

20. **A Windows menu comes with the following:**

    A. Fortune cookies

    B. Gum beneath the tables

    C. Choosable options for making a program do something

    D. Red wine stains

21. **The following steps can help find a lost or covered-up Windows program:**

    A. Press Alt+Tab and look for the program's name on the pop-up list.

    B. Look for the program's name on the taskbar along the bottom of the desktop.

    C. Click on any visible part of the window.

    D. Call the computer salesperson.

22. **If Solitaire's running under the Timed game option, the following animation appears on the deck:**

    A. The robot with the ticking clock

    B. The hand with the card popping out of its sleeve

    C. The bats with the flapping wings

    D. The beach with the floppy-tongued sun

Matching

For the questions in this section, match the lettered items to the corresponding numbered items.

23. **Match up the following keystrokes with the corresponding action:**

    A. F1   1. Bring up the Start menu to load programs.

    B. Ctrl+   2. Undo your last command.
       Esc

    C. Alt+   3. Make unwanted menus and
       Backspace   forms disappear.

    D. Esc   4. Bring up the Windows Help program.

    E. Alt+F4   5. Close down the currently active program.

Part I Test

24. **Match up the action on the bottom with the click location on the top.**

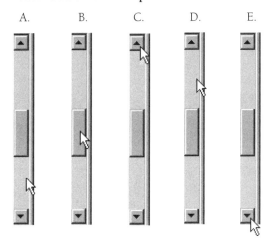

A.   B.   C.   D.   E.

1. Scroll the view down, one page at a time.

2. Scroll the view up, one page at a time.

3. Drag the view to a new place.

4. Move the view up, one line at a time.

5. Move the view down, one line at a time.

25. **Match up the following window parts with their function:**

A.   1. Double-click to close a window.

B.   2. Click to minimize a window.

C.   3. Click to maximize a window.

D.   4. Click to turn a maximized program back into a window.

E.   5. Drag in or out to change the window's size.

Part I Lab Assignment

This is the first of several lab assignments at the end of each part of this book. The lab assignments are designed to provide realistic ways to apply the information that you learned in the part's preceding units.

As opposed to the exercises at the end of each unit, the lab work is more open. That means that you're free to experiment a little bit. It also means that you'll have to figure out more of it for yourself.

In this first lab assignment, you'll start a Windows session, load programs, move windows around with the mouse and keyboard, and close down the session.

Step 1: Load Windows NT and find the Start button and Start menu

Turn on your computer and find the Start menu.

Step 2: Load programs

Load the Solitaire and Calculator programs.

Step 3: Arrange the programs

Arrange your open programs in the following ways:

1. Use the taskbar to tile and cascade the windows across the screen.
2. Use the program's minimize, maximize, and restore buttons to make the windows jump to new sizes.
3. Drag the windows' borders to change their sizes.
4. Drag the windows' title bars to change their locations.
5. Close all the windows.

Step 4: Close down Windows NT

Although you haven't done any work in this particular lab assignment, you'll find yourself creating things in other lab assignments throughout the book. So before shutting down Windows NT, be sure to save your work first.

You got off lucky this time. Part I just teaches Windows NT basics, so this lab assignment doesn't include anything specific. The following ones will make up for it, though.

Working with Your Desktop

Part II

In this part . . .

Windows NT completely computerizes your once-messy desktop. Your manila folders, an In basket, random scraps of paper, a computerized typewriter known as a "word-processor" — even a trendy recycling bin — now live on your computer screen.

In some ways, this new computerized version of a desktop is easier to use. Pencils no longer roll into the black void behind the desk. Desktop need dusting? A wipe of a shirt sleeve across the monitor quickly clears things up.

But in other ways, the Windows NT desktop is more complicated than the traditional mahogany version. Annoying menus pop up with every action. On particularly bad days, your folders will seemingly vanish. You'll often know what *you* want to do — the hard part is making *Windows NT* know what you want to do.

This part of the book teaches you how to move your desktop to your computer screen with a minimum of fuss. You'll learn how to start your work by choosing a program from the Start button — and if your favorite programs don't appear on the Start menu, you'll learn how to put them there.

You'll learn about the icons that sit on your desktop — My Computer, InBox, and Recycle Bin. Plus, you'll learn about the folders and files scattered throughout your computer's innards.

You won't be using all your Windows programs every day or even once a week. But you will find yourself using the information covered in this part of the book several times each day. Don't be afraid to jot lots of notes in the margins in these next several units.

Working with the Desktop, Start Menu, and Taskbar

Prerequisites

▶ Pointing and clicking the mouse (Lesson 2-1)

▶ Moving and sizing windows (Lessons 3-2 and 3-3)

▶ Filling out forms (Lesson 3-5)

Objectives for This Unit

✓ Finding and using the taskbar

✓ Loading programs from the Start menu

✓ Customizing the Start menu

✓ Finding lost programs and files with the Start menu

✓ Making shortcuts to programs and files on the desktop

✓ Using the Recycle Bin

✓ Using the InBox

Whenever Windows NT takes the screen, your computer's hard drive makes whirring noises, and lots of pretty icons jump onto the screen. But then all the action stops, and Windows NT simply sits there, a bureaucrat at heart.

See, Windows NT doesn't manage programs; it merely starts them — and that's if you know the right places to click the mouse. This unit teaches you how to fight back against this lazy nonsense. You'll learn how to find and push the icon that starts your program. Plus, you'll learn the ways in which the Start button organizes its icons on the Start menu. You'll also pick up some techniques for changing the way the Start menu loads programs.

If the Start menu doesn't list your favorite programs and files, you'd better grab a screwdriver. An Extra Credit assignment teaches you how to put an icon there yourself.

Finally, you'll learn about a few other ever-present icons and programs — the taskbar, Recycle Bin, InBox, and My Computer icons.

Figure 4-1: The taskbar normally rests along the bottom of your screen.

| Start | Microsoft Excel - sushi ken. | Microsoft Word - New... | 3:08 PM |

Figure 4-1

Lesson 4-1

Using the Taskbar

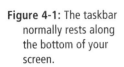

Because the taskbar is almost always on-screen, it's a handy base of operations. The taskbar lets you load programs, close programs, minimize programs while you work on other things and then re-display them again, change your computer's settings, and it can even tell you the time of day. This lesson shows you how to get the most out of the taskbar with minimal effort.

Finding the taskbar

The taskbar, shown in Figure 4-1, can be a handy Windows NT tool — if only finding the darn thing wasn't so hard sometimes.

Normally, the taskbar rests along the bottom of your screen. But if it isn't in plain sight, the following steps usually bring it out into the open:

1 Look for the taskbar along the bottom of the screen.

Most of the time, you'll see the taskbar resting there. It contains the Start button and an icon for each currently running program, as well as a few push-buttons for starting some other programs. Not there? Wait a second to see whether it pops up — it may be running in hidden mode. If nothing happens, move on to Step 2.

2 Look for a little gray border along the bottom of the screen.

Sometimes the taskbar has been dragged off the edge of the screen until it's barely visible. If you spot its edge, point at it with the mouse: The mouse arrow grows two heads, and you can drag and drop the taskbar until it's more visible.

3 Point the mouse at all four edges of the screen, pausing for a few seconds at each edge.

In its fervent desire to let users customize their desktops, Windows NT lets people run their taskbars on the bottom, top, left, or right edge of the screen.

By pointing the mouse at all four edges — or dragging and dropping the taskbar into view if necessary — you can start to make the taskbar do the useful things described in the rest of this lesson.

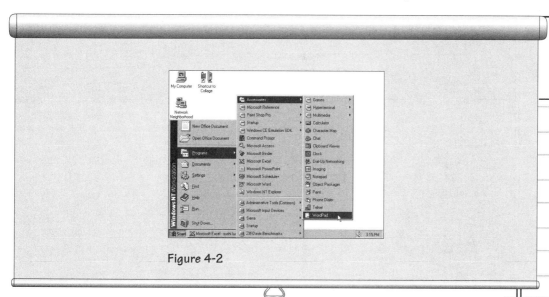

Figure 4-2: Click on a program's name or icon from the Start menu to load that program.

Figure 4-2

Loading a program with the taskbar's Start button

The Windows NT Start menu, found on the edge of the taskbar, would drive diners in a restaurant crazy. Instead of packing all the choices onto a single page, the Start menu constantly shoots additional menus out from its edges. If you're lucky, the menu-within-a-menu system works great, letting you steadily whittle down your choices until you find the right program. If you're not lucky, you're stuck rummaging through annoying menus that list every program but the one you want.

For example, the next steps show you how to load the WordPad word processing program — if everything works out the easy way:

1 **Click on the taskbar's Start button to make the Start menu appear.**

You learned how to find the taskbar in the preceding section.

2 **Click on the <u>P</u>rograms option.**

The Start menu's list of program categories appears.

3 **Click on the Accessories option.**

The Start menu lists the available Accessories programs.

4 **Click on WordPad in the Accessories menu (see Figure 4-2).**

The WordPad program comes to the screen.

5 **Close the WordPad program.**

Unit 3 shows you how to close a program — by clicking on the X in the program's upper-right corner.

So what's the hard part? Well, sometimes the icon you're after is nowhere in sight. That's because some rude programs don't put themselves on the Start menu when you first install them, and you have to find the programs yourself. (Fortunately, this is becoming quite rare.)

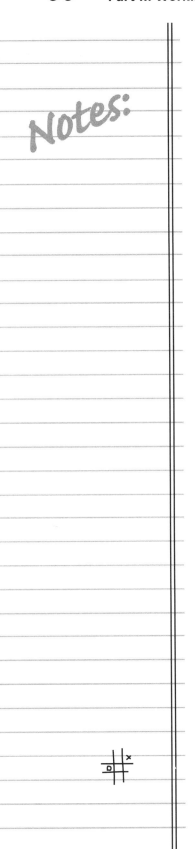

Luckily, the Start menu comes with a Find program that can sniff through your hard drive for lost programs and files. The Find command — and other ways to find and start programs — get coverage in the more extensive Start menu section found later in this unit. (You'll also learn how you can customize the Start menu, putting your favorite programs onto it with a quick drag and drop.)

on the test

The Start menu's Programs menu is merely a list of programs that you can load. By clicking on a program's name or icon in the menu, you start the program.

on the test

See the little black triangles on the right side of some of the Start menu items in Figure 4-2? Holding the mouse pointer over those items makes another, more detailed menu appear.

on the test

Most Windows programs add themselves to the Start menu's Programs menu when you first install them.

Using the taskbar to switch between loaded programs

Whenever Windows NT loads a program, a button for that program appears on the taskbar. Because programs often cover themselves up when running on your crowded computer-sized desktop, the taskbar is an easy way to pluck the program you want from the mix. These steps show you how to move among several programs on your desktop by clicking on their buttons on the taskbar:

1 **Click on the Start button and load the WordPad program.**

You learned how to do so in the preceding section. Notice how the WordPad program's button appears on the taskbar.

2 **Load the Calculator program.**

This program is on the same menu as the WordPad program. And when it's loaded, Calculator's button appears on the taskbar as well.

3 **Load the Notepad program.**

Its button appears, too, making the taskbar look like Figure 4-3.

4 **Click on the WordPad program's button on the taskbar.**

See how the taskbar immediately brings the WordPad program to the forefront?

5 **Click on the Calculator program's button on the taskbar.**

Windows brings Calculator to the top.

The taskbar not only lists all your currently running programs, but it also lets you switch between them.

Tip: To close a Windows program, click on its button on the taskbar with your right mouse button. When the menu appears, select Close. The taskbar shuts down the program, first asking whether you'd like to save any unsaved work.

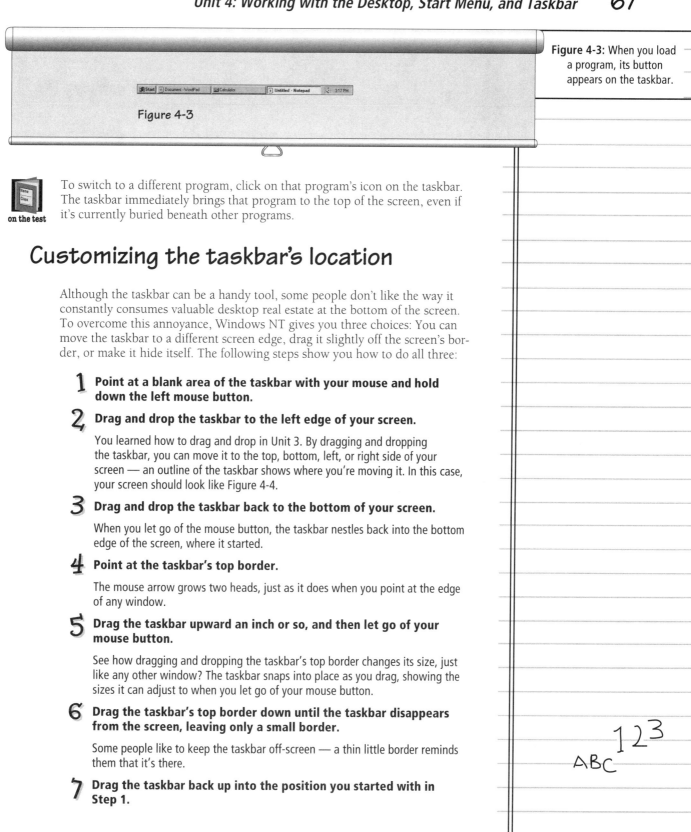

Figure 4-3

Figure 4-3: When you load a program, its button appears on the taskbar.

on the test

To switch to a different program, click on that program's icon on the taskbar. The taskbar immediately brings that program to the top of the screen, even if it's currently buried beneath other programs.

Customizing the taskbar's location

Although the taskbar can be a handy tool, some people don't like the way it constantly consumes valuable desktop real estate at the bottom of the screen. To overcome this annoyance, Windows NT gives you three choices: You can move the taskbar to a different screen edge, drag it slightly off the screen's border, or make it hide itself. The following steps show you how to do all three:

1 **Point at a blank area of the taskbar with your mouse and hold down the left mouse button.**

2 **Drag and drop the taskbar to the left edge of your screen.**

You learned how to drag and drop in Unit 3. By dragging and dropping the taskbar, you can move it to the top, bottom, left, or right side of your screen — an outline of the taskbar shows where you're moving it. In this case, your screen should look like Figure 4-4.

3 **Drag and drop the taskbar back to the bottom of your screen.**

When you let go of the mouse button, the taskbar nestles back into the bottom edge of the screen, where it started.

4 **Point at the taskbar's top border.**

The mouse arrow grows two heads, just as it does when you point at the edge of any window.

5 **Drag the taskbar upward an inch or so, and then let go of your mouse button.**

See how dragging and dropping the taskbar's top border changes its size, just like any other window? The taskbar snaps into place as you drag, showing the sizes it can adjust to when you let go of your mouse button.

6 **Drag the taskbar's top border down until the taskbar disappears from the screen, leaving only a small border.**

Some people like to keep the taskbar off-screen — a thin little border reminds them that it's there.

7 **Drag the taskbar back up into the position you started with in Step 1.**

ABC 123

Figure 4-4: You can move the taskbar to any edge of your screen by using the drag and drop technique.

Figure 4-5: The Taskbar Properties dialog box lets you change the taskbar's appearance and behavior.

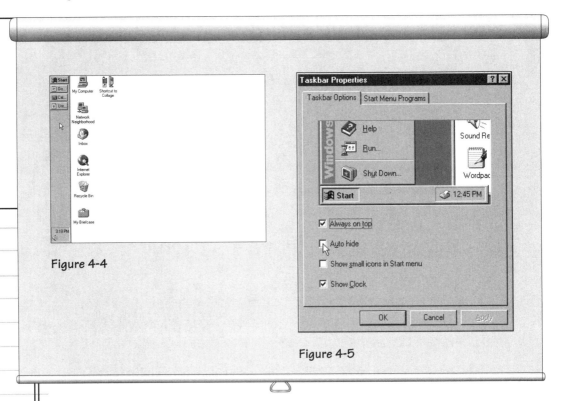

Figure 4-4

Figure 4-5

Notes:

8 **Click on a blank area of the taskbar with your right mouse button.**

Don't click on a button; click on a blank portion of the taskbar, and a menu appears.

9 **Choose Properties from the taskbar's menu.**

The Taskbar Properties dialog box appears, as shown in Figure 4-5.

10 **Click on the A̲uto hide option, and then click on the OK button.**

A check mark appears in the Auto hide box, meaning that you've selected that option. When you click on the OK button at the bottom of the menu, the menu disappears. And when the menu disappears, notice that the taskbar has hidden itself from the desktop as well.

11 **Position the mouse pointer over the bottom edge of the screen.**

The taskbar magically appears whenever you hover the mouse pointer at the edge of the screen containing the taskbar — and that's usually the bottom edge, unless you've moved the taskbar to a different part of your screen, as shown in Step 2.

12 **Repeat Steps 8 and 9, and then disable the A̲uto hide option.**

Tip: Running a lot of programs simultaneously? Then drag the taskbar's edge to make it a little wider. Doing so allows more room for all your buttons and makes it easier to spot the one you're after.

on the test

The taskbar can be on the top, bottom, right, or left edge of your screen.

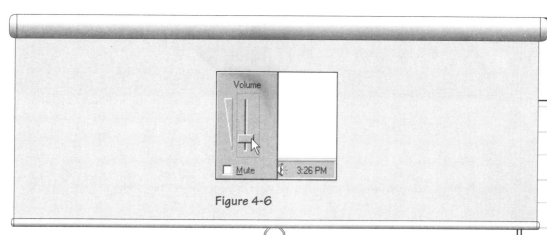

Figure 4-6

Figure 4-6: Slide the little bar up to increase the volume or down to decrease the volume.

Turning the volume up or down

This feature may be the best thing Windows NT has to offer: an easily accessible switch to turn your computer's sound up or down. (It can definitely reduce the nuisance factor in the office.) Here's how it works:

1 **Click on the taskbar's little speaker, located next to the clock.**

A strange-looking menu appears, as shown in Figure 4-6.

2 **With the mouse, drag and drop the little box up and down the shaft.**

When you drop the little box, Windows NT makes a little "ping" sound to show the current volume. Moving the little box up the shaft increases the sound; moving it down the shaft quiets things down.

click on Mute box on volume control to turn off sound temporarily

extra credit

What are the other options in the taskbar's Properties menu?

The Taskbar Properties dialog box, shown in Figure 4-5, offers several options, all explained here:

Always on top: A check mark in this box means that the taskbar is always on top of the screen, no matter how many windows are piled on top of it. If no check mark is present, the taskbar lets itself be buried beneath other open windows. (Pressing Ctrl+Esc always brings the taskbar into view, though.)

Auto hide: As explained earlier in this section, this option makes the taskbar hide itself from view until a mouse pointer rests on it. (Forgotten where you hid your taskbar? Try all four sides, and one will work.)

Show small icons in Start menu: A check mark in this box shrinks the size of the icons in the Start menu. That can be handy if your computer has a lot of programs and the Start menu is getting crowded.

Show Clock: The taskbar normally shows a small digital clock on the edge opposite the Start menu. If no check mark is in this box, you won't see the clock.

Start Menu Programs tab: Click on this tab for options pertaining to your Start menu. These options let you add or remove programs from the Start menu and clear the list of recently opened documents from the Start menu's Documents menu.

☑ **Progress Check**

If you can do the following, you've mastered this lesson:

❑ Load a program from the Start menu.

❑ Switch between running programs with the taskbar.

❑ Move the taskbar to a different part of the screen.

❑ Make the taskbar hide itself automatically.

❑ Use the taskbar to change the computer's volume.

Notes:

By sliding the shaft up or down — and listening to the little ping — you can find the right volume for your current setup.

Tip: Want to turn down that B.B. King CD in a hurry to catch that lunchtime phone call? Click on the Mute box on the Volume control to turn off the sound temporarily.

on the test

Don't forget that the taskbar can also cascade and tile windows across your screen. As described in Unit 3, just click on a blank area of the taskbar with your right mouse button and choose between the two options.

Tip: When you rest the mouse arrow over the clock on the taskbar, Windows NT displays the current day and date.

Lesson 4-2   Using the Start Menu

In its efforts to please, Microsoft tried to make using computers as easy as possible. So Microsoft wants you to click on the Start button to start working in Windows NT; a click of the button brings up the Start menu, which lists everything you might possibly want to do with your computer.

Or does it? What happens if the program you're after isn't listed on the menu? And what are all those other options supposed to do, anyway? This lesson teaches you how to make the Start menu start working for you instead of the other way around.

Finding lost programs and files with the Start menu

Computers are just as good at losing things as they are at creating them. So Windows NT comes with a great Find program that can snoop through all the parts of your computer, looking for lost files. The Find command on the Start menu lets you search for files in several different ways. First, you can simply search for a file based on its name.

Can't remember the name? Find can search for all the files you created yesterday or on any particular time and day.

Don't remember what you called the file or when you created it? Well, the ever-helpful Find program can even search for files containing specific words. By following the next few steps, you should be prepared to find even the most evasive files and programs:

1 **Choose Find from the Start menu, and then choose Files or Folders.**

The Find program appears, as shown in Figure 4-7.

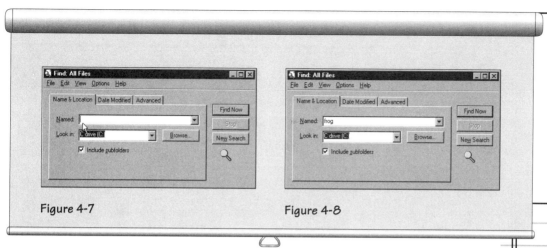

Figure 4-7

Figure 4-8

Figure 4-7: The Find program can seek out and retrieve lost files on your computer.

Figure 4-8: Type the name of a missing file — or a portion of the file's name — in the Named box, and Windows NT searches for it on your hard drive.

2 **Type** frog **in the Named box, as shown in Figure 4-8, and click on the Find Now button.**

Windows NT searches through your computer's hard drive and brings up a list of all the files with the word frog in their names. If you have more than one hard drive, Windows NT searches the C drive.

3 **When you spot your file on the list, double-click on it.**

Windows NT loads the program that created your file, loads the file into the program, and brings them both to the screen. Pretty slick, eh?

If you remember the date on which you created the file but not its name, don't click in the Named box like you did in Step 2. Instead, click on the Date Modified tab. From there, you can tell Windows NT to bring up a list of all files created within a certain number of days or created between certain dates. (Click on the Find Now button to make the Find program start the search.)

To make Windows NT search your computer for files containing certain words, click on the Advanced tab. Type the word or words you're looking for in the Containing Text box, and then click on the Find Now button.

Tip: Before using the Find program, look to see whether your missing file is in the Start menu's Documents list. If you've used the file recently, it's probably listed there, and a double-click on the file's name brings it back into action.

heads up

When using the Find program's Advanced search feature, be sure that you're searching for the exact sequence of words contained in the file. For example, if your missing file contains the phrase *squash and parsnips* and you tell Windows NT to search for a file containing *squash parsnips,* the Find program won't find your file because you left out the word *and.*

Tip: The Find program normally just searches the hard drive on which Windows NT resides. To make Windows NT search your entire computer — including your hard drives, your CD-ROM drive, and any disks currently in your floppy drives — click on the little arrow in the Find program's Look in box, and then choose My Computer from the list that drops down.

☑ Progress Check

If you can do the following, you've mastered this lesson:

❑ Load a program from the Programs menu.

❑ Load a recently used file from the Documents list.

❑ Find a file by using the Find program.

Notes:

extra credit

Quick, what do all those Start menu options stand for?

Most of the time, you use the Start menu for starting programs. But occasionally, you'll want to dip into some of the other menu's options. Although these areas are covered later in this unit and throughout the book, they're described here to cut down the confusion to a more manageable level.

Programs: As you learned earlier in this unit, clicking here lets you start Windows NT programs by clicking on their names from the menus.

Documents: This one's a real time-saver because it lists the last ten files you've worked on. So the next time you sit down at your computer, choose Documents and then click on the name of the file. Windows NT loads the program that created the file, grabs the file, and puts them both on-screen for immediate access.

Settings: This option lets you change your computer's settings. Choose Taskbar,

for example, to customize the taskbar, just as if you'd chosen the taskbar's Properties command, as described in Lesson 4-1. You can also change your printer's settings as well as access the Control Panel. The Control Panel lets you customize just about every aspect of your computer.

Find: This command gets its own section in this lesson. It lets you search through your computer to find misplaced files and programs.

Help: Choosing this option is the same as clicking on your desktop and pressing F1. It simply brings the Windows NT Help program to the screen, ready to answer your questions. (Unit 16 covers the Windows NT Help program more completely.)

Run: Type a program's name here and press Enter, and Windows runs the program. You'll find a few catches, though, and they're covered in Unit 7.

Lesson 4-3   Using the Desktop

Windows NT offers you plenty of ways to do the same thing. That flexibility often makes Windows NT easier to use, because it increases your chance of stumbling across the right way to do something. But it often complicates matters because you have so many things to remember.

The trick? Don't try to remember them all. Just pick out a method that works right for you, and stick with it. The next few sections show you some of the easier ways for working with the Windows NT desktop — the backdrop on the computer screen on which all your windows live. These lessons show you the basics; Unit 15 shows you how to use these tools to customize your desktop and make your work life a little easier.

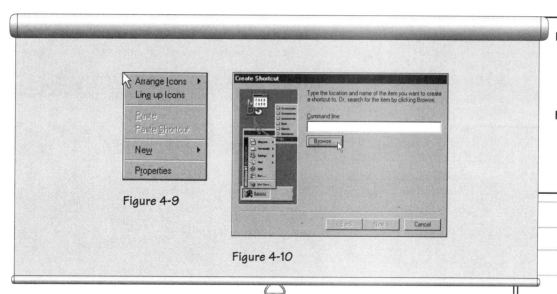

Figure 4-9

Figure 4-10

Figure 4-9: Click on a blank area of the desktop with the right mouse button to see a list of options.

Figure 4-10: Click on the Browse button to select a program to which the shortcut will lead.

Making shortcuts to programs and files on the desktop

Everybody likes a good shortcut; that's why Microsoft stuck so many of them into Windows NT. A shortcut is a quick and easy path to get somewhere fast. Because nobody likes wading through menus in order to load their favorite programs and files, Microsoft made it easy to install shortcuts to those places.

You can even create shortcuts to your favorite folders — areas in which Windows NT stores files. (You'll learn much more about folders in the next unit.)

If you find yourself using the Windows NT Calculator program a lot, for example, you can install a shortcut to the Calculator on your desktop so that it's easier to reach. Here's how:

1 Click on the desktop with your right mouse button.

A menu pops up, as shown in Figure 4-9.

2 Choose New from the menu.

Another menu juts out from the word New.

3 Choose Shortcut from the New menu.

The Create Shortcut dialog box appears, as shown in Figure 4-10.

4 Click on the Browse button, and then double-click on the little "Winnt" folder, as shown in Figure 4-11.

The Browse window subsequently shows you the programs living in the Winnt folder. To see more programs living in that particular folder, click on the little scroll bars — those elevator-mimicking buttons that you learned about in Unit 3.

5 Double-click on the little "system32" folder, as shown in Figure 4-12. (You might have to scroll across to get to it.)

The System32 folder is where a lot of Windows NT's most important programs and files are stashed away, including the Calculator.

Figure 4-11: A click on the Browse button leads to the "Winnt" folder.

Figure 4-12: Next, open the "system32" folder.

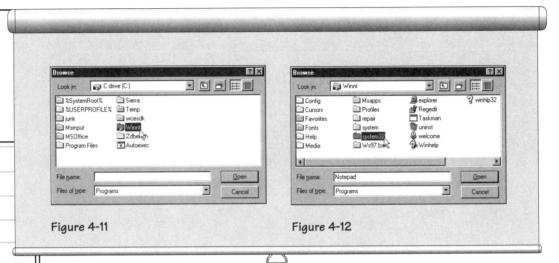

Figure 4-11

Figure 4-12

Notes:

6 **Double-click on the Calculator icon.**

The program is named Calc, and the icon is just to the left of the name, as shown in Figure 4-13.

Finally, Figure 4-14 shows the computer's "path" to the Calc program after you've done all this stuff.

7 **Click on the <u>N</u>ext button.**

Now, type in a name for the shortcut.

8 **Type** Calculator **in the name box, and then click on the Finish button.**

A shortcut to the Calculator program now appears on your desktop, as shown in Figure 4-15, where you can drag and drop it to any convenient location.

When sitting on the desktop, a shortcut looks just like the program it leads to, but there is a big difference. A shortcut is only a push-button that starts a program — it's not the program itself. So when you create or delete a shortcut, you don't affect the program at all. You're simply adding or removing a button that summons that program.

Here's something to think about as well: Remember how the Find command in the last section came up with a list of files matching certain criteria? Well, you can create shortcuts to those files, too. Just point at the file you want, and then drag and drop it onto the desktop. A shortcut to that file immediately appears on the desktop.

Tip: To quickly organize your desktop icons into neat, orderly rows, click on the desktop with the right mouse button and choose the Line up Icons command.

Adding folders to the desktop

The more shortcuts you add to the desktop, the harder spotting the one you want will be. To keep your shortcuts organized, Windows NT lets you create desktop folders. Then just drag and drop your shortcut icons into the folders. It works like this:

recognize
shortcuts by little
arrow in bottom-
left corner

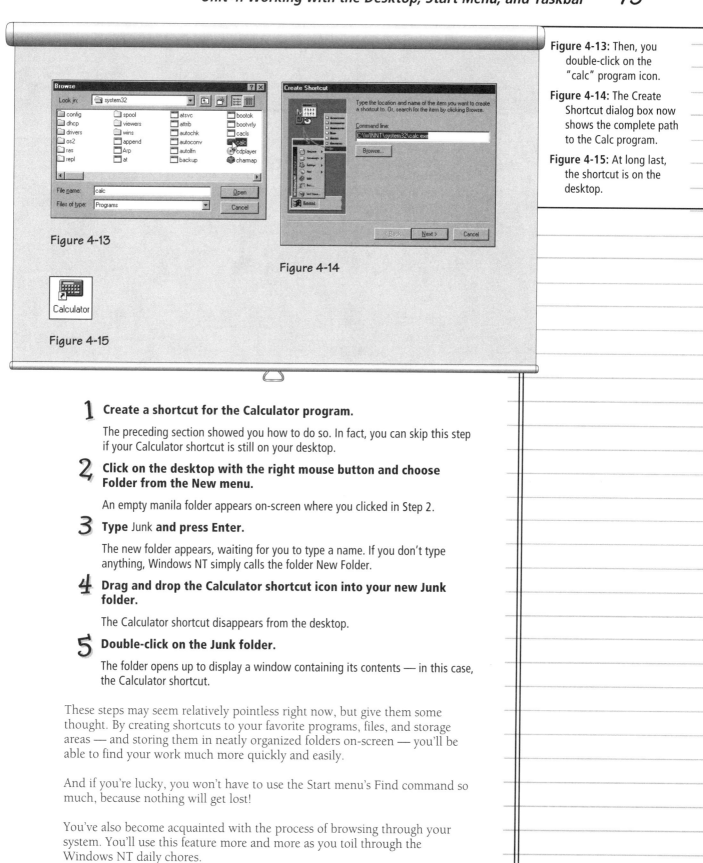

Figure 4-13

Figure 4-14

Figure 4-15

Figure 4-13: Then, you double-click on the "calc" program icon.

Figure 4-14: The Create Shortcut dialog box now shows the complete path to the Calc program.

Figure 4-15: At long last, the shortcut is on the desktop.

1 Create a shortcut for the Calculator program.

The preceding section showed you how to do so. In fact, you can skip this step if your Calculator shortcut is still on your desktop.

2 Click on the desktop with the right mouse button and choose Folder from the New menu.

An empty manila folder appears on-screen where you clicked in Step 2.

3 Type Junk **and press Enter.**

The new folder appears, waiting for you to type a name. If you don't type anything, Windows NT simply calls the folder New Folder.

4 Drag and drop the Calculator shortcut icon into your new Junk folder.

The Calculator shortcut disappears from the desktop.

5 Double-click on the Junk folder.

The folder opens up to display a window containing its contents — in this case, the Calculator shortcut.

These steps may seem relatively pointless right now, but give them some thought. By creating shortcuts to your favorite programs, files, and storage areas — and storing them in neatly organized folders on-screen — you'll be able to find your work much more quickly and easily.

And if you're lucky, you won't have to use the Start menu's Find command so much, because nothing will get lost!

You've also become acquainted with the process of browsing through your system. You'll use this feature more and more as you toil through the Windows NT daily chores.

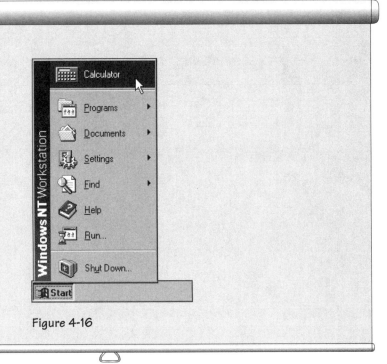

Figure 4-16

put shortcuts to folders, programs, or data files on Start menu by dragging and dropping them onto Start button

Unit 15 shows you how to organize your desktop in several different ways by using shortcuts and folders.

Tip: If you're unsure about what dragging and dropping a file or folder will do, drag and drop with the *right* mouse button. A menu appears, letting you choose whether to move, copy, or create a shortcut to that file or folder.

Customizing the Start menu

This one's pretty simple, actually. The Start menu contains a list of shortcuts that start programs. So to put new programs or files on the Start menu, simply drag and drop shortcuts for those programs and files onto the Start menu. It works like this:

1 Create a shortcut on your desktop for the Calculator program.

If you already have a shortcut for the Calculator program, you can skip this step.

2 Drag and drop the Calculator shortcut icon onto the Start button.

That's it. You've placed the Calculator on the Start menu, as shown in Figure 4-16.

Retrieving Deleted Files from the Recycle Bin

Lesson 4-4

Drop an old letter into a wastebasket, and you have until the next trash day to pick it out again. But computers aren't nearly as forgiving: One press of the Delete key can wipe out a year's worth of work, with no chance of retrieval.

Computer engineers finally listened to the wails of anguished users, and now Windows NT comes with a Recycle Bin. Shown in Figure 4-17, the Recycle Bin is an ingenious way to find deleted files. The following steps show you how to pluck an accidentally deleted file from the Recycle Bin:

1 **Create a shortcut to the Calculator program on your desktop.**

You learned how to do so in the first section of Lesson 4-3.

2 **Drag and drop the Calculator shortcut into the Recycle Bin.**

You can also click on the Calculator shortcut icon with your right mouse button and choose Delete from the pop-up menu. Or you can click on the icon with your left mouse button and press the Delete key. All three methods delete the shortcut from the desktop.

3 **Double-click on the Recycle Bin icon.**

The Recycle Bin window opens, listing all your most recently deleted files, as shown in Figure 4-18.

4 **Drag and drop the Calculator shortcut icon back onto the desktop.**

You can also undelete the file by clicking on its name with the right mouse button and choosing R̲estore.

When the Recycle Bin contains no deleted files, its icon contains no crumpled pieces of paper. After the Recycle Bin starts storing deleted files, however, little pieces of paper appear inside its wastepaper-basket icon.

Tip: Finding deleted files is sometimes easier if they're listed by the date on which they were deleted. To list them that way, choose Arrange Icons from the Recycle Bin window's View menu and select by Delete Date.

on the test

Deleting a shortcut deletes only the push-button that leads to a program, file, or folder; it doesn't delete the program, file, or folder itself.

Tip: Running out of space on the hard disk? Click on the Recycle Bin icon with your right mouse button and choose Empty Recycle Bin from the pop-up menu. The Recycle Bin lets go of all your old, deleted files, creating more space on the hard disk. (The Recycle Bin will continue to save files that you delete in the future; it just won't have room to save as many deleted files before letting them go for good.)

Notes:

Choose Arrange Icons from View menu and select by Delete Date to list files by date they were deleted

☑ **Progress Check**

If you can do the following, you've mastered this lesson:

❏ Delete a file.

❏ Retrieve a deleted file from the Recycle Bin.

Figure 4-17: The Recycle Bin.

Figure 4-18: To protect against accidents, the Recycle Bin stores recently deleted files in case you need to salvage them.

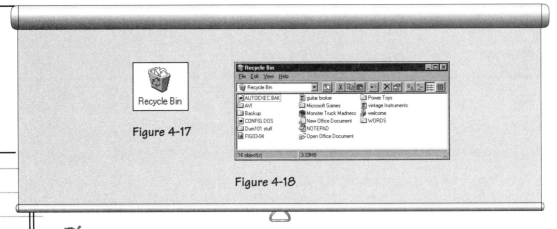

Figure 4-17

Figure 4-18

Notes:

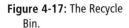

Why do they call it the Recycle Bin?

The name Recycle Bin is a misnomer; Windows NT doesn't really recycle your deleted stuff. It simply moves the deleted files to a secret folder on your hard drive called Recycled. When you open the Recycle Bin, Windows NT is really showing you the contents of the secret Recycled folder.

Pull a file out of the Recycle Bin, and Windows NT pulls the file out of the secret Recycled folder. Or click on the deleted file's name by using your right mouse button and choose Restore from the pop-up menu. The Restore command puts the file back where it lived before you deleted it.

Unfortunately, the Recycle Bin can't hold on to deleted files forever, or your hard drive will fill up. So Windows NT stakes out 10 percent of your hard drive and uses that space for its secret Recycled folder. For example, if you have a 500MB hard drive, Windows NT uses 50MB of that space to store your deleted files. When the Recycle Bin reaches that 50MB limit, Windows NT really starts to delete files. It simply deletes the oldest files in the bin.

Think of the Recycle Bin as a box for you to toss scrap paper into. You can reach into the box and retrieve mistakenly pitched items. But when the box is full, you need to delete things permanently to make room for the new stuff. Because the oldest stuff is in the bottom of the box, that stuff is thrown out first, leaving the freshest — and usually most important — stuff lying on top.

Windows NT handles all this stuff automatically, but you can fiddle with the Recycle Bin's options if you want. Just click on the Recycle Bin icon with your right mouse button and choose Properties from the pop-up menu.

extra credit

What's the Inbox?

Microsoft's Inbox uses *telecommunications* — a fancy word that describes the notoriously difficult world of connecting computers to phone lines and making them talk to each other. Before computers can use phones, however, they need modems — little gadgets that translate computer language into sound.

Windows NT's Inbox comes set up to use The Microsoft Network, and for good reason: Microsoft owns The Microsoft Network. Unfortunately, very few people use The Microsoft Network because, frankly, it pales in comparison to the competition.

Luckily, the Inbox is part of Microsoft Exchange, which lets your computer connect to other online services like CompuServe, America Online, and Prodigy, as well as to the Internet. Because Windows NT comes with files only for The Microsoft Network, you have to contact your online service and ask for an installation disk that lets it work with Microsoft Exchange.

After everything is set up correctly, Microsoft Exchange lets you send and receive e-mail automatically. It can even dial automatically, grab your messages, and hang up.

Unfortunately, the program is too complex to be covered in this book (although Unit 14 gives some basic information). The adventurous will find excellent information in Brian Livingston's *Windows NT SECRETS* (IDG Books Worldwide, Inc.).

Unit 4 Quiz

Circle the letter of the correct answer or answers to each of the following questions. (A few questions have more than one answer, just to keep things lively.)

1. **The Start menu's main job is the following:**

   A. Starting programs.

   B. Losing programs.

   C. Helping you find lost programs.

   D. Starting and closing Windows.

2. **How do you control the windows and folders on your desktop?**

   A. The same way you control other Windows programs and windows.

   B. With a mouse and keyboard.

   C. With the taskbar's Tile and Cascade options.

   D. With joysticks.

Notes:

3. Most Windows programs add themselves to the Start menu's Programs menu when you first install them.

    A. True

    B. False

4. Pointing the mouse arrow at a menu item containing a little black triangle makes even more menu items jump to the screen.

    A. True

    B. False

5. What are shortcuts for?

    A. To provide faster ways to run your programs.

    B. To force you to browse through your entire computer to search for a single file or program.

    C. To find better ways to your destinations, such as the local computer store.

6. Deleting a shortcut from the desktop does the following:

    A. Deletes the shortcut from your computer's hard drive.

    B. Deletes the shortcut and its program, folder, or file from your hard drive.

    C. Deletes the shortcut, its program, folder, or file, and all your other programs from your hard drive.

    D. Removes only the icon from your desktop.

7. Which of these methods deletes a file?

    A. Dragging and dropping the file into the Recycle Bin.

    B. Clicking on the file's name and pressing the Delete key.

    C. Clicking on the file's name with the right mouse button and selecting Delete.

8. You can't add or remove programs from the Start menu.

    A. True

    B. False

9. You can move the taskbar to any edge of your screen.

    A. True

    B. False

10. **To make a hidden taskbar appear, you press these keys simultaneously:**

    A. Alt+Esc

    B. Ctrl+Esc

    C. Alt+Tab

    D. Alt+Ctrl

Unit 4 Exercise

1. Create a new folder called Favorite Programs on your desktop.

2. Put copies of Solitaire (called SOL) and Calculator into the Favorite Programs folder.

3. Delete the folder.

4. Retrieve the shortcuts from the Recycle Bin.

5. Find all the files on your hard drive that contain the word distance, and then create shortcuts to them on your desktop. (*Hint:* Use the Start menu's Find command.)

6. Create a new folder on your desktop named Long, and drag and drop all your new distance file shortcuts into it.

7. Delete your Long folder and all the shortcuts that it contains.

Working with Files and Folders in My Computer and Windows NT Explorer

Prerequisites

▶ Opening a program (Lesson 4-2)

▶ Choosing an item from a menu (Lesson 3-4)

▶ Pointing and clicking with a mouse (Lesson 2-1)

▶ Opening, closing, and moving windows (Lessons 3-1, 3-2, and 3-3)

▶ Dragging and dropping with a mouse (Lesson 2-1)

Objectives for This Unit

✓ Understanding files, folders, disks, and drives

✓ Viewing files, folders, disks, and drives

✓ Understanding the My Computer program

✓ Understanding the Explorer program

✓ Creating folders

✓ Opening files and folders

✓ Copying and moving files and folders

✓ Copying floppy disks and folders

✓ Deleting files and folders

✓ Formatting a floppy disk

✓ Moving a file from one folder to another

✓ Using Explorer

on the CD   ▶ Joe's Lament

After you work with Windows NT for a while, your files will pile up, just like they do on any other desktop. In a good-faith effort to help you organize your work, Windows NT offers you a computerized file cabinet system for storing the important stuff. This stands as a metaphor on your computer for the daily work routines at the office.

Windows NT offers two completely different computerized file cabinets; one's called My Computer, and the other's called Windows NT Explorer. The intricacies of these two "file cabinets" can be a bit frustrating, and they are probably the most complicated parts of Windows NT. After you learn how to use the Windows NT Explorer and My Computer, you'll be able to find your work when you need it.

Lesson 5-1 — Understanding File Management

To create and store files, you need to understand four basic areas of computer life: *files, folders, disk drives,* and *disks* (both floppy disks and hard disks). Think of your computer as a big file cabinet with many drawers, and all this stuff becomes a little easier to understand.

Just as you need to organize a file cabinet, moving related items into clearly labeled folders, you need to organize your computer's files. And that's where the My Computer and Explorer programs come in: They let you create folders, label them, and move your files into them.

Both the My Computer and Explorer programs put buttons, windows, and folders across your screen so that you can access your computer's files, folders, disks, and drives — all described in this lesson. Figure 5-1 shows the My Computer program with its parts labeled; Figure 5-2 shows the Explorer program. Both programs display your computer's innards, but they do so in very different ways. You'll want to refer to both figures as you read the next few sections.

This particular lesson doesn't have much hands-on stuff, but don't worry — after you get the information in this lesson, the *real* hands-on stuff will come up quickly.

Understanding files

In keeping with the file cabinet metaphor, a *file* is a batch of computerized information stored in a file cabinet's file folder.

Files can contain many different things: memos, love letters, company presentations, programs that people in your company create, or spreadsheets containing the financial numbers for your department — *anything* that you can store on a computer is stored in a file. Whenever you want to store information — or use information that's already been saved — you need to use a file. Files come in all sizes, from empty to amazingly huge, depending on the amount and type of information stored in them.

Windows NT itself dumps many hundreds of files onto your computer; as time goes by, you'll probably add a few hundred yourself.

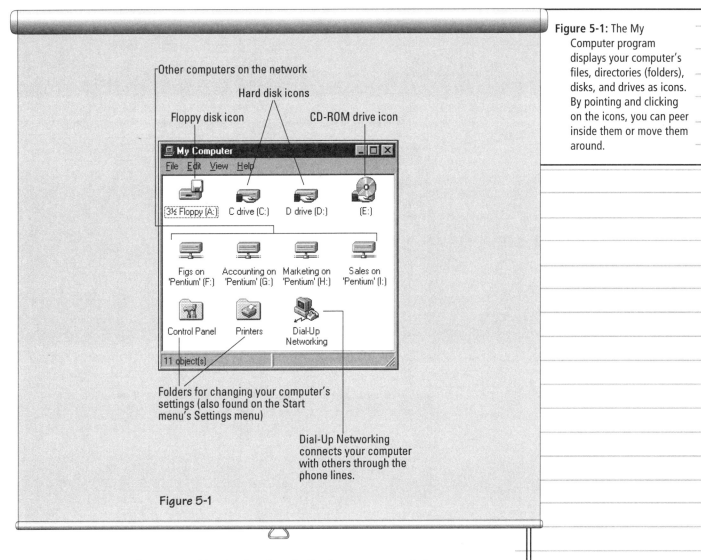

Other computers on the network

Hard disk icons

Floppy disk icon

CD-ROM drive icon

Folders for changing your computer's settings (also found on the Start menu's Settings menu)

Dial-Up Networking connects your computer with others through the phone lines.

Figure 5-1

Figure 5-1: The My Computer program displays your computer's files, directories (folders), disks, and drives as icons. By pointing and clicking on the icons, you can peer inside them or move them around.

Figure 5-2 shows some files displayed in the Explorer program; their names are displayed next to small icons that basically indicate the *type* of file that they are. As you grow more accustomed to seeing this kind of thing, you'll be able to tell identify a file's type by the shape of its icon. (Don't worry about that right now, however.)

Understanding folders and directories

on the test

After the files start adding up, you'll want to keep them stored neatly away inside *folders*. In computer country, folders are usually called *directories*; Windows NT breaks tradition by sticking with the term *folders*. Folders let you store related files for easy access.

To keep things orderly, folders store files that have related information. You can store all your word processor files relating to the office in a separate folder, your personal letters can go in yet another folder, and your secret resumes can

Figure 5-2: The Explorer program displays much of the same information as the My Computer program, but in a completely different format.

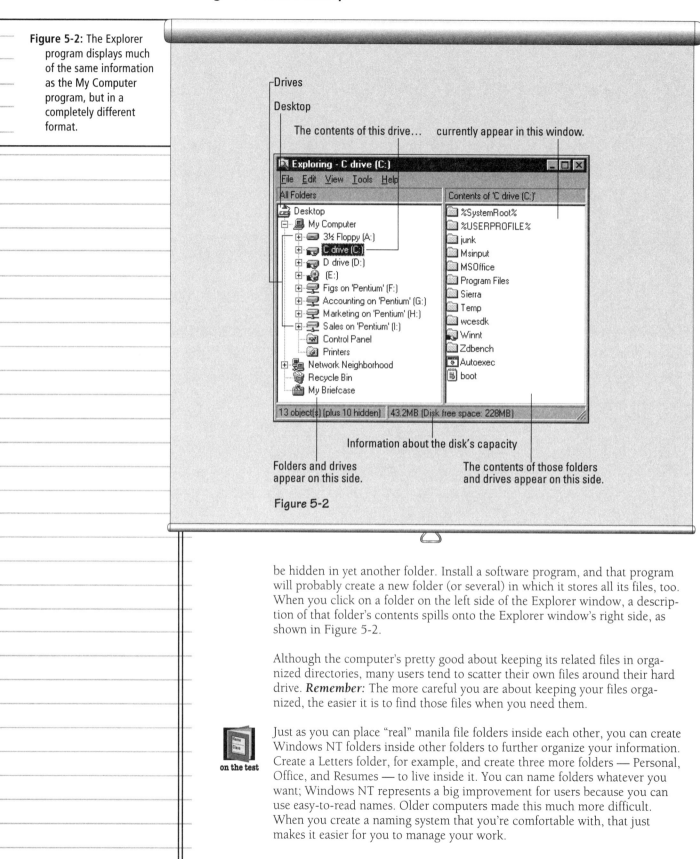

Drives

Desktop

The contents of this drive... currently appear in this window.

Exploring - C drive (C:)

File   Edit   View   Tools   Help

All Folders

Desktop
My Computer
3½ Floppy (A:)
C drive (C:)
D drive (D:)
(E:)
Figs on 'Pentium' (F:)
Accounting on 'Pentium' (G:)
Marketing on 'Pentium' (H:)
Sales on 'Pentium' (I:)
Control Panel
Printers
Network Neighborhood
Recycle Bin
My Briefcase

Contents of 'C drive (C:)'

%SystemRoot%
%USERPROFILE%
junk
Msinput
MSOffice
Program Files
Sierra
Temp
wcesdk
Winnt
Zdbench
Autoexec
boot

13 object(s) (plus 10 hidden)   43.2MB (Disk free space: 228MB)

Information about the disk's capacity

Folders and drives appear on this side.

The contents of those folders and drives appear on this side.

Figure 5-2

be hidden in yet another folder. Install a software program, and that program will probably create a new folder (or several) in which it stores all its files, too. When you click on a folder on the left side of the Explorer window, a description of that folder's contents spills onto the Explorer window's right side, as shown in Figure 5-2.

Although the computer's pretty good about keeping its related files in organized directories, many users tend to scatter their own files around their hard drive. *Remember:* The more careful you are about keeping your files organized, the easier it is to find those files when you need them.

on the test

Just as you can place "real" manila file folders inside each other, you can create Windows NT folders inside other folders to further organize your information. Create a Letters folder, for example, and create three more folders — Personal, Office, and Resumes — to live inside it. You can name folders whatever you want; Windows NT represents a big improvement for users because you can use easy-to-read names. Older computers made this much more difficult. When you create a naming system that you're comfortable with, that just makes it easier for you to manage your work.

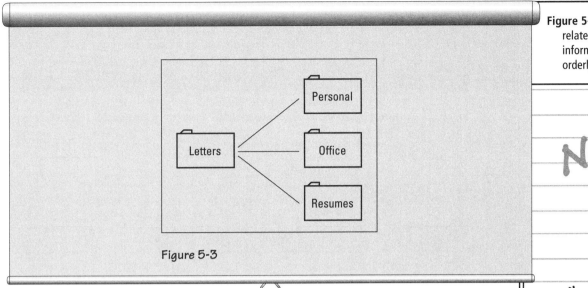

Figure 5-3

Notes:

easily created and easily deleted, folders make finding files easier later on

Note: Don't be afraid to create new folders for new programs or incoming files; doing so makes it easier to find the files later.

extra credit

What's a root folder?

Figure 5-3 shows a typical directory "tree" with folders sprouting from each other; the files grow more closely related as the branches extend outward. With real trees, everything grows outward from the roots: A trunk leads to branches, which lead to clusters of leaves. In keeping with this tree business, the Official Computer Name for the computer's first folder — the folder that everything branches from — is the drive's *root folder.* (I'm not making this up.)

When you double-click on your drive C icon in the My Computer program, My Computer brings a new window showing the contents of drive C to the screen. That window shows the root folder of drive C.

Of course, this stuff is pretty technical. But if a program ever bugs you about the *root folder,* now you'll know where to find it: It's the first window that appears when you double-click on a drive's icon in My Computer.

Understanding disks

A file cabinet stores its folders and files in big drawers. A computer, by contrast, stores its folders and files on *disks.*

on the test

For the most part, computers store their information on four types of disks: *floppy disks, hard disks, removable disks,* and *compact discs,* often referred to as *CD-ROMs.* Floppy disks are those square, plastic things that look like coasters. Compact discs look just like the ones you use in your stereo (one is included in the back of this book). Hard disks live permanently inside computers where

keep floppy disks
away from magnets
and moisture

Notes:

nobody can see them. Removable disks are a special case. They vary a great deal in their size and in how much they can hold, and are often used as an excellent backup drive or means of saving lots of files (more than a floppy disk could ever hold) in a safer place.

Yawn. At least you have to learn this stuff only once. And mainly, just remember this about floppy disks and removable disks: Keep them away from magnets and moisture. (Both are disk killers.)

Also, disks come in different sizes, shapes, and capacities. Table 5-1 gives the rundown.

Table 5-1	Common Computer Disks		
Drive Letter	*Type*	*Content*	*Popularity*
Usually A or B	5¼ Floppy	360K	Obsolete
Usually A or B	5¼ Floppy	1.2MB	Obsolete
Usually A or B	3½ Floppy	720K	Very rare
Usually A	3½ Floppy	1.44MB	Very common
C or above	Hard	From 512MB	Very common to 5,000MB or more!
D or above	Compact Disc or CD-ROM	Up to 600MB	Very common
D or above	Removable	From 100MB to 9GB	Increasingly popular

extra credit

Q/A session

Question: What do K and MB stand for?

Answer: Computers store their information in nuggets called *bytes.* A byte is pretty much like a character or letter in a word. For example, the words *pig's eye* contain nine bytes. (The space and the apostrophe count as one byte each, too.) Computers use the metric system, so bytes are measured in kilos (approximately 1,000), megas (1,000,000), and gigas (always incredibly large).

Question: What is a Zip drive?

Answer: Zip drives are taking the computer world by storm. They're a popular type of removable disk drive that uses small diskettes that look a lot like a floppy disk but hold 100MB of information. Zip drives are fairly cheap, portable, and offer a nice way to back up large folders of data pretty fast, since Zip drives are fairly quick. (Otherwise they wouldn't be named "Zip," I guess.)

Remember: Keep track of how much free space you have on your disks; sometimes they won't have enough room to store all the information you'd like.

Understanding drives

on the test

The terms *disk* and *drive* are usually used interchangeably. *Drives* are the parts of computers that read or write information onto disks. The floppy drive, for example, is that slot into which you insert a floppy disk. CD-ROM drives suck in compact discs like a home stereo does. And hard drives sit inside your computer, out of sight.

All drives do their work in the background, so just remember a few things:

- **Floppy drives** can't store much information on their own disks. Although the disks don't hold much information, they're cheap and portable, making them ideal for moving information to other computers.

- **Hard drives** can read and write a lot of information quickly, so they're used most often. (In fact, whenever you save a file, your computer writes that file's contents to your hard drive.) Hard drives can't be moved to other computers easily, though.

- **CD-ROM drives** can read a lot of information, but more slowly than hard drives. Most CD-ROM drives can't write information onto compact discs (although the more expensive ones now can), so don't try to store any files there. No, you'll probably be storing all your information on your hard drive. (CDs are more handy for installing new programs on your machine, which is why most large programs like Microsoft Office and Corel Office come on CDs.)

- **Removable drives** come in all shapes and sizes, including the 100MB Zip drive and continuing up to larger than you'll ever need. Leave them to the office administrator to fiddle with.

Most new computers come with at least one floppy drive and one hard drive. Almost all modern PCs (basically, anything manufactured since 1995) also have a CD-ROM drive. Any additional drives depend on the size of the computer owner's pocketbook (or how well the company's profit/loss statement was last quarter).

on the test

Finally, in Windows NT, files and folders all have similar names that consist of up to 255 characters; on the other hand, drives use a single letter. For example, your floppy drive is probably called *drive A*, and your hard drive is probably called *drive C*. As another example, Figures 5-1 and 5-3 show drive letters that go all the way up to *I*. For a Windows NT computer, especially in an office environment, this isn't as rare as you'd think.

---

to see available disk space, click on drive with right mouse button in My Computer and choose Properties from menu

☑ Progress Check

If you can do the following, you've mastered this lesson:

❑ Understand how Windows NT stores files.

❑ Understand different kinds of disks and disk drives.

Notes:

extra credit

Q/A session

Question: Why does my computer use up to 255 characters in its file and folder names, but my friend's computer can use only eight characters?

Answer: For years, most IBM-compatible computers could store only files with names using eight or fewer letters or numbers. Windows NT, by contrast, can use up to 255. Although those extra characters make thinking up descriptive filenames a lot easier, they can cause problems when you swap files with friends who don't use Windows NT.

For example, if you give your friend a disk containing a file named Incredible Thoughts, that file will appear to be named INCRED~1 on a computer that uses Windows 3.1.

Then, if your friend copies the file to her hard drive, adds some incredible thoughts of her own, and copies the file back to the floppy, be prepared for a surprise when you get the file back: It will still be named INCRED~1.

Lesson 9-2 contains more information about naming and saving files.

Question: Why does someone's computer have all those drive letters, like the ones shown in Figure 5-1?

Answer: Windows NT is widely used in offices and businesses for one good reason: It has very good *networking* capabilities. This means that you can hook up other peoples' computers together and have them share things between them. The result? Windows NT can look very different on different people's desktops. Don't be surprised if the pictures in this book differ from the version of Windows NT on your own computer. They're really the same thing.

Lesson 5-2   # Working with Drives

If you were looking to retrieve a particular piece of paper that you'd filed away somewhere, you would walk to the file cabinet, grab the handle of the appropriate drawer, and give it a pull.

Retrieving information in Windows NT works pretty much the same way. By opening the right drive, you can access the folders and files stored on that drive.

Drives come in several varieties and sizes, but this lesson includes some hands-on work with your CD-ROM drive so that you can see what's stored on the CD that comes with the book.

Finding out what's stored on a drive

Windows NT makes it fairly easy to peer inside your computer and look at files. We've already mentioned, at the start of this unit, how Windows NT organizes itself around two "file cabinets": Windows NT Explorer and My

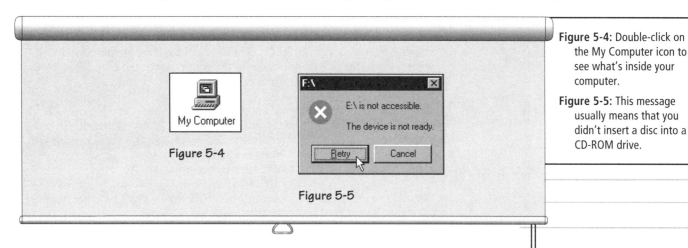

Figure 5-4

Figure 5-5

Figure 5-4: Double-click on the My Computer icon to see what's inside your computer.

Figure 5-5: This message usually means that you didn't insert a disc into a CD-ROM drive.

Computer. To see what's inside your computer, you use the My Computer icon, shown in Figure 5-4. (Windows NT Explorer works just as well, but My Computer may be slightly easier for beginners.)

The following steps teach you how to use My Computer to see the files and folders on your computer's drives:

1 Open My Computer.

Double-click on the My Computer icon — that picture of a computer shown in Figure 5-4 — and the My Computer window appears on-screen (refer to Figure 5-1). Each gray icon in the My Computer window represents a disk drive or CD-ROM on your computer; the three folders contain other information. In Figure 5-1, the computer has one floppy drive (A), two hard drives (C, and D), a compact disc drive (E), and four networked drives. Notice how each type of drive has a different type of icon? (Your screen will certainly look different, of course. But you will probably have most if not all of those drive types in My Computer on your system as well.)

2 Put this book's CD in your CD-ROM drive.

Your CD-ROM drive is one of the slots in the front of your computer; push the disc into the drive with the disc's labeled side facing up.

3 Double-click on the appropriate disc drive icon.

For example, if you put your disc into drive E, move the mouse until its arrow hovers over the E icon, as shown in Figure 5-1, and then double-click on the left mouse button.

My Computer opens a new window that shows you the disc's contents.

If you didn't put a disc in there, just to see what would happen, Windows reprimands you with a message like the one in Figure 5-5. Put the disk in the drive and then click on the Retry button, and the computer tries again.

4 Double-click on the C drive icon.

Notice how the My Computer program brings up another window, this time showing the contents of drive C — your hard drive?

5 Click on the remaining icons to see all the drives in your computer.

double-click on any folder in My Computer to see its contents

Notice how My Computer uses something that should be awfully familiar now: windows. See the telltale little icons in the windows' corners? See the scroll bar and title bar that you were introduced to in Unit 3?

The windows in My Computer work just like all the other windows you've read about in this book. You can have several open at once, for example, displaying the contents of several drives simultaneously. Or you can minimize or maximize them for better views of other windows. (You'll get to practice that stuff later in this unit, so don't get carried away now.)

You can even drag and drop files and folders from window to window in order to copy or move things around. (You'll hear plenty more about that later in this unit, too.)

One last thing: Opening all those folders probably left a lot of open windows cluttering your desktop. You can close those extra windows the same way you close any other window: click on the little X in their upper-right corner.

dragging and dropping disk drive icons from My Computer onto desktop makes easily accessible shortcuts to them

extra credit

How can I get more information about a disk or drive?

Sometimes you need to know more information about a drive than its current inventory. How much information can the drive hold, for example? And more important, how much space does the drive have left for storing your information?

You find out this information with a trick that should be getting familiar by now: Click on the drive's icon with your right mouse button and choose Properties from the pop-up menu. A window pops up, as shown in Figure 5-6, listing the drive's total storage capacity, the amount of space that's currently being used, and the amount of space left over.

The Label box lets you name your drive as well. Plus, if the drive is acting funny, the window's Tools tab lets you check the box for errors. Close the window like any other, by clicking on the X in its upper-right corner.

on the test

Remember: When you put a new floppy disk in a drive, My Computer often forgets to update its view. Yep, it still shows you the files that were stored on the old disk. To make it update its view, press F5. In fact, make it a habit to press F5 every time you view a floppy by using My Computer, and you'll be safe.

on the test

To make My Computer display files and folders on a particular drive, double-click on that drive's icon in the My Computer window.

to tell how much space a drive has left on its current disk, click on it with right mouse button and choose Properties from menu

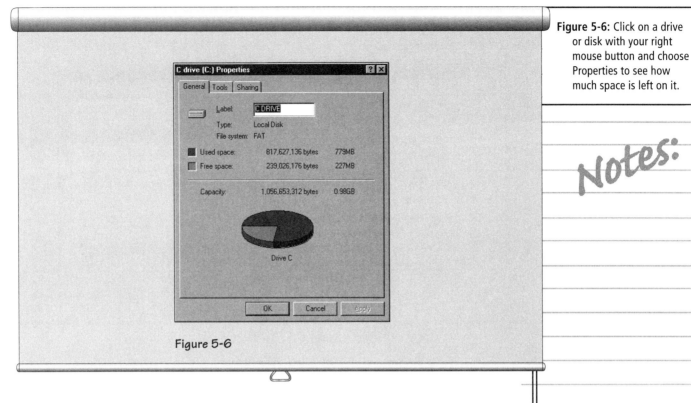

Figure 5-6

Figure 5-6: Click on a drive or disk with your right mouse button and choose Properties to see how much space is left on it.

Notes:

Deleting a drive

heads up

Deleting a computer's drive is impossible unless you have a screwdriver and some patience. You can't drag a drive's icon to the Recycle Bin. If you click on the drive icon with the right mouse button, the word Delete doesn't appear, either. (You can delete a drive's contents, though, so be careful when pointing and clicking at folders and files.)

Working with Folders

Lesson 5-3

Folders let you store files in easily relocated places. Whenever you open a drive and peek inside, My Computer displays the folders stored on that particular drive. The next few sections teach you how to open (known in technical terms as "peek inside"), create, copy, move, and delete folders.

Looking inside a folder

on the test

If you want to see what's inside a different folder, just double-click on it. Here's an example for practice:

1 **Open My Computer.**

Figure 5-7: Click in a folder with your right mouse button to see a list of things that you can do with that folder.

Figure 5-8: When choosing a name for your new folder, use only letters, numbers, and the most common symbols for best results. Keep the names brief so that they're easier to work with.

Figure 5-7

Figure 5-8

Notes:

2 **Double-click on the C drive icon.**

My Computer brings a window to the screen, showing the files and folders stored on your C drive.

3 **Double-click on the folder labeled Winnt.**

The files and folders contained in your computer's Winnt folder appear on the right side of the screen. If you can't find your Winnt folder, try clicking on the scroll bar in the C drive window until the Winnt folder appears. (Lesson 3-4 covers scroll bars.)

Tip: When you double-click on a folder, My Computer normally opens a separate window to show that folder's contents. Digging deep into several folders results in a string of open windows across your screen, each displaying a folder's contents. To make My Computer use the same window that changes each time you double-click on one of its folders, hold down Ctrl while double-clicking.

Creating a folder

Sooner or later, your life will branch off; you'll create some new files, and you'll need a new folder to hold them all. The following steps show you how to create a new folder on your C drive:

1 **Open My Computer.**

2 **Click on the C drive icon.**

A window appears, displaying all the files and folders on the C drive.

3 **With the right mouse button, click anywhere in the background of the newly opened C drive window.**

A menu pops up, as shown in Figure 5-7.

4 **Choose Folder from the New menu.**

A new folder appears, as shown in Figure 5-8.

5 **Type** Temporary Trash **as the name for your new folder, and then press Enter.**

Why Temporary Trash? Because that way, you'll have a folder to store files temporarily until you decide where to file them. (Remember: Folders, like files, can't have names longer than 255 characters.)

When you press Enter, your new folder appears on-screen.

You can put a new folder inside any of your existing folders in the same way: Simply open a folder, click on it with the right mouse button, and choose Folder from the New menu.

Copying or moving a folder

You won't want to copy or move a folder very often, but the procedure is simple because it uses one of the most basic Windows tricks: the drag and drop.

Follow these steps to create a folder and then move that folder to the Temporary Trash folder that you created in the preceding set of steps:

1 **Create a folder called Junk on your C drive.**

2 **Drag and drop the Junk folder to the Temporary Trash folder.**

You learned how to drag and drop in Lesson 2-1, but if you need a refresher, here goes: Point at the Junk folder and, while holding down your left mouse button, point at the Temporary Trash folder. Then let go of the mouse button.

Windows NT does something pretty dumb to confuse people, though. It makes you follow different rules when copying or moving folders — nothing wrong with that. But it *reverses* those rules when you're copying or moving folders to different disk drives. Table 5-2 helps you keep track.

Note: Windows NT won't let you put two folders with the same name into one folder. For example, you can't have two folders called Pig's Breath in one Barnyard Hygiene folder. If you try, Windows NT gently stops you, saying that you already have a file named Pig's Breath in that folder, and you have to change the name Pig's Breath to something else.

Table 5-2	Moving Files and Folders Around
To Do This . . .	*Do This . . .*
Copy a file or folder to another location on the same disk drive	Hold down Ctrl and drag it there.
Copy a file or folder to a different drive	Drag it there.
Move a file or folder to another location on the same drive	Drag it there.
Move a file or folder to a different drive	Hold down Alt and drag it there.

to be safe, always drag and drop with right mouse button to make Windows NT bring up menu of choices

Figure 5-9: If you're sure that you want to delete the folder, click on the Yes button.

Notes:

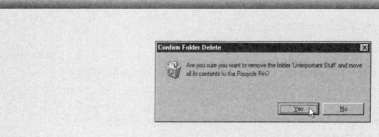

Figure 5-9

extra credit

Q/A session

Question: How can I copy a folder to a different drive?

Answer: Just drag and drop it there. For example, open My Computer and find the folder you want to copy. Then find the icon for the drive onto which you want to copy the folder. You may need to put each folder in its own window and drag the windows around on-screen until they're both clearly visible. And remember, if you drag and drop something with your right mouse button, Windows NT puts a menu listing your movement choices on-screen.

When you can see the folder's target, drag it there and let go.

Deleting a folder

heads up

This one's easy — so easy, in fact, that it can be dangerous. Before deleting a folder, give it a good ogle with both eyes open to make sure that you're not deleting anything important inside it.

1 **Create a folder on your desktop called Unimportant Stuff.**

You need something unimportant to delete.

2 **Click on the Unimportant Stuff folder's name in My Computer.**

My Computer highlights the folder's name.

3 **Press the Delete key.**

Depending on your computer's setup, My Computer does one of two things. It may just delete the folder immediately. Or it may toss a warning message, like the one in Figure 5-9, in your face.

If you prefer less long-winded deletion methods, skip Step 2. Instead, just drag and drop the Unimportant Stuff folder to the Recycle Bin.

Changing a folder's name

1 Click on the folder you'd like to rename — perhaps the Temporary Trash folder that you created earlier in this unit.

2 Click on the folder's name to highlight it.

3 Type the new name and press Enter.

The new name replaces the old name.

Pretty easy, eh?

heads up

This is a big-time gotcha. Windows NT programs always look for pieces of themselves to be located in specific places on the system. When it can't find 'em, it *really* doesn't like that and will refuse to work. If you change the name of a folder, Windows NT might not be able to find a program or file and will become cranky.

A good rule of thumb: Only change the names of folders you personally use in your computer for your own files. Leave everything else alone.

And for goodness sake, don't change the name of the folders named Winnt, Temp, or Programs. Your computer won't forgive you easily.

Working with Files

Lesson 5-4

In Lesson 5-1, you learned why your computer uses files, folders, disks, and drives for storing information. For the most part, you'll be using files, so be sure to pay careful attention to this lesson.

Opening a file

Opening a file in Windows NT is pretty easy — if you can find the file you're after. As you learned earlier, you not only need to know the file's name, but you also need to know its *location:* the name of the folder in which the file's sitting and the name of the drive on which that particular folder lives.

After you find the file, you can open it by double-clicking on its name. The following steps show you how to open the letter called Joe's Lament that was written in WordPad and supplied on the CD that came with this book.

on the CD

1 Open My Computer.

2 Click on the drive C icon to switch the view to drive C.

3 Click on the Dummies 101\Windows NT folder.

4 Double-click on the Joe's Lament file.

Windows looks at the Joe's Lament file and figures out that it was created in WordPad. So it automatically loads WordPad and loads the file into that program.

Notes:

Tip: For a quick look inside a file, click on it with the right mouse button and choose Quick View from the menu. Windows NT shows you the file's contents, whether they were created by a word processor, spreadsheet, or other type of program. (Unfortunately, Quick View works better with Microsoft products than with those created by other companies.)

Copying or moving a file

This procedure works just like copying or moving a folder, described in Lesson 5-3. Nonetheless, here's a quick refresher to make sure that you've got it down pat:

1 **Create a folder called Temporary Junk on your desktop.**

2 **Open My Computer and double-click on the drive C icon.**

3 **Open the Winnt folder.**

4 **Choose the Winnt and Winnt256 files.**

on the test

Hold down Ctrl while clicking on the names of the two files. By holding Ctrl while you click, you enable My Computer to highlight more than one file. (If you mess up and click on the wrong file, continue holding the Ctrl key and click on the file again to "unhighlight" it.)

5 **With your right mouse button, drag and drop the files onto the Temporary Junk folder.**

6 **Choose Copy Here from the menu.**

By dragging and dropping with your right mouse button, you can choose between copying or moving files each time you drag them. Or if you have a good memory, memorize Table 5-2, which lets you know when dragging and dropping a file copies it and when dragging and dropping a file moves it. (You'll find an irritating difference.)

extra credit

Q/A session

Question: How come Windows automatically loads some files when you double-click on them, but it doesn't load others?

Answer: When a Windows NT program creates a file, it usually tacks three hidden letters onto the end of its name. Save a file in Paint called Pistachio, for example, and Paint puts the letters *BMP* on the end of the filename. WordPad uses the letters *WRI*, and Notepad uses *TXT*. With these three-letter code words, Windows NT can register files with the programs that created them.

That means two things: First, Windows NT can use the right icon when displaying the file in My Computer. For instance, any file created with Notepad uses the Notepad icon. Second, Windows NT can look at the hidden three letters, decide which program created the file, and — when you double-click on the file — bring the file to the screen inside the program that created it.

If Windows NT doesn't recognize the three-letter association, however, it uses a boring, generic icon and subsequently gives you an error message when you double-click on the file.

Deleting a file

No longer using a file? Then delete it — in the same way you delete folders:

on the CD

1 **Click on Joe's Lament to highlight the file's name.**

2 **Press the Delete key.**

Poof. My Computer wipes the file off your hard drive or floppy drive and puts it in your Recycle Bin (from which you can salvage it if you deleted it by mistake). You can't delete files and folders from compact discs, however; those CDs just won't let go.

3 **Click Yes when the Confirm File Delete box pops up.**

4 **Open the Recycle Bin, click on Joe's Lament with the right mouse button, and select <u>R</u>estore.**

Doing so brings the file out of the trash and puts it back on your hard drive. (You'll need the file for later lessons.)

extra credit

Q/A session

Question: I want to copy some files from one floppy to another, but I have only one floppy drive.

Answer: If you want to copy a few files or folders from one floppy disk to another, just create a new folder called Junk on your desktop; then copy the floppy's files to that Junk folder. When you're done copying the files to your desktop, remove the first floppy disk, insert the second one, and move the files from the Junk folder to the second floppy.

Remember, you can hold down Ctrl while clicking on the names of files, and My Computer will select more than one file. That way, you can delete, copy, or move a whole bunch of files at once.

You can delete program files as well as files you've created, but doing so often causes problems. Programs rarely come in neat packages, and they tend to spread themselves across your hard drive. You should probably invest in an *Uninstaller* program that handles all the background issues involved in removing a Windows program from your computer. (In fact, Windows NT comes with a built-in Uninstaller. And the CD that comes with this book includes an uninstall program as well.)

Changing a file's name

You change the name of a file in the same way you change a folder's name: click on the file, click on the file's name, type the new name, and press Enter.

heads up

Just watch out; don't move too fast, or Windows NT will mistake your two single clicks for one double-click and try to load your file.

heads up

Here's another big gotcha: Don't change the name of any file that the system needs to do its work. Your safest bet is to avoid changing the names of any files that you didn't create. They're just like folders: Don't change the names of any program files or they may not work!

Lesson 5-5

Working with Floppies and CDs

Like spouses and Kahlua cheesecakes, floppies and CDs require special care. This lesson shows you how to keep them happy and functioning well.

Formatting a floppy disk

When you first take them from the box, floppy disks may not be ready to be used. You need to *format* them first — a process that gets them ready for storing data. How do you know whether a disk needs to be formatted? Well, if you try to use the floppy and see the message shown in Figure 5-10, you know that you're dealing with an unformatted disk. Go ahead and click yes to format the disk.

If you're stuck with a box of unformatted floppy disks, follow these steps to format them:

heads up

1 Slide the floppy disk into the floppy disk drive.

Formatting a floppy disk erases all the information it contains. Look at the disk's contents in My Computer to make sure that it doesn't hold anything important before you proceed.

2 With the right mouse button, click on the floppy disk drive's icon in My Computer and select Format.

A box appears, as Figure 5-11 shows.

3 Choose the capacity of the disk from the Capacity box.

Floppy disks can hold different capacities, as described back in Table 5-1. If you have a newer computer, you're probably using the high-capacity 1.44MB, 3½ inch disks.

4 Click on the Start button.

Follow the computer's on-screen instructions to finish the process.

Note: When you buy a box of new floppy disks, take the time to format them all. That way, you won't be stuck with an unformatted floppy when you're in a hurry to copy some important information. Most floppies you buy nowadays are already formatted, so you won't usually have to worry about this.

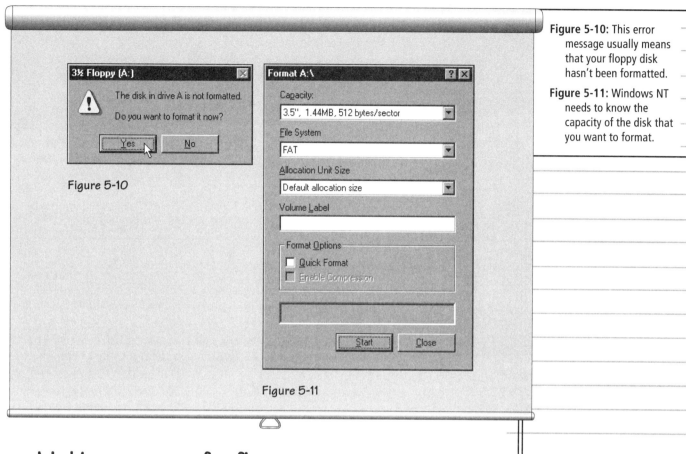

Figure 5-10

Figure 5-11

Figure 5-10: This error
    message usually means
    that your floppy disk
    hasn't been formatted.

Figure 5-11: Windows NT
    needs to know the
    capacity of the disk that
    you want to format.

Making a copy of a floppy

Sometimes you'll want to make an exact duplicate of a floppy disk. Some
computers come with different sizes of drives, complicating matters.

If you have two floppy drives that are the same size and capacity, stick your
original floppy in one drive and your second floppy in the second drive. Then
use what you learned in Lesson 5-4 to copy the files from one disk to the
other.

But if you have only one floppy drive — or just one floppy drive that can
handle your type of floppy disk — you have to follow these steps. (And
actually, they're a little easier than those in Lesson 5-4, anyway.)

1 **Open My Computer and click on the floppy disk's icon with your
    right mouse button.**

2 **Choose Copy Disk from the pop-up menu.**

A window like the one in Figure 5-12 appears, letting Windows NT know what
disk you want to copy and what disk you want to copy the information to.

Figure 5-12: Windows NT can make a direct copy of a floppy disk, even if you have only one floppy drive.

Notes:

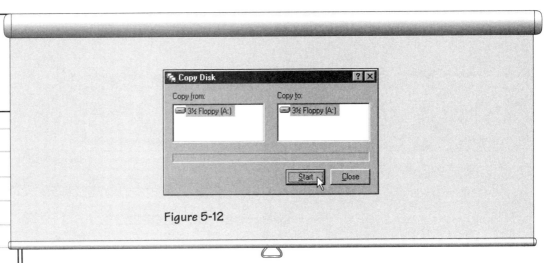

Figure 5-12

heads up

In the process of making an exact duplicate of a disk, Windows NT formats the second disk, so make sure that your second disk doesn't contain any valuable information. Luckily, Windows NT warns you that you'll erase all information on the second disk.

3 **Make sure that Windows NT displays your original disk on the left side of the window and the duplicate on the right side of the window.**

Windows NT can make a duplicate of a floppy disk even if you have only one floppy drive, so both sides of the window can be your A floppy drive. (You just have to switch the original floppy with the duplicate a few times while Windows NT is making the copy.)

4 **Click on the Start button.**

Windows NT starts reading all the information from the disk.

5 **When instructed, insert the second disk and press Enter.**

6 **Follow the instructions on-screen.**

Windows NT may make you swap the two disks once or twice until it's through copying all the information from one to the other. That's why keeping track of which disk is the original and which is the duplicate is important. Finally, be sure to put a label on your new disk so that it doesn't immediatily get lost in the box of unlabelled floppies.

on the test

The Copy Disk command wipes out any information stored on the floppy disk to which you copy information.

Formatting a hard disk

heads up

Please don't do it. Formatting a hard disk wipes out any and all information stored on your computer.

Get a second opinion before even thinking about formatting your hard disk. (Then have the person who gave you the second opinion do the actual dirty work if a reformat is truly necessary.)

What am I trying to say here? Only that hard disks usually need to be formatted only once, and that's when you first stick them inside the computer. Almost any other time, you're asking for trouble.

Working with Explorer

Lesson 5-6

By now, you've learned what files and folders are supposed to do and which buttons you need to push to move them around. You learned how the My Computer program lets you peer inside your computer's hard drives, where you can see your folders and the files stored inside them.

But just as some people like pineapple on their pizza and others don't, Windows NT comes with an alternative program for people who don't like My Computer. Called *Explorer,* the program lets you look at your files, folders, and disk drives in a different way.

This lesson shows you how to make Explorer do the same things as My Computer; by the end of the unit, choose to use the program you find less confusing.

Looking in folders and files with Explorer

Windows NT Explorer and My Computer do the same things, but in different ways. Because the two programs are so similar, you shouldn't find it too surprising that you can launch NT Explorer directly from the My Computer program. The following section shows you how to load Explorer and perform some of the tasks described earlier in this unit.

Don't think that you can skip this stuff because you already know how to use My Computer. Explorer and My Computer use the same commands and many similar techniques, so almost everything you learn in this lesson applies to the My Computer program, too.

on the test

1 **Click on My Computer with your right mouse button, and then choose Explore from the menu.**

Or you can choose Windows NT Explorer from the Start menu's Programs menu. Or you can right-click on any folder and then choose Explore. Any of these three actions brings Explorer to the screen, as shown in Figure 5-13.

2 **Click on the C drive icon in Explorer's left window.**

Explorer changes its view and displays the contents of your C drive in its right window, as shown in Figure 5-14. The folders and files in the right window should look familiar; they're the same ones you see when you first open the My Computer program. However, the icons are smaller.

☑ Progress Check

If you can do the following, you've mastered this lesson:

❏ Find information about your drives, disks, folders, and files.

❏ Copy and move files to different drives and folders.

❏ Create, copy, move, and delete folders.

❏ Format floppy disks.

❏ Make copies of floppy disks.

❏ Use Explorer's Find feature to find lost files.

Figure 5-13: The left side of Explorer shows your computer's drives and folders; the right side shows the contents of those drives and folders.

Figure 5-14: Click on a folder or disk drive on Explorer's left side, and Explorer displays the contents of that folder or disk drive.

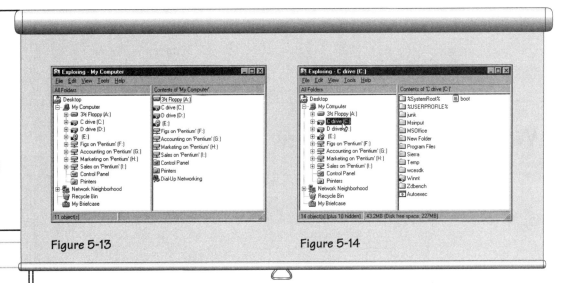

Figure 5-13   Figure 5-14

3 **Choose Large Icons from Explorer's View menu.**

Windows NT folders can display their contents by using large icons, small icons, a list of small icons, or a detailed list of file information — the file's size, type, and creation date. My Computer starts out by displaying large icons, just as Explorer is doing now.

4 **Double-click on the Windows folder.**

The right side of Explorer displays the contents of your C drive's Windows folder.

5 **Choose List from Explorer's View menu.**

List view often makes dealing with large groups of files easier.

6 **Click on the file named Forest with the right mouse button and choose Quick View from the File menu.**

Explorer displays the contents of the Forest file.

7 **Close your opened windows.**

Like other windows, you close the Explorer and Quick View windows by clicking on the X in their upper-right corner.

Although the Explorer program, the My Computer program, and the folders on your desktop look very different, they share an almost identical menu for displaying files and folders. For example, all three use the same View menu for changing the size of the icons they display. They all let you sort the display by the icons' name, size, type, or creation date through the View menu's Arrange Icons command.

And most important, they all let you copy, move, or delete folders and icons by dragging and dropping them to different locations on the desktop: Dragging and dropping to other folders moves or copies objects, and dragging and dropping objects to the Recycle Bin deletes them. You can even drag and drop files and folders from My Computer to Explorer and vice versa.

Tip: Can't find a file? Choose Find from Explorer's Tools menu. Doing so brings up the same Find program that you learned about in the Start menu.

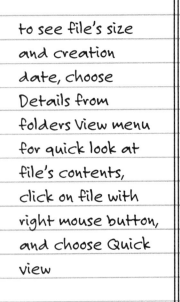

to see file's size and creation date, choose Details from folders View menu for quick look at file's contents, click on file with right mouse button, and choose Quick view

Unit 5 Quiz

Circle the letter of the correct answer or answers to each of the following questions. (Just like before, some questions have more than one answer to keep things from being too easy.)

1. **Computers use this name for their file folders full of information:**

   A. File folders

   B. Manila danglers

   C. Folders

   D. Directories

2. **Your computer's folders do this:**

   A. Store files for easy access.

   B. Organize related files.

   C. Lose files.

   D. Create films.

3. **Files and folder names can't exceed this number of characters:**

   A. 8

   B. 11

   C. 255

   D. 64

4. **Computers store their information on these types of disks:**

   A. Floppy disks

   B. Compact discs

   C. Hard disks

   D. Frisbee-brand flying disks

5. **Computers use drives to read and write information to disks.**

   A. True

   B. False

6. **Drives are named with one letter, and most computers have a hard drive called *drive C*.**

   A. True

   B. False

Notes:

Notes:

7. **My Computer displays this folder when you first open it:**

    A. Root folder

    B. Branch folder

    C. Currant folder

    D. Current folder

8. **Do this to make My Computer bring a new window to the screen, displaying files and folders on a certain drive:**

    A. Click on that drive's icon with your right mouse button.

    B. Wipe off your monitor with your sleeve.

    C. Beg.

    D. Double-click on that drive's icon with your left mouse button.

9. **Do this to make My Computer display a certain drive's files and folders in its currently open window:**

    A. Double-click on that drive's icon.

    B. Wipe off your monitor with your sleeve.

    C. Beg.

    D. Hold down Ctrl while double-clicking on that drive's icon.

10. **To make sure that My Computer is displaying the current contents of your floppy disk, you press this key:**

    A. Alt

    B. Del

    C. F1

    D. F5

11. **Do this to see a folder's contents:**

    A. Double-click on its folder in Explorer.

    B. Double-click on its folder in My Computer.

    C. Double-click on its folder on the desktop.

    D. Click on the folder with the right mouse button and choose Open from the menu.

12. **Do this to *move* a folder to a new location on the same drive:**

    A. Drag and drop its folder.

    B. Hold down Ctrl while dragging and dropping its folder.

    C. Pick it up and carry it.

    D. Toss it across the room.

13. Do this to *copy* a folder to a new location on the same drive:

    A. Drag and drop its folder.

    B. Hold down Ctrl while dragging and dropping its folder.

    C. Pick it up and carry it.

    D. Toss it across the room.

14. To select more than one file at a time, hold down Shift while clicking on the files' names.

    A. True

    B. False

15. My Computer's <u>C</u>opy Disk command wipes out any information stored on the floppy disk to which you copy information.

    A. True

    B. False

Unit 5 Exercise

1. Load My Computer.

2. Put a disk in drive A and view its folders.

3. Create a folder on the disk in drive A.

4. Move the newly created folder to drive C.

5. Delete the newly created folder from both drives.

6. Format a blank floppy disk.

7. Close My Computer and all its open windows.

8. Open Explorer and view the contents of the C drive's Windows folder.

9. Using the View menu's Arrange Icons command, sort the files alphabetically and find all the files in your Windows folder that begin with the letter C.

10. Using Quick View, view the Clouds file in your Windows folder.

11. Close Explorer and open My Computer.

12. Drag and drop each drive onto your desktop to create shortcuts.

Unit 6

Talking to Other Computers on a Network

Objectives for this Unit

- ✓ Using Network Neighborhood to find other computers
- ✓ Using The Explorer to find other computers
- ✓ Using the Find feature to locate other network resources
- ✓ Placing Network Resources in the My Computer group (Mapping a network drive)
- ✓ Placing a network drive icon on the desktop
- ✓ Transferring files between your system and another user's system
- ✓ Setting up your hard disk so that it can be shared on the network

Prerequisites

- ▶ Pointing and clicking the mouse (Lesson 2-1)
- ▶ Moving and sizing windows (Lessons 3-2 and 3-3)
- ▶ Filling out forms (Lessons 3-5)

on the CD

▶ Readme

Windows NT 4.0 is becoming an extremely popular operating system in corporations. The biggest deal about NT is its powerful networking features. Without networking, Windows NT 4.0 would just be a slower and less-friendly copy of Windows 95. Networking is so important in NT, in fact, that I simply had to include a chapter on it in this book.

But networking is scary. Luckily you can save most of its ugliness for the office network administrator. Nevertheless, every user can benefit from knowing how to use the basic networking features of NT Workstation. This book shields you from all the really hard stuff, letting you concentrate on things without interrupting your work flow.

Notes:

Things that have to do with configuring the network, assigning passwords, gaining permission to access someone else's system or printer, and similar things are always best left to the administrator and are nothing that you should ever have to worry about.

(A good tip for office politics: Always make friends with one of the network administrators at your company. That way, if something goes wrong or something needs to be done, the way will be a lot smoother for you. I've done this at every company I've been at, and it does make things easier — and also widens your social circle.)

When you start up your computer at the beginning of the day, you're required to *log on*. This means that you tell the system who you are so you can use it. You've already done this in Unit 1. But there's another more important objective that logging in does: It gives you access to the *network* — the other computers you're connected to.

After you log on, you can use Network Neighborhood to find the other computers that you can access on the network. Network Neighborhood is an extremely important feature of Windows NT Workstation, and it's where you'll be spending most of your time in this unit.

Lesson 6-1

Opening and Exploring Network Neighborhood

Network Neighborhood is a cheery-sounding program that lists the other computers attached to yours through the office network. By opening Network Neighborhood, you can access those computers — provided the office Network Administrator has tweaked the appropriate settings so that you can *share* those computers.

If your system is fully set up by the administrator, here's how to open Network Neighborhood and start peeking:

1 Double-click on the Network Neighborhood icon on the Windows NT desktop.

Network Neighborhood appears, listing the computers connected to your own computer through the network. In Figure 6-1, for example, three computers appear: 486, Pentium, and Pentium pro.

The computers listed on your own system will almost certainly be different. *Entire Network* is shown as a little globe icon, and it contains all the resources that you can use on the network.

Note: If someone's system shows up in your Network Neighborhood but you can't access it — and you're supposed to be able to — the other person's network setup hasn't been done properly. Better call over the Network Administrator for this one.

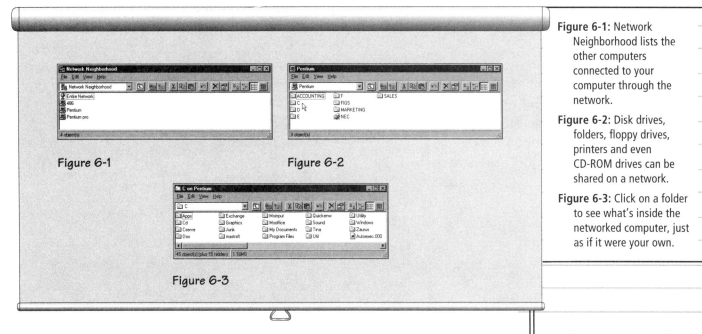

Figure 6-1

Figure 6-2

Figure 6-3

Figure 6-1: Network Neighborhood lists the other computers connected to your computer through the network.

Figure 6-2: Disk drives, folders, floppy drives, printers and even CD-ROM drives can be shared on a network.

Figure 6-3: Click on a folder to see what's inside the networked computer, just as if it were your own.

2 **Double-click on a computer icon in the Network Neighborhood.**

Figure 6-2 shows an example of what you'll see.

heads up

In the Network Neighborhood, everything in someone else's computer is shown as folders that you can open, even another computer's hard disk. Notice how more than one resource can be available from a machine, as seen in Figure 6-2.

Note: CD-ROMs, removable drives, hard disks, and even floppy drives can be shared across a network, just as you see in Figure 6-2.

3 **Double-click on any folder icon in the window you've just opened.**

A bunch of folders (and, perhaps, files) will be displayed in a new window, as shown in Figure 6-3.

You've just finished locating other computers on the network. Simple as that.

Using Windows NT Explorer to Open Network Resources

Lesson 6-2

You can also use the Windows NT Explorer to do much the same thing as you did in the previous unit: Locate and open resources on the network. Here's how:

1 **Click on the Start button.**

2 **Choose Programs and then Windows NT Explorer.**

The Explorer program comes up on your screen, as shown in Figure 6-4.

3 **Double-click on the Network Neighborhood icon.**

A list of the currently available network resources appears underneath. As shown in Figure 6-5, you'll probably see the same computer icons that you found in Network Neighborhood.

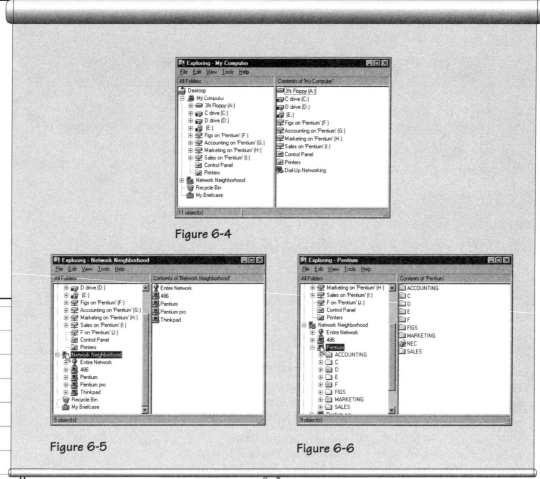

Figure 6-4

Figure 6-5

Figure 6-6

4 **Double-click on any of the icons under Network Neighborhood in the Explorer.**

You see a list of all the resources from each computer that have been designated by the Network Administrator for sharing with your computer, as seen in Figure 6-6. They're all shown as folder icons in the list.

Any of those folder icons can be opened and explored just as though they were part of your own computer.

Lesson 6-3

Using the Windows NT Find Feature to Locate Other Network Resources

If a network resource doesn't show up in the Explorer, or in Network Neighborhood, there's a good chance that you can still find it and use it. How? By running the Find feature from the NT Start menu.

1 **Click on the Start button.**

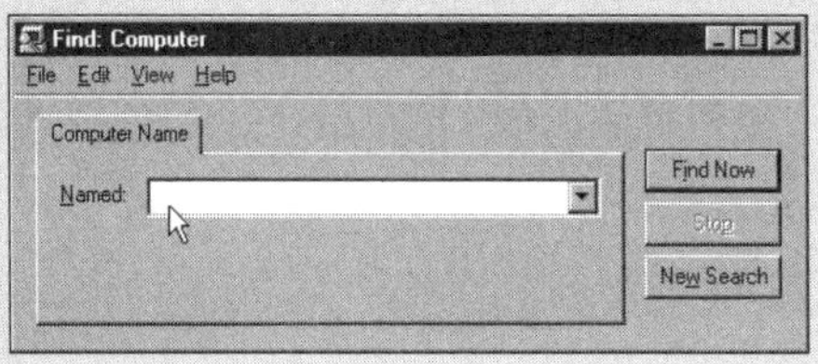

Figure 6-7

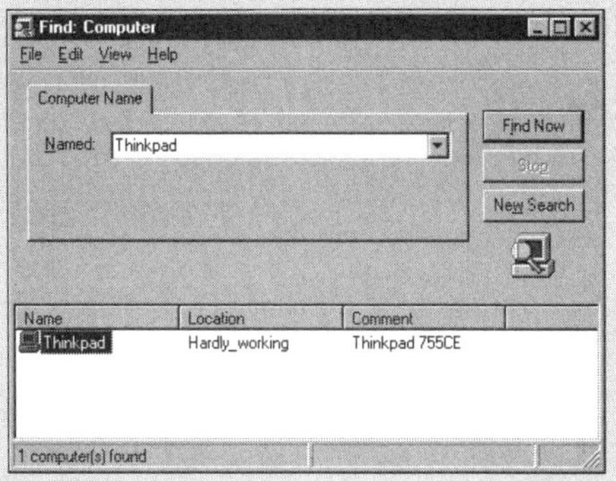

Figure 6-8

Figure 6-7: The Find program not only ferrets out missing files but can identify all the computers on your network.

Figure 6-8: The name of the missing computer appears in the Name box, where you can create a shortcut to it by dragging it to the desktop.

Notes:

2 **Choose Find and then Computer.**

The Find Computer dialog box appears, as seen in Figure 6-7.

3 **Type the computer's name in the box (which should be the name that the Network Administrator has already assigned to it) and click on the Find Now button.**

If the resource can be found, it pops up in the dialog box, as shown in Figure 6-8.

4 **Close the Find program.**

5 **Open Network Neighborhood or the Windows NT Explorer, and the new system icon should appear there.**

Note: If someone has removed a computer from the network for some reason and then put it back on later (perhaps they have a laptop, for example), you may be able to access that computer again through the Explorer but not through Network Neighborhood. Using the Find feature can help fix this (assuming, of course, that the other computer is fully reconnected in the network).

Placing Network Resources in the My Computer Group (Mapping a Network Drive)

Lesson 6-4

One of the best things about networking with Windows NT is that it allows you to have a lot more things available to you than what is just in your own computer. If someone else's computer is linked to yours on the network, you can make their hard disk, CD-ROM drive, or removable drive look like it's another device in your own machine. This is called *mapping a network drive*.

1 **Open Network Neighborhood.**

Figure 6-9: "Mapping a network drive" means to make another computer on the network appear as a disk drive on your own computer.

Figure 6-10: Type the name you want to use for the drive.

Figure 6-11: The new drive and its icon appear in your computer's window.

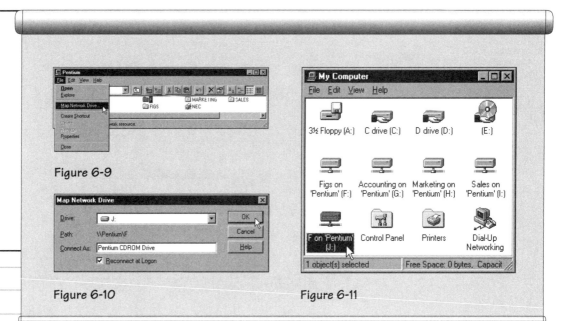

Figure 6-9

Figure 6-10

Figure 6-11

Notes:

2 **Double-click on one of the computers listed in the Network Neighborhood box.**

A new window appears on the screen, showing the folders representing the hard drives, CD-ROMs, or other resources available on the other computer.

3 **Select a folder in the new window.**

4 **From the File menu in the new window, select Map Network Drive, as shown in Figure 6-9.**

Figure 6-10 shows the Map Network Drive dialog box. It automatically defaults to the first available drive letter on your computer. (Computer gurus who understand network "path language" will note the words //Pentium/F listed above the drive's label. This is the network's path to the drive on the other system.)

5 **In the Map Network Drive dialog box, enter a desired title in the Connect As box.**

The drive in Figure 6-10 is called Pentium CDROM Drive.

heads up

You can also select another drive letter from the Drive list, but don't try to use one that's already taken by another network resource — the system will actually let you do it, but will display a prompt that the device is already connected to another drive. Unless the Administrator allows this, it isn't a good idea.

6 **Click on OK. (Your computer accesses the drive and displays its contents in a new window.)**

After you've mapped the network drive, it will appear in other parts of your system such as My Computer.

7 **Close the Network Neighborhood and open My Computer.**

As shown in Figure 6-11, the new drive has been added to the window as (J:). (The drive letter will probably be different on your computer.) This means that the other computer's drive has been successfully mapped into your own system for easy access. It's shown as a little drive icon with a pipeline connected to it, denoting a network drive.

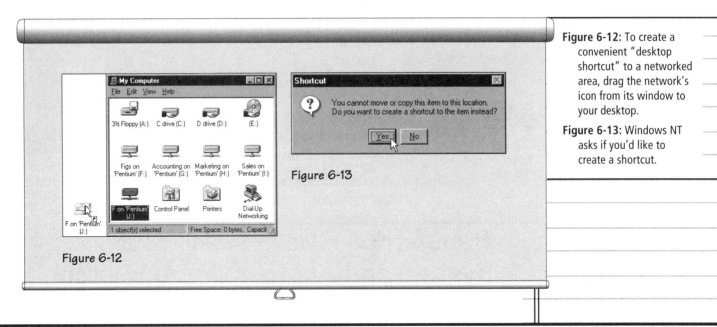

Figure 6-12

Figure 6-13

Figure 6-12: To create a convenient "desktop shortcut" to a networked area, drag the network's icon from its window to your desktop.

Figure 6-13: Windows NT asks if you'd like to create a shortcut.

Placing a Network Drive Icon on the Desktop

Lesson 6-5

There are some other benefits to mapping network drives. If you want really fast access to a network resource without fumbling through Network Neighborhood or the Explorer, you can drop a shortcut icon that points to the resource onto your NT desktop. Here's how:

1 Open My Computer.

2 Select a network drive icon that appears in My Computer.

3 Drag the network drive icon to the desktop.

The mouse cursor changes to a ghosted image of the dragged icon, as shown in Figure 6-12.

Windows NT displays a dialog box, shown in Figure 6-13, reading "You cannot move or copy this item to this location. Do you want to create a shortcut to the item instead?"

4 Choose Yes.

Figure 6-14 shows the results. A new drive icon appears on the desktop, labeled as a shortcut. Double-clicking on it opens a window displaying the contents of the network resource. You can also name the shortcut whatever you'd like.

You can also do this from Network Neighborhood.

heads up

You can also click the right mouse button on the network drive icon in My Computer to bring up the Shortcut Menu. A Create Shortcut menu option is offered there, as shown in Figure 6-14. When you select this option, you'll see the same dialog box that's shown in Figure 6-13 in this exercise.

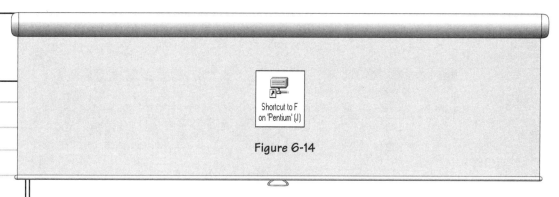

Figure 6-14

Figure 6-14: The new shortcut appears on your desktop.

Lesson 6-6

Transferring Files between Your System and Another User's System

☑ Progress Check

If you can do the following, you've mastered this unit:

❑ Locate network resources in Network Neighborhood.

❑ Locate network resources in the Windows NT Explorer.

❑ Use the Find command to locate network resources.

❑ Map a network drive.

❑ Create a shortcut on your desktop to a network resource.

❑ Copy files from your computer to another place on the network.

Why bother with the often complicated mechanics of networking? Well, a big part of it is not having to copy files to a floppy disk and then lumber over to a coworker's computer to feed it the information. This method, called "Sneaker-Net," is becoming increasingly obsolete with the more efficient networking features of Windows NT.

1 Open Network Neighborhood.

2 Open a network resource, such as someone's hard disk that is connected to the network.

on the CD

3 Insert the *Dummies 101: Windows NT* disc into the compact disc drive. Open My Computer and double-click on your compact disc's icon to show the disc's contents.

4 Drag the file titled ReadMe from the compact disc's window to the window for the network drive.

The computer displays a brief message stating that it's copying the file over. It's that simple. You can also open two different network resources and copy stuff between them.

heads up

If you try to copy a file over to a network drive that happens to be a CD-ROM, you won't be able to, because CD-ROMs are read-only devices: You can read from them, but you can't write to them. Strangely enough, you'll get a "Network Access is Denied" error message, which doesn't really tell you what the problem is.

extra credit

Cut down on those windows!

When you browse down several layers in the Network Neighborhood, you may find yourself with a hopelessly cluttered screen, because you'll have a huge number of windows open on the screen. There's a pretty easy way to fix this, and you can do this in Network Neighborhood.

1. **Open Network Neighborhood.**

2. **From the <u>V</u>iew menu in Network Neighborhood, choose <u>O</u>ptions.**

3. **In the Folder tab, select the "Browse folders by using a single window that changes as you open each folder" option.**

4. **Click on OK.**

5. **Now, the Network Neighborhood window will change its contents to show whatever drive and/or network resource you want it to display.**

How do you move your view back up again, traveling to the windows you came from? Press the backspace key, and Windows takes you up one more "notch" of a window level.

Notes:

Unit 6 Quiz

Circle the letter for the correct answer or answers to the following questions. As usual, a question may have more than one right answer.

1. **What is Network Neighborhood used for?**

   A. Locating other computer resources on the network

   B. Browsing network resources for files and programs you want to use

   C. Copying and moving items between your computer and others

   D. Browsing the Internet

2. **What can the Windows NT Find command be used for?**

   A. To locate resources on the network

   B. To locate files on your computer or on other computers connected to the network

   C. To locate a specific folder on your computer or on the network

   D. To find a good Chinese restaurant near the office

3. **Mapping a network drive means:**

   A. Assigning a drive letter to a network resource

   B. Making a different computer's hard drive appear as a new drive letter on your computer

   C. Putting a network drive on the map of the United States

4. **You can use a network to copy files between computers.**

   A. True

   B. False

   C. True, if the system administrator sets them up that way

   D. Only if it's worth your while to do so

5. **What types of network drives can you copy files to?**

   A. Hard Disks

   B. CD-ROMs

   C. Floppy Drives

   D. Removable Drives

Unit 6 Exercise

1. Open Network Neighborhood.

2. Open an available system on the network.

3. Drag a network folder onto the desktop. (This creates a shortcut.)

4. Rename the folder icon shortcut.

5. Open the new shortcut to view the network resources that it points to.

6. Now, close the window opened by your new shortcut.

7. In Network Neighborhood, right-click on the same network folder you previously created a shortcut from. The shortcut menu appears.

8. From that shortcut menu, select Map Network Drive.

9. Select a drive name, if necessary, from the dialog box.

10. Close the dialog box and open My Computer. A new network drive icon should appear there.

11. Drag the new network drive icon onto the desktop to create a new shortcut. Rename the new shortcut if desired.

12. Open the new shortcut and the one you created just before and compare their contents.

Part II Review

Unit 4 Summary

▶ **The taskbar:** The taskbar is a strip that runs across the edge of your screen. It lists currently running programs, making them easy to find: Click on a program's icon, and its window rises to the top of the screen. The taskbar can be dragged and dropped to any side of the screen, although it's usually found along the bottom.

▶ **Start menu:** Clicking on the Start button (found on the taskbar) brings the Start menu to the screen. The Start menu lets you load programs, find misplaced files, change your computer's settings, open recently used documents, and perform other computer chores.

▶ **Loading programs:** Most programs automatically list themselves by name in the Start menu's Programs area. Click on a program's name, and Windows NT brings that program to the screen.

▶ **The desktop:** All your work in Windows NT takes place on your desktop — the background of your screen. Windows on the desktop can be *maximized*, where they fill the screen, or *minimized*, where they appear as icons along the taskbar. Almost all windows have scroll bars and menus, which lets you move and resize them all by using the same methods.

▶ **Shortcuts:** Sometimes digging through menus for frequently used items can be frustrating. To speed things up, Windows NT lets you create shortcuts to those items. By double-clicking on the shortcut's icon, Windows NT behaves just as if you'd double-clicked the frequently used item itself. You can create shortcuts to programs, files, and folders.

▶ **Deleting a shortcut:** Deleting a shortcut doesn't delete the shortcut's target — it just deletes the push-button that takes you to that target, be it a file, program, or folder. The file, program, or folder itself stays on your computer's hard drive.

▶ **Recycle Bin:** To delete a file or folder, drag and drop it on the Recycle Bin — that little trash can on your desktop. If you accidentally delete something, double-click on the Recycle Bin. You can usually salvage recently deleted files by dragging them out of the Recycle Bin and onto the desktop or into another folder.

Unit 5 Summary

▶ **The computer's four main tools:** When handling information, your computer uses four main tools: *files, folders* (also known as *directories*), *disk drives,* and *disks.* The My Computer and Explorer programs let you manipulate all four of these tools.

▶ **Files:** Windows NT stores its information in files. Files are stored in folders, so they're easy to find later. Files and folders are stored on disks. Drives read and write files to those disks.

▶ **Windows:** The My Computer program displays its information by using windows — just like any other Windows NT program. Each window shows the files and folders that live on a particular folder on a particular drive.

▶ **Copying and moving files and folders:** You can move and copy files and folders to different places on your hard drive by dragging and dropping them. They can be dragged and dropped among My Computer, Explorer, and your desktop.

▶ **My Computer and Explorer are like file cabinets:** My Computer and Explorer work like big file cabinets, where information is packed into folders; the folders are packed onto disks, which can hold hundreds of folders. Also, you can put folders inside each other, further organizing your information.

Part II Review

▶ **Naming files and folders:** Files and folders have specific rules about their names: The names can use only letters, numbers, and certain symbols; plus, they can't be longer than 255 characters. Older versions of Windows can use only 8 characters, often causing problems if you swap files with friends who don't have Windows NT.

Unit 6 Summary

▶ **Network:** A network is a collection of computers strung together with wires or the phone lines so they can share information.

▶ **Network Neighborhood:** Just as a disk drive icon lists the folders inside that drive, the Network Neighborhood icon reveals the computers available for networking.

▶ **Find:** The Find command, located in the Start menu, can find networked computers by name, just as it can locate missing files.

▶ **Mapping Drives:** If you find yourself using a networked area frequently, create a shortcut to it on your desktop. Or, to make that area show up in your program's list of disk drives, create a "mapped network drive." That fools the computer into thinking another computer is merely a disk drive.

Part II Test

The questions on this test cover all the material presented in Part II, Units 4, 5 and 6.

True   False

T   F   1. A drive can always read and write information to a disk.

T   F   2. After you delete a file, you can never retrieve it.

T   F   3. You can control the folders and windows in My Explorer just like you do the windows on your desktop.

T   F   4. Double-clicking on an program's name on the Start menu starts that program.

T   F   5. Programs usually put their names on the Start menu so that you can launch them easily.

T   F   6. You can use Windows NT without a mouse.

T   F   7. Deleting a shortcut from the desktop deletes that shortcut's target, be it a file, program, or folder.

T   F   8. My Computer and Explorer perform the same functions, but in slightly different ways.

T   F   9. Many floppy disks must be *formatted* before you can use them.

T   F   10. You can move or copy files and folders by *dragging and dropping* them into other places in My Computer or Explorer.

Part II Test

T   F   11. You can move or copy files and folders from other computers by dragging and dropping them into other places in My Computer or Explorer.

T   F   12. The Network Neighborhood lists the computers attached to your computer.

Multiple Choice

For each of the following questions, circle the correct answer or answers. Remember, each question may have more than one right answer.

13. **The My Computer program is often compared to this common object:**

   A. A trash can.

   B. A nail file.

   C. A file cabinet.

   D. A television set.

14. **My Computer lets you drag and drop the following items:**

   A. Files, folders, and drives onto the desktop.

   B. Folders into other folders.

   C. Files onto floppy disks.

   D. Carrot peelings into the trash.

15. **Both My Computer and Explorer can do the following tasks:**

   A. Load your programs.

   B. Delete your programs.

   C. Create folders.

   D. Create icons.

16. **What is a root folder?**

   A. A big folder on a disk that contains all the other folders.

   B. A folder that's usually named after the drive it lives on.

   C. A book that's popular with farmers.

   D. The first folder that appears when you open My Computer.

17. **These disks can hold the most computer information:**

   A. Floppy disks.

   B. Hard disks.

   C. Compact discs.

   D. Vinyl disks.

   E. Removable disks.

18. **These things can damage floppy disks:**

   A. Sticky fingers.

   B. Magnets.

   C. Foul smells.

   D. Moisture.

Part II Test

19. The following step(s) can help find a lost or covered-up window on the desktop:

    A. Click the taskbar with the right mouse button and choose Cascade or one of the Tile commands.

    B. Press Alt+Tab.

    C. Click on any visible part of the window.

    D. Call home.

20. My Computer lets you use a mouse for the following tasks:

    A. Changing a window's size and location.

    B. Loading programs.

    C. Feeding cats.

    D. Deleting icons.

Matching

21. Match up the following keystrokes with the corresponding action:

    A. F1   1. Brings up a list of currently running programs.

    B. F5   2. Cancels an action.

    C. Alt+Tab   3. Brings up the Windows Help program.

    D. Esc   4. Makes My Computer and Explorer take another look at a newly inserted floppy.

    E. Enter   5. Opens or loads the highlighted item.

22. Match up the icon for the drive with the drive's type.

    A. ▭   1. CD-ROM drive

    B. ▭   2. Floppy disk drive

    C. ◉   3. Hard drive

    D. ▭   4. Mapped network drive

Part II Lab Assignment

This lab assignment gets to the nitty-gritty of Windows NT — the sort of stuff that you'll find yourself doing on a day-to-day basis. You'll start a Windows NT session, create folders, copy files, load programs, and close down the session.

Step 1: Create a folder for a project

Create a new folder called Today's Work on the desktop.

Part II Lab Assignment

Step 2: Create a shortcut to your book's disk folder

Make a shortcut on your desktop that leads to the folder where this book's disk is installed.

(**Hint**: The folder is called Windows NT, which lives in a folder called Dummies 101, which lives on your C drive. So using your right mouse button, drag and drop the Windows NT folder out of My Computer's Dummies 101 folder and onto your desktop. Then select Create Shortcut Here from the menu.)

Step 3: Close all your desktop's open windows

Step 4: Double-click on the Dummies 101 shortcut

The folder containing your book's disk files opens up on-screen.

Step 5: Copy a file into your desktop's folder

Find the Eau de Froggie file, and then copy that file into your new Today's Work folder.

Step 6: Load and close a program

Double-click on the Eau de Froggie icon in the Today's Work folder, and then close Paint.

Step 7: Delete a file, shortcut, and folder

Delete the Eau de Froggie file from the Today's Work folder. Then close the Dummies 101 window and delete its shortcut from the desktop. Finally, close the Today's Work window and delete its folder from the desktop.

Step 8: Retrieve a deleted file from the Recycle Bin

Double-click on the Recycle Bin and drag the Eau de Froggie file back onto the desktop.

Step 9: Double-click on the Network Neighborhood icon

The Network Neighborhood window appears, showing all the computers you can access. Because everybody has a different network setup, the exercise stops here. Ask your Network Administrator if your company has a handbook or manual explaining which computers are to be used for which purposes. (You might have to simply bug a coworker; Network Administrators are notoriously busy.)

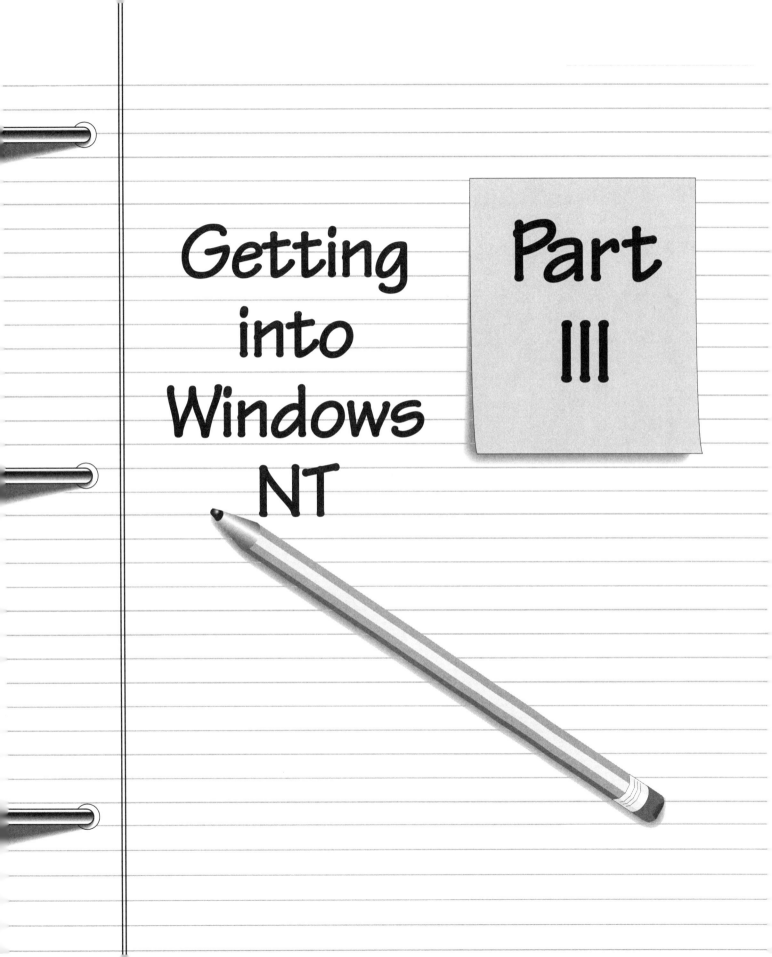

Getting into Windows NT

Part III

In this part . . .

The first half of this book taught the basics of Windows NT: moving a mouse, moving boxes around on-screen, and pushing the correct keys and buttons at the right times. Plus, you learned how to make the My Computer and Explorer programs do your bidding, as well as how to sneak over to the different computers strewn over the office network.

Congratulations! You're over the hill, so to speak, and the rest of this book has all the easy stuff. Because you've learned the basics, it's time to break things down into specifics. The next few units teach you how to start a program and load a file into it. After you fiddle with the file for a while, you'll learn how to save your work. Finally, you'll learn how to print the thing — if you decide that it's worth putting on paper.

Starting a Program

Objectives for This Unit

✓ Starting a program from the Start menu

✓ Starting a program from the desktop

✓ Starting a program in My Computer

✓ Starting a program in Explorer

✓ Starting a program in a Run box

Windows may be a computerized desktop, but it starts out as an awfully empty one. Just as you need to pull the stapler out of the drawer before you can start stapling papers, you need to load programs before you can start working in Windows.

This unit shows you how to reach into the right drawers for grabbing programs out of your computer. Several main ways are available, but you'll use the method in the first lesson the most often. (The others are listed for those people who like to know *everything*.)

Lesson 7-1   Opening a Program from the Start Menu

By the time you've reached this part of the book, you're probably already familiar with loading programs through the Start menu. But in case you need a refresher — and because it's nice to have all the program-loading methods in one place — here's what to do. The following steps load the WordPad word processing program:

1 Click on the Start button and choose Programs from the Start menu.

A list of programs squirts out the side of the menu.

2 Choose Accessories from the menu.

3 Choose WordPad from the Accessories menu.

WordPad comes to the screen.

When installed, most programs automatically add their names to the Start menu, so this method is usually the easiest and quickest way to load a program. (Click on the X in WordPad's top-right corner to close the program and move to the next lesson.)

Lesson 7-2   Opening a Program from the Desktop

The desktop lets you open programs in three main ways:

▶ First, you can double-click on any icon — like the Recycle Bin — and the desktop opens it.

▶ Second, you can create a shortcut to a program and double-click on it. (Creating a shortcut leaves a handy push-button for opening that program in the future.)

▶ Last, you can click on the desktop with the right mouse button and choose from the programs listed on the menu that suddenly appears. The next few steps teach all three methods.

Loading a program from a desktop icon

1 Double-click on the My Computer icon.

Windows NT opens the My Computer program.

2 Close the My Computer program.

See how easy things can be if your program already has an icon on the desktop? That's why shortcuts, described in the very next section, come in so handy. By creating shortcuts to your most frequently used programs and files, you can access them almost instantly.

Creating a desktop shortcut and loading a program

If your program already has a shortcut on the desktop, you can load that program quickly and easily. If you'll be loading the program only once, don't bother creating a shortcut; load it by using one of the other methods described in this unit. But if you'll be accessing the program a lot, the shortcut will save you some time. Follow these steps:

1 **Click on the desktop with your right mouse button.**

2 **Choose Shortcut from the New menu.**

3 **Click on the Browse button.**

A box that vaguely resembles the Windows NT Explorer appears. Just as with Explorer, the Browse box lets you double-click on folders to open them. And to look at other drives, click on the Look in box near the top of the box.

4 **Double-click on the Winnt folder.**

I'll use the Winnt folder as an example because it contains a lot of programs.

5 **Double-click on the explorer file.**

6 **Click on the Next button.**

7 **Type** explorer **in the box and then click on the Finish button.**

A handy shortcut for the Explorer program appears on your desktop. Double-click on the shortcut, and the Explorer program comes to the screen. Feel free to move the shortcut to any convenient place on-screen. You can even create a folder full of shortcuts that lead to your favorite files and programs.

Loading a program from the desktop menu

Some programs put themselves on the desktop's secret menu — the one that appears from nowhere when you click your right mouse button on a blank area of the desktop. Here's how the process works:

1 **Click on the desktop with your right mouse button.**

The secret menu appears. (It's not really a secret, though, because you saw the same menu in the preceding section.)

2 **Choose New from the menu.**

Windows NT gives you a choice of new things to create, as shown in Figure 7-1.

3 **Select Text Document from the menu.**

Windows NT immediately brings the Notepad program to the screen, ready for you to start typing some quick words.

Many programs add themselves to the desktop's right-click menu, which provides an easy way to summon them quickly.

Notes:

dragging and dropping programs from My Computer or Explorer onto desktop creates quick and easy shortcuts

Figure 7-1: Clicking on the desktop with the right mouse button gives you access to a number of options.

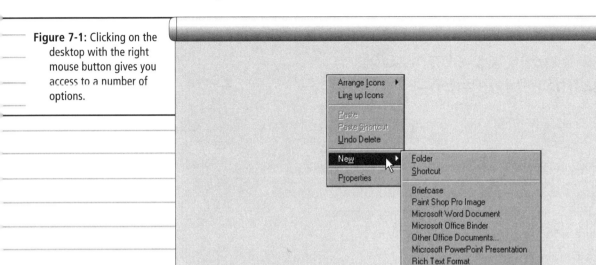

Figure 7-1

Lesson 7-3 Opening a Program in My Computer

holding down Ctrl while double-clicking folders in My Computer keeps all activity in current window — My Computer won't open new window for each opened folder

Opening a program in My Computer is pretty easy; the hard part is finding the program. If you know which folder the program lives in, here's how to launch the program:

1 **Double-click on the My Computer program.**

The program opens on-screen, displaying your computer's disk drives.

2 **Double-click on the C drive icon.**

3 **Double-click on the Winnt folder.**

4 **Double-click on the Explorer icon.**

The Explorer program loads itself and comes to the screen. If you don't know which folder your program lives in, however, the program may be hard to find. In fact, your best bet may be to use the Find program, covered in Unit 4.

Lesson 7-4 Opening a Program in Explorer

Opening a program in Windows NT Explorer is almost identical to opening a program in My Computer. That means that they're both difficult to use if you don't know the folder in which the program lives. Explorer can be a little

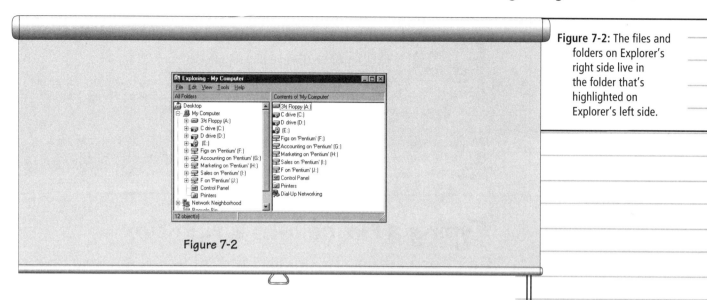

Figure 7-2

Figure 7-2: The files and folders on Explorer's right side live in the folder that's highlighted on Explorer's left side.

quicker, however, and it has a key feature: It doesn't leave trails of windows across your screen as it moves from folder to folder.

If you know the name of a program's folder, here's how to bring the program to the screen:

1 Click on the My Computer program with your right mouse button.

2 Choose Explore from the menu.

The Windows NT Explorer program leaps to the screen, as shown in Figure 7-2.

3 Click on the C drive icon on the Explorer window's left side.

Explorer shows the contents of the C drive on the right side.

4 Double-click on the Winnt folder on the right side.

Explorer lists the contents of the Winnt folder on the right side.

5 Double-click on the system32 folder on the right side.

You'll probably have to slide the window's scroll bars to see all the folders and files inside some of these folders. (The Scroll Bar Sliding Class took place in Unit 3.)

6 Double-click on the Calc icon on the right side.

The Calculator program loads itself and comes to the screen. Difficult? Yes. Just as with My Computer, loading programs can be difficult in Explorer if you don't know the location of the program's folder.

7 Close the Calculator program.

Click on the X in its upper-right corner.

8 Double-click on the C drive's Dummies 101 folder.

The Dummies 101 folder's contents — in this case, the Windows NT folder — spills out into the window's right side. (The Dummies 101 folder contains the goodies that came with this book, and it's located right off your C drive.)

9 Double-click on the Windows NT folder.

click on My Computer with right mouse button and choose <u>F</u>ind to load Start menu's <u>F</u>ind command

choose Tools from Explorer's menu and click on <u>F</u>ind to load Start menu's <u>F</u>ind command

on the CD

10   Double-click on the Eau de Froggie file.

Doing so shows you a second way of opening programs that works throughout Windows NT: Double-click on a file, and Windows NT loads the program that created the file and brings them both to the screen.

on the test

A program's name and its filename are two different things. The program's *name* — Calculator, for example — is designed for people to use. The program's *filename* — Calc, for instance — is for the computer to use.

Lesson 7-5   Typing a Name into a Run Box

You probably won't have to deal with this one, but I'm sticking it in just in case. It's sort of a throwback to that DOS stuff that the computer oldsters rave about. See, back in the old days, people didn't just point and click at pictures to run their programs. Instead, they typed the program's name and pressed Enter. Windows NT lets the old-school folks type a program's name in a Run box when loading programs in the Run section of the Start menu. The following steps show you how, if you're still interested:

1   Click on the Start button.

2   Choose Run from the menu.

A box similar to the one shown in Figure 7-3 appears.

3   Type the program's filename and path in the box and click on OK.

on the test

Here's where this task gets complicated. You not only need to know the program's filename, as described earlier, but you also need to know its path. Its *path* is its location on your hard drive, and it works as a road map that helps the computer find the file.

First, a path contains the letter of the disk drive, followed by a colon. Next, the path lists which folders the computer must look through to find the file. For example, say you're looking for the Spreadsheet program that's in the Accounting directory. The Accounting directory lives in the Office directory, which is in the Downtown directory. And all this stuff is on your C drive.

Whew. One more thing, though: All the folders and names need to be separated by the \ (backslash) character.

So the path for your Spreadsheet program would be C:\Downtown\Office\Accounting\Spreadsheet, and that's what you'd type in the box in Figure 7-3.

When you click on OK, the Start menu uses that path as a road map to find the Spreadsheet program. When the Start menu finds the program, it loads that program and brings it to the screen.

You'll rarely use the Run boxes in Windows NT, but they're there. And now you know what a path does.

☑ **Progress Check**

If you can do the following, you've mastered this unit:

❑ Load a program from the Start button menu.

❑ Load a program from the desktop.

❑ Load a program from My Computer.

❑ Load a program from Explorer.

❑ Load a program from a Run box.

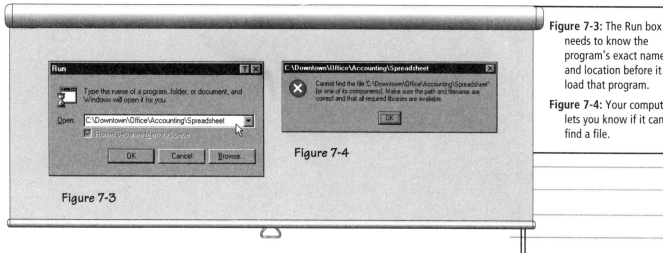

Figure 7-3: The Run box needs to know the program's exact name and location before it will load that program.

Figure 7-4: Your computer lets you know if it can't find a file.

Figure 7-4

Figure 7-3

Oh, one last thing: If the computer doesn't find your program — make just one mistake in the path, and the computer gets confused — it comes back with an error message like the one shown in Figure 7-4.

on the test

Browse boxes, like the one used in Lesson 7-2, also let you type in a path to avoid wading through a bunch of menus to find your file or program.

Unit 7 Quiz

Circle the letter of the correct answer or answers to each of the following questions. (Remember that some questions have more than one right answer to keep things from being too easy.)

1. **How do a program's name and its filename differ?**

    A. One is for people to use; the other is for the computer to use.

    B. One can be longer than 255 characters; the other can't.

    C. One is a trademark; the other isn't.

    D. One got teased in school; the other didn't.

2. **Loading programs is easiest to do by using this program:**

    A. Start menu

    B. Explorer

    C. My Computer

    D. UNIX

3. **Windows NT can create shortcuts to these items:**

    A. Programs

    B. Folders

    C. Files

    D. Success

4. **When you double-click on a file's name, Windows does this:**

    A. Sends an error message

    B. Loads the file

    C. Loads the file if it can figure out which program created the file

    D. Writhes in agony

5. **A path serves this purpose:**

    A. Holds cookie crumbs

    B. Gives the computer directions to a file's location

    C. Lists a file's current folder

    D. Lists a file's current drive

Unit 7 Exercise

By completing this exercise, you practice loading the WordPad program in each possible way. Close WordPad after each step so that you can bring it to the screen again in the next step.

1. Double-click on the WordPad icon from the Accessories area of the Start menu's Programs area.

2. Type **C:\Winnt\system32\Write** in the Run box and press Enter.

3. While in My Computer, double-click on the following icons in this order: the C drive icon, the Winnt folder, the system32 folder, and the the Write file.

4. While in Explorer, double-click on the Write file located in that same C:\Winnt\system32 folder.

5. Double-click on the Joe's Lament file in the C:\Dummies 101\ Windows NT folder.

on the CD

6. Create a shortcut on the desktop to Joe's Lament in your C:\Dummies 101\Windows NT folder. (Hint: You can type **C:\Dummies 101\ Windows NT** in the Browse box instead of choosing Browse and pointing and clicking through the folders.)

Unit 8

●●●●●●●●●●●

Opening or Creating a File

Objectives for This Unit

✓ Loading a file into a program

✓ Loading a file by using My Computer or Explorer

✓ Creating a file from the desktop

Prerequisites

▶ Using a mouse (Lesson 2-1)

▶ Moving and controlling on-screen windows (Unit 3)

▶ Opening My Computer and Explorer (Unit 5)

▶ Loading WordPad (Lesson 7-1)

▶ Joe's Lament
on the CD

When a painter finishes creating a painting, the painting is done. There's no need to mess with it anymore — the paint's dry, and the work's complete. Computers aren't nearly as static as a painting hanging in a gallery. After you finish creating a file and saving it to disk, you'll probably want to open it again someday. You may want to print the file's contents again. Or you may want to modify an angry letter to your boss and turn it into a more constructive letter before somebody else on the network gets hold of it.

This unit shows you how to load files into programs, something you'll find yourself doing over and over again.

Loading a File into a Program

Lesson 8-1

on the CD

Feeling like a poodle? Here are the hoops that WordPad makes you leap through before it lets you play with a file. Luckily, most programs use an identical scheme. In this case, you'll open a letter file called Joe's Lament from the folder created by the CD in the back of this book.

Figure 8-1: When Windows programs open files, they let you choose the file's drive, folder, type, and name.

Figure 8-2: Double-clicking on the C drive reveals the folders and WordPad files living on that drive.

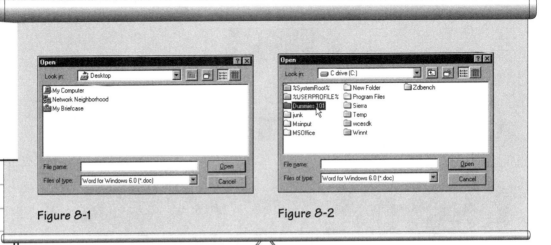

Figure 8-1   Figure 8-2

Notes:

1 **Click on the Start button.**

2 **Load WordPad from the Accessories area of the Programs menu.**

Click on the WordPad icon — the one that looks like a little quill pen hovering over a notepad.

3 **Choose Open from WordPad's File menu.**

A box somewhat like the one in Figure 8-1 appears. Notice how it has four main areas: folders and drives are listed in the big area of the window, while two little boxes along the bottom let you specify filenames and types. Because different computers are set up differently, your screen may look slightly different than the one in Figure 8-1.

The Files of type area is WordPad's way of filtering out all files that it didn't create. See, whenever WordPad creates a file, it secretly tacks on the letters *DOC* to the end of the file's name; that lets WordPad locate the file more easily later.

Windows NT hides those DOC letters, known as a *file extension,* because normal, healthy-minded people don't need to know about them. Only WordPad (and a few computer engineers) really care about the whole concept.

4 **Click on the Look in box.**

This lets you choose the drives and folders for WordPad to peer into.

5 **Click on the C drive icon from the Look in box.**

Because you're after a file that lives on the C:\ drive, select that drive, as shown in Figure 8-2. WordPad displays the files and folders on drive C.

6 **Choose the Dummies 101 folder.**

The box changes views to show the files and folders living in the Dummies 101 folder, as shown in Figure 8-3.

7 **Choose the Windows NT folder.**

Doing so moves to the folder containing the CD files that came with this book.

8 **Double-click on the Joe's Lament file.**

That double-click tells WordPad to load the file.

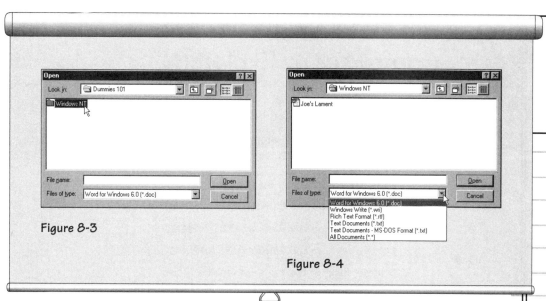

Figure 8-3

Figure 8-4

Figure 8-3: Double-click on the folder in which your sought-after file lives.

Figure 8-4: The Files of type area lets you filter out all but certain types of files.

Note: When you first tell WordPad to open a file, it displays the files and folders living on the *current* folder — the last folder to be accessed. If the file you're after lives in the current folder, you see it right away. If the file doesn't appear, you have to do a little spelunking to find it, looking in different drives and folders.

When you choose the Open command from a program's File menu, the program automatically displays all the files it has created that live in the current folder. Although programs normally display only files that they've personally created in the Open box, you can display other files by choosing other options in the Files of type box.

To view files in other folders or drives, click in those folders or in the Look in box and choose other areas to search.

extra credit

Q/A session

Question: By clicking on folders, I can delve deeper into my computer's mass of folders. But how do I move back out and start over if I started clicking on the wrong ones?

Answer: Each time you double-click on a folder or drive from within a program's Open window, the program shows you the contents of that folder or drive. By continually double-clicking on folders,

you eventually reach a dead end. If your file isn't there, you have to turn around and go back.

To go back, folder by folder, click on the little folder with the arrow on it, located immediately to the right of the Look in box. Each click on that folder moves you up another step in your folder structure; eventually, you'll see the My Computer icon, and you can start down a different path.

Lesson 8-2

Loading a File from within My Computer or Explorer

Notes:

you can start
program by clicking
on names of files
that program has
created

Hey, I'm not going to punish you twice; you already learned this trick back in Lesson 5-4. If you were out sick that day and want to try and fake it, however, here's a rough sketch. Use this lesson to do what you did in Lesson 7-4: load a file into WordPad.

1 **Load My Computer or Explorer.**

2 **Double-click on the C drive icon.**

3 **Double-click on the Dummies 101 folder.**

4 **Double-click on the Windows NT folder.**

5 **Double-click on the Joe's Lament file.**

on the CD

Windows NT recognizes the secret file extension, loads WordPad, and tosses the Joe's Lament file into WordPad for your use.

If this method seems a little weird, head back to Lesson 5-4.

extra credit

Q/A session

Question: How do I load a file into WordPad if its filename doesn't end in DOC?

Answer: When you tell a program to load a file, that program automatically displays the files that it knows it has personally created. For example, WordPad always tacks the letters DOC onto the end of its files' names, so it automatically displays files ending in DOC. But what if you're trying to load a file into WordPad and WordPad *didn't* create it? For example, the file FLAPPER.TXT won't show up in the box because it ends in the letters TXT. The fix? Use the Files of type area in the Open box. Click on the little downward-pointing arrow and choose among the other types;

as shown in Figure 8-4, each line lets you filter out all but a certain type of file.

If you want to see *all* the files in a certain folder, choose the *.* option. Be careful, though. Because different programs tend to save their files in different formats, you usually can't open other types of files in your program.

One last caveat: Microsoft likes to link its programs so integrally that people wouldn't even think about buying something from another company. So Microsoft Word for Windows and WordPad both use DOC as their identifying file extension. Don't be surprised to see Word come up when you want WordPad or vice versa.

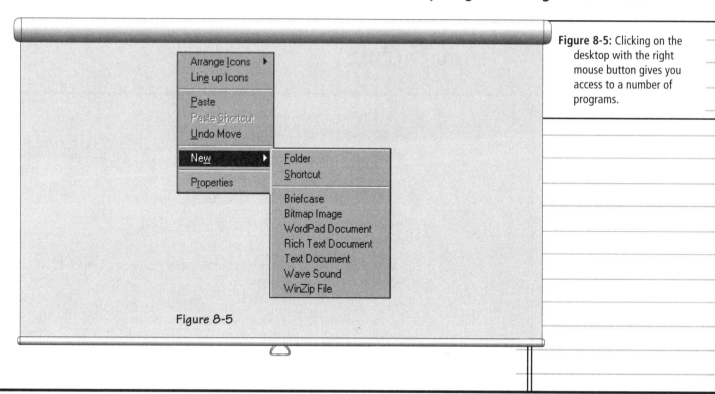

Figure 8-5

Figure 8-5: Clicking on the desktop with the right mouse button gives you access to a number of programs.

Creating a File from the Desktop Menu

Lesson 8-3

You're really getting off easy with this unit, because you've already learned how to do this task, too. Back in Unit 7, you learned how to load a program straight off the desktop. That trick works when creating files, too, and the following steps show you how:

1 Click on the desktop with your right mouse button.

The secret menu appears. (By now, it shouldn't be a secret; it's an integral part of Windows NT.)

2 Choose New from the menu.

Windows NT gives you an option of new files to create, as shown in Figure 8-5.

3 Choose Text Document from the menu.

Windows NT immediately brings the Notepad program to the screen, ready for you to start typing some quick words.

Many programs add themselves to the desktop's right-click menu, which provides you with an easy way to summon them quickly.

Tip: To create a text file, record a sound, draw a picture, or access some of your other programs, click on the desktop with your right mouse button and choose New from the pop-up menu.

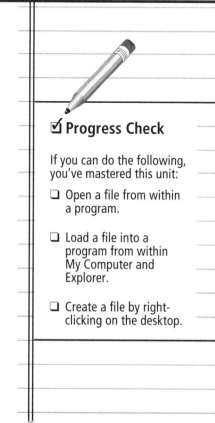

☑ Progress Check

If you can do the following, you've mastered this unit:

❏ Open a file from within a program.

❏ Load a file into a program from within My Computer and Explorer.

❏ Create a file by right-clicking on the desktop.

Unit 8 Quiz

For each question, circle the letter of the correct answer or answers. Remember, each question may have more than one right answer.

1. **The Open command from a program's File menu displays this:**
   A. All the files on your computer
   B. All the files the program has created
   C. All the files stored in the program's currently open folder
   D. Nothing

2. **Double-clicking on the folders or drives in a program's Open files window lets you view these:**
   A. The files and folders inside those folders
   B. The files and folders inside those drives
   C. The contents of files
   D. Files the computer didn't create

3. **Choose this option in the Files of type box to make a program display all the files in the current folder:**
   A. Show All
   B. Documents
   C. $.$
   D. All files (*.*)

Unit 8 Exercise

on the CD

You've hired the most trendy artist in New York to come up with the new label for this season's perfume fragrance. In this exercise, you experiment with several different ways to open the Eau de Froggie file in the Paint program by using the methods you learned in this unit. Got the art on the screen? Keep your fingers crossed while the rest of the corporate board gives it a high-pressure look.

1. Open the Start menu.
2. Load Paint.
3. Load Eau de Froggie into Paint from the Windows NT folder (which lives in the Dummies 101 folder on your C drive).
4. Close Paint.
5. Load Eau de Froggie by double-clicking on its name in My Computer.
6. Close Paint.
7. Load Eau de Froggie by double-clicking on its name in Explorer.
8. Close Paint.

Unit 9

• • • • • • • • • • •

Saving a File

Objectives for This Unit

✓ Learning where to save your work

✓ Saving your work

✓ Saving in different formats

Prerequisites

▶ Pointing and clicking a mouse (Lesson 2-1)

▶ Manipulating windows (Unit 3)

▶ Opening folders (Lesson 5-3)

▶ Opening a Windows program (Lesson 4-2)

▶ Loading a file (Lesson 8-1)

Y ou know how your most important thoughts can drift away if you don't write them down. Computers do the same thing.

When a computer saves a file, it writes the information onto a disk so that it can grab the information later. And if the information doesn't get written down, it drifts away like the promise of a raise with next week's paycheck.

heads up

The problem is that most computer programs don't save your work automatically — you have to give them a nudge every so often. How often? The answer's easy: *Save your work whenever you think of it.* You never know when the power might go out, somebody might accidentally kick the power cord, or your computer might simply expire. (Fortunately, this doesn't happen very often.)

So if you're word processing, try to save your work after every paragraph. If you've just come up with a killer sentence, save your work. And of course, be sure to save your work after you finish writing the document.

Windows NT usually reminds you to save your work before it lets you exit your program, so you get off easy there. Nevertheless, this unit teaches you how and where to save your work in Windows NT. Once again, you'll be using the WordPad program since it's always handy.

Lesson 9-1

Knowing Where to Save Your Work

You learned this trick back in Lesson 5-1, but here it is again: When storing files on a computer, store them in related folders. For example, keep all your correspondence in a Letters folder. And if you start getting a lot of business letters from Acme International and Acme United, make two additional folders in your Letters folder, one for Acme International and one for Acme United. Then divide up the files according to income or expenses, putting each one in its appropriate folder.

Still too much correspondence? Then start making even *more* folders and start dividing them by date. Doing so will make finding that letter you wrote back in June 1992 (the one asking a company to explain why they're charging you for all their "business" trips to Key West) a lot easier. You're pretty much unlimited in the number of folders you can have and the number of levels under which you can have them.

The following steps show you how to create a system of folders as I've just mentioned:

1 **Open My Computer.**

   Double-clicking on the My Computer icon opens it up for viewing.

2 **Open the C drive.**

   Again, a double-click does the trick.

3 **Click on a blank area of the C drive folder with the right mouse button.**

   A familiar-looking menu appears.

4 **Choose Folder from the New menu.**

   A new folder appears, waiting for you to type in a name.

5 **Type Letters and press Enter.**

6 **Double-click on the new Letters folder.**

   The Letters folder opens up.

7 **Click inside the new Letters folder with your right mouse button and choose Folder from the New menu.**

8 **Name the new folder Acme International.**

9 **Repeat Step 7, but name the folder Acme United.**

By following those steps, you have a Letters folder on your C drive, and the Letters folder contains two additional folders, one for Acme International and the other for Acme United. After you get the hang of creating folders, it's not as hard as it appears.

folders can be dragged and dropped inside each other even when you're saving a file

extra credit

Q/A session

Question: Why can't I just keep all my folders on the desktop?

Answer: The desktop itself is a tempting place to put new folders, but it's not the best place. No, reserve the desktop for shortcut icons that point to the folder's *real* location on your hard drive or shortcuts to important programs you often use. Doing so keeps your desktop free of clutter and lets you "nest" folders on your hard drive.

Feel free to create folders on the desktop, like the Letters example I just explained, which you broke down into Acme International and Acme United folders. But after you create the Letters folder on your desktop, create a folder on your C drive called Words and move the Letters folder into it.

Saving Your Work

Lesson 9-2

All Windows programs work the same way when it comes to saving a file. The following steps save a file in WordPad, but you follow the same steps for any Windows program:

1 Load WordPad from the Start menu.

WordPad is in the Start menu's Accessories area (which is located in the Programs area).

2 Type a sentence in WordPad.

You can use your imagination here. Type the words **Aphids suck plant juice** if you're having trouble thinking of something. You've got an excuse to fool around at work: You just need something to save.

3 Choose <u>S</u>ave from WordPad's <u>F</u>ile menu.

If you had saved that file previously, the program would simply save the file using all the information you gave it before. But because you're saving this file for the first time, a questionnaire appears in a box, as shown in Figure 9-1.

4 Choose your C drive from the Save <u>i</u>n box.

As Figure 9-1 shows, the Save in box that runs along the top of the window explains where WordPad will stuff your file if you don't choose anything else. But because you want the C drive, click on the little black triangle at the end of the Save in box, and choose the C drive from the list of drives and folders that appears. That same list may also appear directly in the box; if so, just double-click on the C drive to open it up, as shown in Figure 9-2.

(You can save your work on any drive, but for this example you're using drive C.)

The Save As box changes its view to display all the folders living on your C drive.

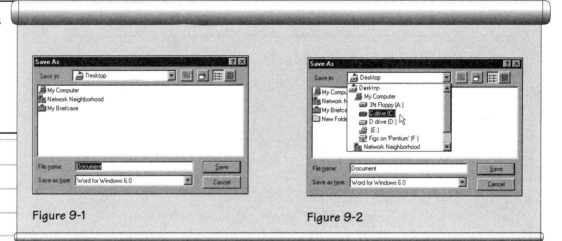

Figure 9-1: You fill out this form when saving a file for the first time.

Figure 9-2: Choosing the C drive from the Save in box reveals the folders living on that drive.

Figure 9-1   Figure 9-2

Notes:

5 **Double-click on the Dummies 101 folder.**

See the Dummies 101 folder listed in the box? Double-click on that folder to choose it. Windows NT opens the folder and shows what's inside.

6 **Double-click on the Windows NT folder.**

That opens up the Windows NT folder, which lives inside the Dummies 101 folder. As before, Windows NT opens the folder and shows what's inside.

extra credit

Q/A session

Question: The Save File window doesn't let me create a new folder for storing my new file!

Answer: For years, Windows programs didn't let you create new folders while you were trying to save your file. For example, say you just drew an ad-agency picture of a trendy, lime green cigar in Paint and want to save it in your age-old Cigar folder. But you've drawn a picture of a *Cuban* cigar, so you want to save it in a new folder called Cuban. How can you create a Cuban folder inside your Cigar folder at the same time you save your new file?

Windows NT lets you create new folders on the fly when you're saving a file for the first time. First, open the Save File window and move to your Cigar folder. Then, with the Save As window on-screen, as shown in Figure 9-1, click on the little folder icon with the little shining explosion on its upper-right corner. (Can't tell which folder icon has the explosion? Hold your mouse pointer over each folder icon until a little box that says Create New Folder appears.) A new folder appears in the window and asks you for a name. After you name the new folder, double-click on it to open it up and save your program inside.

Tip: Lost? Clicked too far into some of your folders and need a way out? Click on the little folder along the top with the arrow in it — the folder closest to the Save in box — to make Windows NT back out of your current folder. Keep clicking that little folder with the arrow, and you'll eventually see all your listed drives; then you can start over.

7 **Ignore the Save as type box.**

Because you're saving the file in the WordPad program, WordPad automatically saves the file in its special *Word for Windows 6.0* format (and that's why it tacks on the letters *DOC* to the end of the file). WordPad, as well as some other Windows programs, can get sneaky and save files in other formats, but we cover those later.

8 **Type** Study in Aphid Sucking **in the File name box, replacing the word** *Document.*

Here's some good news about the file's name. For years, IBM-compatible PCs could use only eight characters when naming their files. That meant that people had to use names like REPORT12 and 950122.

Windows NT lets you use 255 characters, so you can name your file Study in Aphid Sucking because you've written about aphids sucking plant juice.

9 **Click on the Save button.**

The computer saves the Study in Aphid Sucking file in the Dummies 101\ Windows NT folder on your computer's C drive.

Now, because you've assigned a name, folder, and drive to that particular file, you'll only have to perform Step 3 when saving that file in the future: just choose Save from WordPad's File menu, and WordPad automatically saves your file using the same name and location that you used before.

on the test

Filenames can be 255 characters long and can contain letters, numbers, and some common symbols. You can't use the following symbols in filenames: . , " / \ [ ] : * | < > + = ;

extra credit

Q/A session

Question: What if I don't choose a drive, folder, or name when saving my file?

Answer: If you don't choose a drive or folder when saving a file, the program simply saves the file in the *current folder,* or the drive that happens to be open at the time. Usually, this means that the program saves the file in the same drive and folder

that the program itself lives on, which makes the file harder to find in the future.

Programs almost always make you choose a name when saving a file for the first time, however. If you don't choose a name, they'll make up a name like nondescript Unnamed File or New Text Document.

---

to save files quickly, press Alt+F+S

Lesson 9-3

Saving in Different Formats
(The Save As Command)

Notes:

People in different countries often speak different languages; foreigners don't know what they're saying. So it's only natural that computer programs do the same thing when storing files: They store them in different formats that other programs can't read.

But just as some people can understand more than one language, some Windows programs can read and write in other computer programs' formats. Plus, some wise computer engineers came up with a computerized *Esperanto* — a file format that a whole bunch of computer programs can understand. (The language is called *ASCII* — pronounced *ASK-ee* — if you ever see that word and wonder what it means.)

You save files in different formats with the Save as type command. To teach you how the process works, this lesson shows you how to create a file in WordPad and store it in a format that Notepad, another Windows program, can read. First, you see what happens when you try to open a WordPad file in Notepad:

1 Load Notepad.

The Notepad icon is that little green spiral-bound notebook in the Accessories menu of the Start menu's Program area.

2 Choose Open from Notepad's File menu.

A box appears, as shown in Figure 9-3.

3 Choose drive C from the Look in box.

The window shows you the files and folders on your C drive.

4 Choose the Dummies 101 folder and then open the Windows NT folder that lives inside it.

Now, Notepad lists the files in that folder *if* they are stored in the proper Notepad format. However, you stored Study in Aphid Sucking in WordPad format, so that file won't be listed in the box.

5 Choose Cancel and close Notepad.

Now, reload the Study in Aphid Sucking file into WordPad and save it in a format that Notepad can understand:

1 Load WordPad.

2 Choose Open from WordPad's File menu and load Study in Aphid Sucking.

Loading a file is covered in Lesson 8-1; the file is in the Windows NT folder, which lives in your C drive's Dummies 101 folder.

3 Choose Save As from WordPad's File menu.

A box appears that lets you save the Study in Aphid Sucking file in a different format (see Figure 9-4).

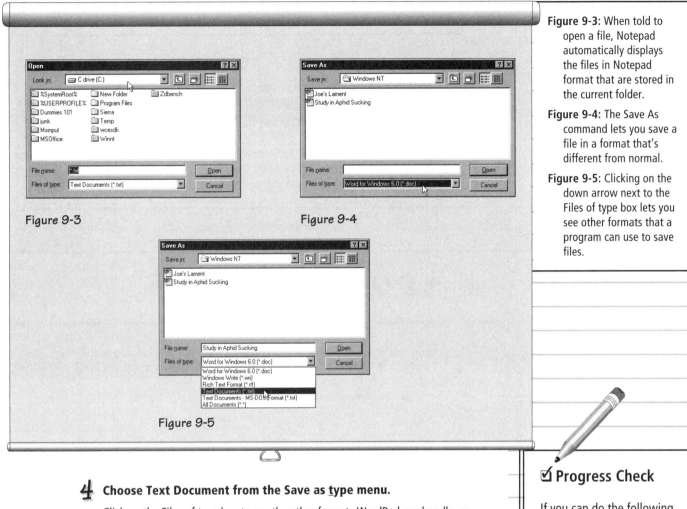

Figure 9-3

Figure 9-4

Figure 9-5

Figure 9-3: When told to open a file, Notepad automatically displays the files in Notepad format that are stored in the current folder.

Figure 9-4: The Save As command lets you save a file in a format that's different from normal.

Figure 9-5: Clicking on the down arrow next to the Files of type box lets you see other formats that a program can use to save files.

4 **Choose Text Document from the Save as <u>type</u> menu.**

Click on the Files of type box to see the other formats WordPad can handle, as shown in Figure 9-5. Then choose the Text Document option to save the Study in Aphid Sucking file as an ASCII file — a text file that Notepad can read — rather than as a WordPad file, which Notepad can't handle. This is shown in Figure 9-5.

5 **Change the Study in Aphid Sucking file's name to Study in Aphid Sucking.txt.**

That way, Notepad can recognize the file as being readable. See, Notepad's not smart enough to look at the file before deciding whether or not it can read it. It looks only at the last three letters of the file's name — which Windows NT normally hides. So by tacking the letters TXT to the end of the file's name, you tell Notepad to make an effort to read it.

6 **Load Notepad.**

7 **Load Study in Aphid Sucking into Notepad.**

Now, because you've saved the file as a text file and added the letters TXT to the end of its filename, Notepad recognizes the file as something it can handle. So it lists Study in Aphid Sucking as a file it can open — something it couldn't do back in Step 4 of this lesson's first section.

☑ **Progress Check**

If you can do the following, you've mastered this unit:

❑ Know when to save a file.

❑ Save a file.

❑ Save a file in a different format.

Save as command comes in handy for saving files in formats that other programs can read

extra credit

Q/A session

Question: Couldn't I save some tIme by renaming Study in Aphid Sucking to Study in Aphid Sucking.txt and then loading the file into Notepad that way?

Answer: No. Simply renaming the file by choosing the Rename command would allow it to appear on Notepad's menu of readable files, and Notepad would make an effort to load it. But it would spit the file back out as indigestible when it discovered that it wasn't stored in true Notepad format. In other words, changing the last three letters of the filename won't change the essential nature of the file format.

Unit 9 Quiz

Circle the letter of the correct answer or answers to each of the following questions. (A few questions may have more than one right answer.)

1. **Save your work at these intervals:**

   A. When you've completed work on a project

   B. After you write a page

   C. After you write a unit

   D. Whenever you think about it

2. **Windows NT programs let you create a new folder at the same time you save a file.**

   A. True

   B. False

   C. Sometimes

   D. Never

3. **Filenames can contain up to this number of characters:**

   A. 8

   B. 16

   C. 64

   D. 255

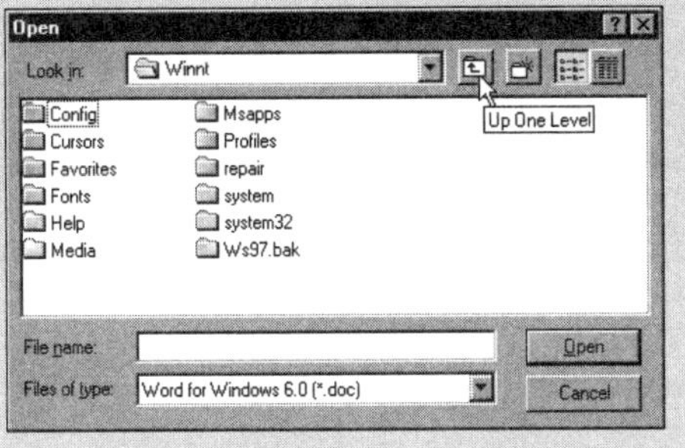

Figure 9-6: Double-clicking on closed folders moves you deeper into your folder hierarchy; clicking on the little folder icon with the right-angle arrow moves you back out folder by folder.

Figure 9-6

4. **Filenames can't contain these symbols:**

   A. , " / \

   B. [ ] : * |

   C. < > + = ;

   D. @ ! # $ %

5. **Changing a filename's last three letters allows other programs that use different formats to read that file.**

   A. True

   B. False

   C. Sometimes

   D. Never

Unit 9 Exercise

1. Create a file in WordPad and save it in Rich Text Format.

   (Rich Text Format is like the "Rich Man's ASCII" format. Many programs can read it, and unlike ordinary ASCII, Rich Text Format preserves much of a document's formatting, including bold, italics, margin settings, and other features.)

2. Choose Open from WordPad's File menu. When the Open box appears (refer to Figure 9-3), practice double-clicking on all the folders in the Open box — both the open ones and the closed ones — until you've looked inside every folder on your hard drive.

   To move deeper into your folder hierarchy, double-click on the folders again. To move out, click on the little folder icon with the "right-angle" arrow on it, as shown in Figure 9-6.

Printing a File on Your Computer's Printer

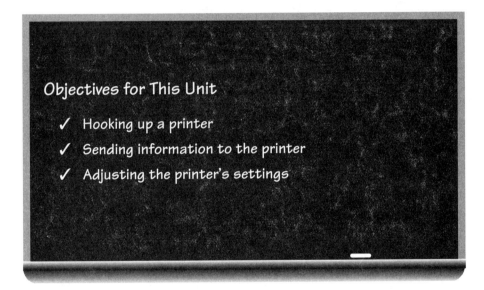

Objectives for This Unit

✓ Hooking up a printer

✓ Sending information to the printer

✓ Adjusting the printer's settings

Prerequisites

▶ Loading a Windows NT program (Unit 7)

▶ Opening a Windows NT file (Unit 8)

▶ Navigating windows with a mouse (Lesson 2-1)

▶ Joe's Lament

on the CD

Windows NT makes printing pretty easy, unless the paper gets jammed. (And if the paper does get jammed a lot, take the beast to the repair shop for a thorough cleaning. Believe me, doing so will save you a lot of aggravation.)

This unit takes you through the process of transporting your thoughts from the computer's monitor onto paper so that you can pass them around, post them, or if you really messed up, make paper airplanes out of them.

If you don't have a printer or won't be doing any printing yourself, you can jump ahead to Unit 11. This book's not like college, which forces people to take courses in Medieval Literature even though they just want to be tax attorneys.

Hooking Up a New Printer

Lesson 10-1

Follow these steps if you've brought a new printer into the office and are hooking it up for the first time.

Figure 10-1: Double-click on the Printers folder in My Computer to find the Add Printer icon.

Figure 10-2: Double-click on the Add Printer icon to begin the process of installing a printer in your Windows NT system.

Figure 10-3: The Add Printer Wizard takes you through the steps of installing a new printer in Windows NT.

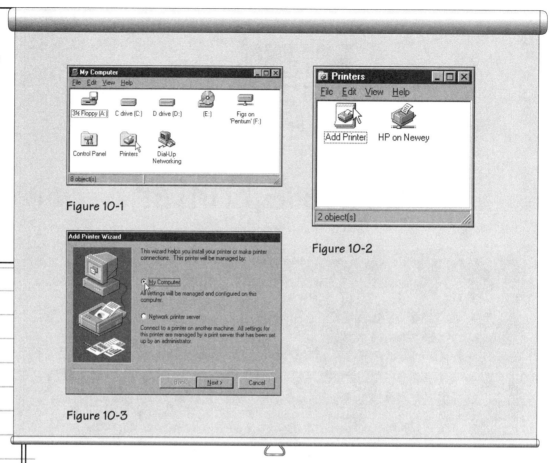

Figure 10-1

Figure 10-2

Figure 10-3

Before plugging anything into your computer, be sure to save any current work in progress, shut down Windows NT, and turn off your computer.

heads up

1 Put the printer on a desk near your computer.

It doesn't have to be on the same desk; just make sure that it's close enough for the printer cable to reach your computer. (The cables are usually six feet long or less.)

2 Plug the printer cable from the printer into your computer's parallel port.

The parallel port is in the back of your computer; it's usually the biggest port back there, and it has 25 pin-sized holes. (Count 'em if you don't trust me.)

3 Turn on your computer, log on to Windows NT, and double-click on the Printers folder from the My Computer program (shown in Figure 10-1).

Or click on Printers from the Start menu's Settings menu; both actions bring up the Printers window, shown in Figure 10-2.

4 Double-click on the Add Printer icon.

The Add Printer Wizard pops into action, as Figure 10-3 shows. The mystical Wizard takes you through the printer installation steps, pitching in some tips when things go wrong.

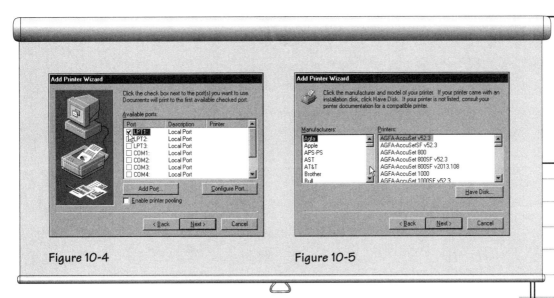

Figure 10-4

Figure 10-5

Figure 10-4: Select the LPT1: port checkbox if your printer is connected to your computer's parallel port.

Figure 10-5: Use the Wizard to help select the correct printer driver.

5 **Click on the Next button.**

The Add Printer Wizard will display a list of connection spots called "ports" that are available on your computer. Your printer needs to be connected to one of these ports.

Normally, if you're hooking up a printer directly to your computer, you'll be using the LPT1: port, as is shown at the top of the list in Figure 10-4. LPT1: designates your computer's parallel port. (Why don't they just *call* it your computer's parallel port? Who knows?)

6 **Click on the LPT1: checkbox if you have connected the printer to the parallel port on your computer.**

7 **Click on the Next button.**

The Printer Wizard now brings a huge menu to the screen, shown in Figure 10-5, listing printer manufacturers on the left and printer model names on the right.

8 **Click on the manufacturer of your new printer, and then choose the model from the right side of the box.**

You may need to scroll up or down the list of manufacturers by using the scroll bar along the list's right side. (Scroll bars were covered in Lesson 3-4, if you skipped that one.) When you find the manufacturer's name, click on it — and choose your printer's model from the list that appears in the window's right side. (This installs a piece of software called a *printer driver*, which enables your computer to use the printer properly.) Printer not listed? Head to the upcoming "Q/A session" sidebar for more information.

9 **Click on the Next button.**

Now, type in your preferred name for your printer. (Your office may assign a name for you to use, or you can stick with the name Windows NT automatically tosses in for those who can't be bothered with such details.)

The box also asks you a question, as shown in Figure 10-6:

Do you want your Windows-based programs to use this printer as the default printer?

Figure 10-6: Specify the name for your printer, and whether it's going to be your default printer.

Figure 10-7: Is your printer going to be shared with other users? You decide those settings here.

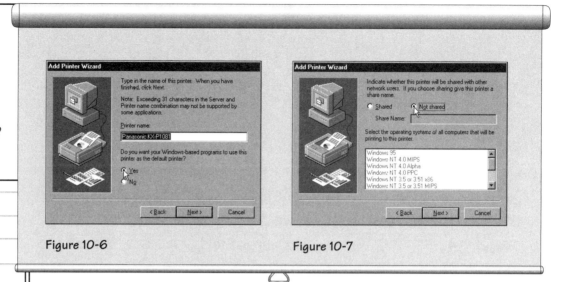

Figure 10-6   Figure 10-7

10 **If you'll be using that printer a lot, make sure that the <u>Y</u>es button is highlighted, and then click on the Next button.**

Because you want Windows NT to use your new printer as the *default printer* — the printer that Windows NT automatically chooses if you don't choose something else — choose the <u>Y</u>es button. Choose the <u>N</u>o button if you'll be using several printers and plan to switch among them manually each time you print.

11 **Click the Next button again and choose N<u>o</u>t shared.**

The next step in the Wizard indicates an important aspect of printing with Windows NT: networked printing. This step allows you to indicate whether or not the printer you're installing can be shared with other users who are hooked up to you. For the present, we'll assume your printer is not going to be shared with other users; so make sure the N<u>o</u>t shared button is selected, as shown in Figure 10-7, and click the Next button again. (Networking printers and how to use them is covered later in this book, in Unit 11.)

extra credit

Q/A session

Question: What if my new printer isn't listed on the Add list?

Answer: If Windows NT doesn't list your new printer on the list of printers, choose the Have Disk button. Then look in the new printer's package for a floppy disk. (Windows NT needs information from it in order to know how to speak to your computer.) Some printers come with installation programs that bypass this stuff altogether. I hate to say this, but you may have to read your printer's manual to figure this one out.

12 **Make sure that the Yes button is highlighted, and click the Finish button.**

That tells Windows NT to print a test page to your printer so that you can tell whether it gets along well with your computer.

on the test

Before trying to use a printer, make sure that it's plugged in and turned on. Also, Windows NT works with most printers on the market.

Sending Information to the Printer

Lesson 10-2

Sending information to a printer is one of the easiest Windows tasks, as you'll see by following these steps:

on the CD

1 **Load WordPad.**

2 **Open the Joe's Lament file from the Windows NT folder in your Dummies 101 folder.**

3 **Choose Print from WordPad's File menu.**

WordPad tosses a dialog box in your face, as shown in Figure 10-8.

Printing options differ in different programs. Some let you print out more than one page; others can tell the printer to use different sizes of paper for certain tasks. (Lesson 10-3 runs you through the most common printer settings.)

4 **Click on OK.**

When you click on OK, WordPad tosses your file to a place called the *print queue,* described in the Extra Credit sidebar "What's the print queue?"

extra credit

What's the *print queue* or *spooler*?

The print queue or spooler, shown in Figure 10-9, is a traffic controller of sorts, keeping too many files from trying to worm their way into the printer at the same time. See, you can send files to the printer a lot faster than the printer can print them. To avoid traffic jams, the print queue stacks the files in order and sends them to the printer, one after the other.

The print queue — also known as a *spooler* — works in the background, so you'll probably just notice it as a tiny printer icon that sits next to the digital clock along the bottom of your screen

while you're printing. But if you want to be tricky, you can tell the print queue to change the order of the files you're print-ing. Just double-click on the tiny icon to bring the print queue to the screen, then "drag and drop" a file from near the bottom of the queue's list to near the top of the list, and the print queue lets that file have cuts in line.

The print queue lets you cancel print jobs as well: Click on the listed file with your right mouse button and select Cancel Printing from the menu that pops up.

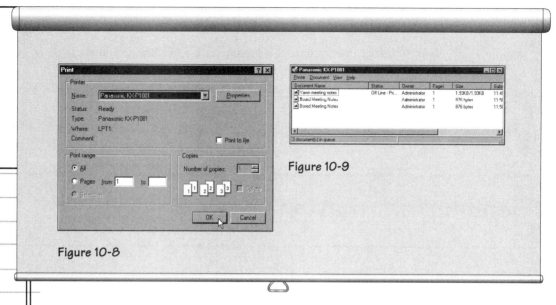

Figure 10-8: WordPad asks some questions before allowing you to print a file.

Figure 10-9: The print queue is a traffic controller that carefully routes files to the printer.

Figure 10-9

Figure 10-8

Lesson 10-3   Adjusting the Printer's Settings

Sometimes you want something a little extra from your printer. For example, maybe you have more than one printer hooked up to your system and want to switch to a different printer.

Maybe you want to change paper sizes, print sideways, or take advantage of some of your particular printer's other "sexy" features. That's all done through the Print command, found in the File menu of most programs.

heads up

Here's a warning, however. Because different brands of printers work differently and have different features, your Print command will probably work differently than the one described here.

Nevertheless, here's how to adjust the settings on an NEC Silentwriter laser printer. Your printer's settings will probably be similar, yet a little different.

1 Load WordPad.

Any program will do, but use WordPad because you probably know how to load it quickly.

2 Choose Print from the File menu.

A box like the one in Figure 10-10 appears.

3 Adjust your printer's settings and click on OK.

Table 10-1 shows you what some of these settings mean; some of the settings are on the first window, others appear when you click on that page's Properties button.

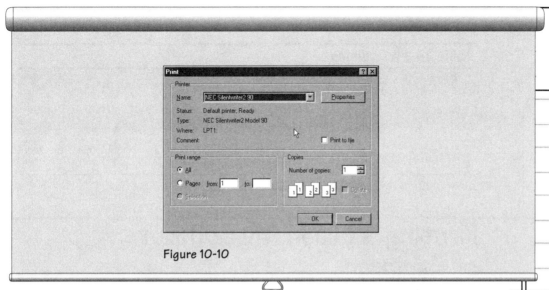

Figure 10-10

Figure 10-10: Adjust a printer's settings with the Print command from a program's File menu.

Notes:

Table 10-1	Print Commands
This Setting	*Does This*
Name	People who have more than one printer connected to their computer can choose a particular printer here. The *default* printer is the one that Windows NT always uses unless you tell it otherwise.
Print range	Normally, you choose All so that WordPad prints all your pages. But if you want to print only a few — pages 3 through 6, for example — you can set that up here.
Number of copies	Yep, this works just like a copy machine. Type in the number of copies you'd like here.
Print to file	Windows asks for a filename and then prints your page to a file. (Not used frequently.)
Options	If you have this button, click on it to take advantage of your particular program's advanced features.

Click on the Print menu's Properties button for these additional choices:

Paper size	Here, you can choose among the different sizes of paper that your printer can use.
Layout	Some printers can squeeze two or even four pages of text onto a single page. If your printer can handle it, you'll see the feature listed here.
Orientation	*Portrait* means to print on the paper normally — like a portrait of a person hanging on a wall. *Landscape* means to print on the paper horizontally, as if you were printing a wide picture of a landscape.

(continued)

Table 10-1 *(continued)*

This Setting	Does This
Paper source	Does your printer have a top tray? Bottom tray? Choose the one you want to use here.
Resolution	Found in the Graphics menu, this option adjusts the way your graphics appear on paper.

Lesson 10-4

Printing a File in My Computer or Explorer

You can print a file from the desktop or the My Computer or Explorer program, but you won't have a chance to change your printer settings, as you'll see in the following steps:

on the CD

1 Load My Computer and find the Windows NT folder in your Dummies 101 directory.

2 Click on the Joe's Lament file with your right mouse button.

3 Choose Print from the menu.

Windows NT immediately sends Joe's Lament off to the printer without giving you a chance to examine and adjust any of your printer settings. You won't be able to choose the number of copies, for example, or choose among the printers you have connected to your computer.

If you think of any last-minute changes that you'd like to make, you're stuck; if you click on Cancel to cancel the print job, you aren't left in WordPad, where you can make your last-minute fixes. No, the print queue simply disappears, leaving you to load WordPad yourself and fix the changes there.

If you just want to dash off a quick copy of a letter, printing directly from the desktop or the My Computer or Explorer programs might be a decent alternative. But unless you're sure that everything's set up correctly, printing directly may be more of a hassle than it's worth.

Tip: Most Windows programs use *WYSIWYG.* Pronounced *wizzy-wig,* it stands for *What You See Is What You Get,* meaning that the images you see on-screen are the same as the images you see on the printer.

☑ Progress Check

If you can do the following, you've mastered this unit:

❑ Hook up a printer.

❑ Send information to the printer.

❑ Adjust the printer's settings.

Unit 10 Quiz

Circle the letter of the correct answer or answers to each of the following questions. (A question may have more than one right answer.)

1. **Do these things before using a printer:**

    A. Make sure that it's plugged in.

    B. Make sure that it's turned on.

    C. Make sure that your program is set up to print to the right brand of printer.

    D. Wash your hands.

2. **Windows NT works with most printers on the market.**

    A. True, when the printer is plugged in, turned on, and set up properly

    B. False

    C. Sometimes

3. **Windows NT can print files from the desktop and the My Computer and Explorer programs.**

    A. True

    B. False

4. **What is a *print queue* or *spooler*?**

    A. A place where your printing jobs are stashed until the printer can deal with them.

    B. A traffic controller for your various print jobs.

    C. A line outside your cubicle of people waiting to use your printer.

Unit 10 Exercise

on the CD

1. Load Paint.
2. Open Eau de Froggie from the Windows NT folder in your Dummies 101 folder.
3. Print Eau de Froggie.
4. Quit Paint.

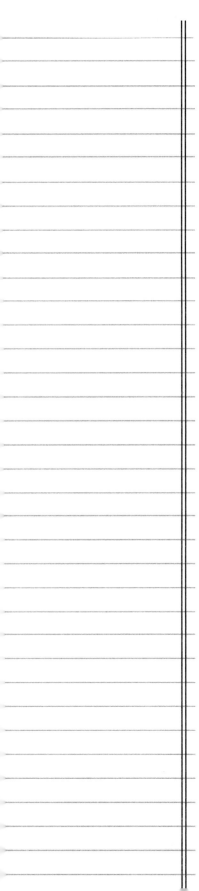

5. Load My Computer.

6. Print Eau de Froggie from the My Computer program.

7. Load Explorer.

8. Print Joe's Lament from the Explorer program.

9. Close all open files.

Printing on a Network

Prerequisites

▶ Using a Mouse in Windows NT (Unit 2)

▶ Loading a Windows NT Program (Unit 7)

▶ Opening a Windows NT File (Unit 8)

▶ Printing in Windows NT (Unit 10)

▶ Talking to Other Computers on a Network (Unit 6)

Objectives for this Unit

✓ Using the Add Printer Wizard to locate and install network printing resources

✓ Setting up your Windows NT Workstation for network printing

✓ Printing to a network printer.

▶ Joe's Lament

This chapter builds on skills that you've learned in Units 10 and 6. It actually combines them into a unit on how to set up and use networked printers on your computer. Any printer that you can normally hook up to a Windows NT computer can be networked so that others can share the printer. (And you can tweak your computer so people can't share the printer, too, if you want to cause problems around the office.)

It boils down to two jobs. First, your computer needs to know that the printers exist on the network and are up for grabs. You'll perform that job in the first lesson. The second lesson shows how to send documents to the printer once it's hooked up to the network.

Finally, the Network Administrator must set up the printers so that your system can see them across the network. This requires setting up the printer's Sharing features on the system that it's connected to, which will not be your job in this book. (Whew.)

Figure 11-1: Double-click on the Add Printer icon to attach a new printer to your computer.

Figure 11-2: The Add Printer Wizard helps attach the printer by making you fill out the right forms.

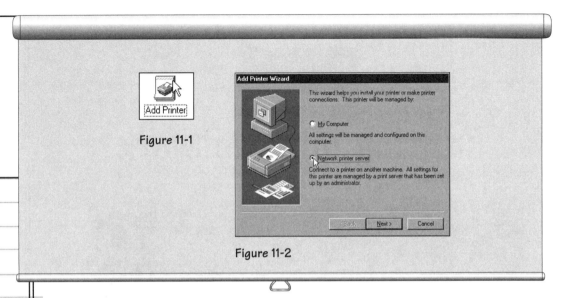

Figure 11-1

Figure 11-2

Lesson 11-1

Using the Add Printer Wizard to Locate and Install Network Printing Resources

Windows NT comes with a friendly wizard to help introduce your computer to an office printer and get them communicating along the wire pathways. Here's how to make the initial connection:

1 Open My Computer.

2 Double-click on the Printers icon.

The Printers window opens.

3 Double-click on Add Printer, as shown in Figure 11-1.

The Add Printer Wizard appears as shown in Figure 11-2.

4 Select the Network printer server option button.

5 Click on Next.

The Connect to Printer dialog box appears. It provides a list of all the computers that are connected to your system, as shown in Figure 11-3.

6 In the Connect to Printer dialog, double-click on any of the computers listed.

If a printer has been hooked up to a networked computer and set up for sharing, it will appear in the list.

7 Select a printer on the list.

The printer that you select appears in the Printer box of the dialog box.

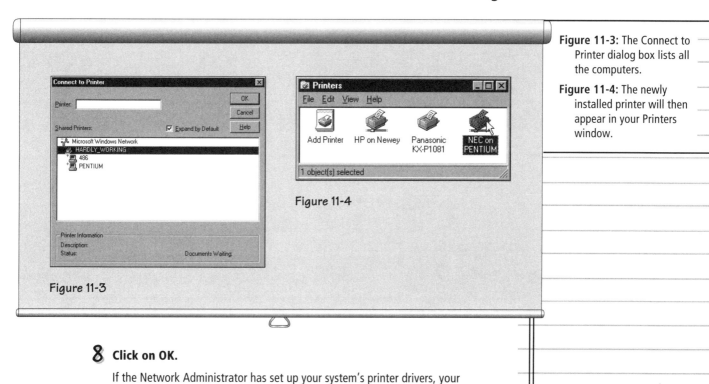

Figure 11-4

Figure 11-3: The Connect to Printer dialog box lists all the computers.

Figure 11-4: The newly installed printer will then appear in your Printers window.

8 **Click on OK.**

If the Network Administrator has set up your system's printer drivers, your system accesses the hard disk for a moment and then a new printer icon appears in your Printers window (shown in Figure 11-4), and Windows NT notifies you that the new network printer has been successfully installed.

heads up

Here's where things can get a little tricky. Whenever you want to set up a networked printer on your computer, you still need to have a special piece of software called a *printer driver* on your system, whether the printer is hooked up directly to your computer or to someone else's on the network. If you don't have a driver installed for that printer, Windows NT will ask you to install one. Because that is beyond the scope of this book, it's time to find your old pal the Network Administrator. . . . (Chances are that you won't have to be doing this stuff anyway.)

Sending Information to a Network Printer

Lesson 11-2

Now that you've set up your computer to use a network printer, it's time to actually *use* the printer. The process is fairly simple, and here you'll run the NT WordPad application to print a file from the companion CD of this book. You must have gone through the previous lesson in this unit to do this successfully.

1 **Click on the Start button.**

2 **Choose Programs, then Accessories, and then WordPad.**

Figure 11-5: Load the file called Joe's Lament into WordPad.

Figure 11-6: The Print dialog box lets you adjust your printer's settings.

Notes:

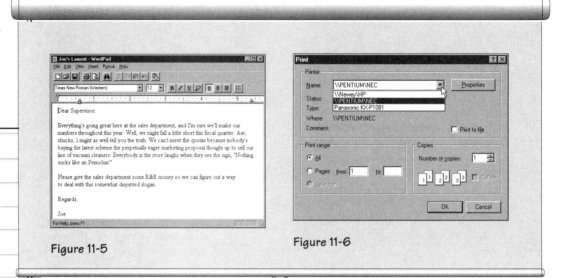

Figure 11-5

Figure 11-6

on the CD

3 **Load the file Joe's Lament into WordPad from the Windows NT folder (which lives in the Dummies 101 folder on your C drive).**

Figure 11-5 shows what the file should look like.

4 **Choose Print from WordPad's File menu.**

The Print dialog box appears, as shown in Figure 11-6.

5 **In the Name box of the Print dialog, make sure the printer you set up in Lesson 11-1 is selected.**

Figure 11-6 shows the printer entry NEC — the one on the networked Pentium computer — as an example.

6 **Click on OK to print the file.**

As you can see, the process of printing to a networked printer is pretty much the same as for one that's hooked up directly to your machine. The key thing is that the setup is a bit different. The next lesson discusses the various ways that you can change the settings for your networked printer.

extra credit

Locating printing resources in Network Neighborhood

Need to know if any of the other people in the office have a networked printer? Here's how to find out:

1. Double-click on the Network Neighborhood icon.

2. Double-click on a computer that is connected to you in the network.

If a networked printer is connected to the computer you've selected, you will see a listing for it, denoted with a small printer icon, as shown in Figure 11-7.

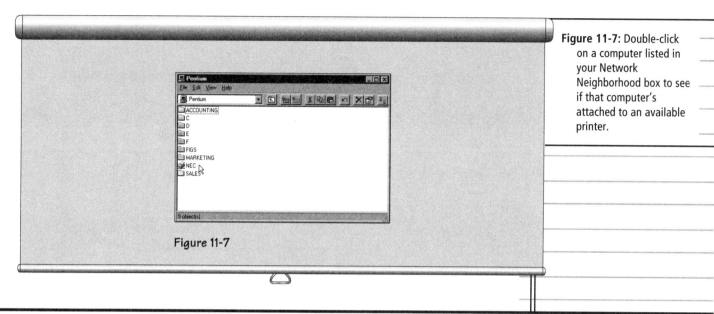

Figure 11-7

Figure 11-7: Double-click on a computer listed in your Network Neighborhood box to see if that computer's attached to an available printer.

Adjusting the Network Printer's Settings

Lesson 11-3

When you use a networked printer, you can modify its settings in the same way as you would for a printer connected to your own system.

1 Load WordPad.

You can use any program that can print documents, but because WordPad is featured in this unit, it will work fine.

2 Choose Print from the File menu.

A box like the one in Figure 11-6 appears. For a quick review of its features, refer to Unit 10 of this book.

3 Click on the Properties button.

The printer's Document Properties box appears, similar to Figure 11-8. Your screen probably looks different, depending on your printer. Figure 11-8 shows a Hewlett Packard DeskJet. Two tabs are shown: Page Setup and Advanced.

4 For more settings, click on the Advanced tab.

Advanced settings change depending on the type of printer you're working with, Figure 11-9 shows the Hewlett Packard Deskjet's advanced settings.

5 To access any of the settings, simply click on a plus sign and navigate through the list.

Settings that can be changed are displayed in blue text. Clicking on a setting displays a Change box for defining a new value or selecting between options, as shown in Figure 11-10.

6 Click on OK after making any desired changes.

Figure 11-8: The Properties button comes with two tabs: one to adjust the Page Setup and the other for the printer's more Advanced features.

Figure 11-9: The more advanced settings control more specific areas of a printer's features.

Figure 11-10: Click on a feature that's displayed in blue to change its value.

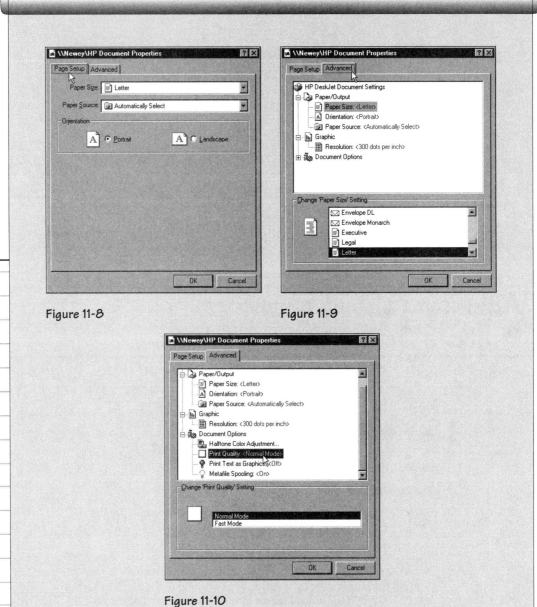

Figure 11-8

Figure 11-9

Figure 11-10

Notes:

heads up

In the Advanced tab, if you're not sure about what any particular printer feature does, click on it with the right mouse button. A What's This? button appears. Click on it, and you see a description of the printer feature. (That's always a good first step before bugging a coworker — and that helpful hovering arrow feature appears throughout Windows NT.)

Unit 11 Quiz

Circle the letter for the correct answer or answers to the following questions. As usual, a question may have more than one right answer.

1. **In Windows NT, printers are automatically installed on the network.**

   A. True. Windows NT installs network printers automatically.

   B. False. The Network Administrator must set the printer up on the network; then, you must run an Add Printer wizard to tell your computer that it's available.

   C. Sometimes

   D. Printers can't be networked in Windows NT.

2. **Any printer that you can run under Windows NT can be networked.**

   A. True

   B. False

3. **You can locate network printers from within the Network Neighborhood, or use the Add Printer Wizard within the My Computer Printers group.**

   A. True

   B. False

   C. Neither

   D. Printers can't be networked in Windows NT.

4. **What printer settings can be changed in the Advanced tab of the Document Properties box?**

   A. Printer Resolution

   B. Paper Size

   C. Paper Orientation

   D. None of the above

Unit 11 Exercise

on the CD

1. Load WordPad.

2. Open the Joe's Lament file from the Windows NT folder in your Dummies 101 folder.

3. Print Joe's Lament.

4. Quit WordPad.

5. Open My Computer.

6. Locate the Joe's Lament file on the hard disk and print it from My Computer.

7. Load Windows NT Explorer.

8. Print Joe's Lament from the Windows NT Explorer program.

9. Close all open files.

Unit 12

• • • • • • • • • • •

Sharing Information (That "Cut and Paste" Stuff)

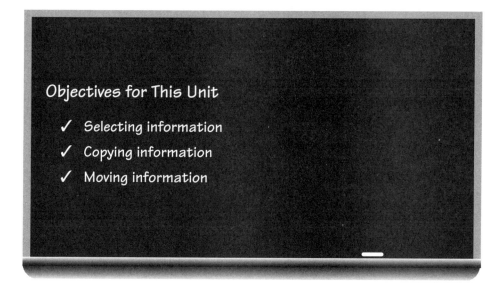

Objectives for This Unit

✓ Selecting information

✓ Copying information

✓ Moving information

Prerequisites

◗ Loading programs (Unit 7)

◗ Loading files (Unit 8)

◗ Navigating windows with a mouse (Lesson 2-1)

on the CD

◗ Joe's Lament

◗ Fax Cover

Big corporations often despise each other. Oh, sure, competing CEOs will sit together in big rooms, smoke cigars, and share guffaws, but they're silently plotting to bat each other over the head with their humidors.

Computer programs used to be like that. Each software company thought that it had come up with the best way to save information. So when you tried to move information from one program to another, the receiving program choked. The programs wouldn't cooperate, and you had to suffer for it.

With Windows NT, however, everybody gets along, more or less. To move information from one program to another, you simply "cut and paste," just like a preschooler. Or if you're feeling less drastic, you can "copy and paste," creating a second copy of your information to spread around.

This unit shows you how to grab, cut, copy, move, and paste your work without any hard feelings.

Lesson 12-1

Selecting Information

In Windows, you can move just about all information from one program to another. You can copy words and paragraphs from one letter to another. You can create a "multimedia" postcard by pasting sounds, pictures, and movies into a letter. You can grab a chart from a spreadsheet, paste it into a report, and add a gasp sound as well.

But first, you have to *select* the information you'd like to grab. The process works slightly differently in different programs, but basically it involves *highlighting* the information with a mouse. The following steps show you how to select information in WordPad; after you select the information, you can cut or copy it to a new location, as the subsequent lessons show.

on the CD

1 Load WordPad.

2 Load the Joe's Lament file from the Windows NT folder in your Dummies 101 folder.

3 Point at the start of the first paragraph.

As Figure 12-1 shows, the mouse cursor is at the beginning of the first word of the first paragraph.

4 Hold down the left mouse button and, while dragging the cursor down and across the screen, point at the end of the first paragraph.

See how the first paragraph is highlighted, as in Figure 12-2? That means you've selected it, and it's ready for further action.

Highlighting text by sliding the mouse cursor over it can be awkward at times, so Table 12-1 shows you a few shortcuts that some (but not all) Windows programs use.

Table 12-1	Shortcuts for Highlighting Information
To Do This	*Do This*
Highlight a word	Double-click on it
Highlight a paragraph	Double-click next to it in the left margin
Highlight a sentence	Hold down Ctrl and double-click on the sentence
Highlight an entire document	Hold down Ctrl and double-click in the left margin

heads up

Note: Be very careful when you've highlighted something, because you can accidentally delete it. Anything you type — even an accidental keystroke — replaces the highlighted information.

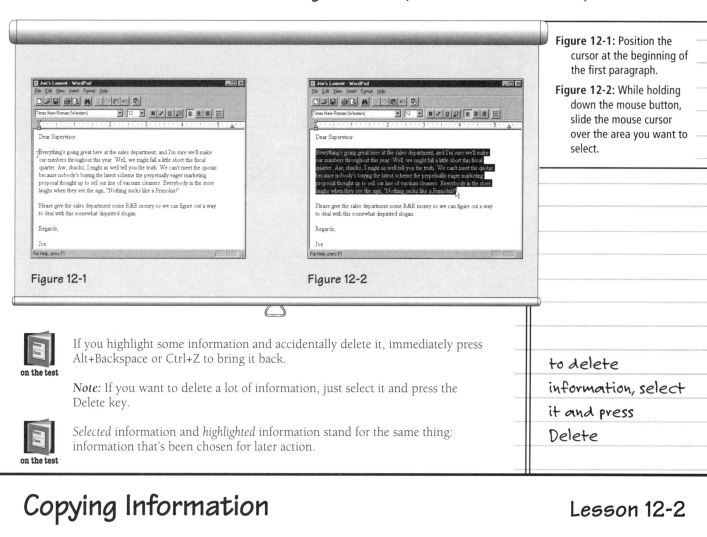

Figure 12-1: Position the cursor at the beginning of the first paragraph.

Figure 12-2: While holding down the mouse button, slide the mouse cursor over the area you want to select.

Figure 12-1   Figure 12-2

on the test If you highlight some information and accidentally delete it, immediately press Alt+Backspace or Ctrl+Z to bring it back.

Note: If you want to delete a lot of information, just select it and press the Delete key.

on the test *Selected* information and *highlighted* information stand for the same thing: information that's been chosen for later action.

to delete information, select it and press Delete

Copying Information   Lesson 12-2

Copying information from one place to another is easy, after you get over the fact that everything happens in the background: You won't be able to see anything happen on-screen, but here's how the process works:

1   Follow Steps 1 through 4 in Lesson 12-1.

Following these steps highlights the first paragraph of the Joe's Lament file in WordPad.

2   Choose Copy from WordPad's Edit menu, as shown in Figure 12-3.

Or if you don't like using the menus, press Ctrl+C to do the same thing. Pressing Ctrl+Insert has the same effect, too. Choose whichever method is easiest for you to remember.

Watch the screen carefully, and prepare yourself for a surprise: Nothing happens. At least, it doesn't *look* like anything happens. But Windows NT grabs your highlighted information and sticks it in a special place called the *Clipboard,* where it can be transported to wherever you'd like to put it. Trust me; the information has been copied.

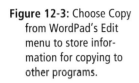

Figure 12-3: Choose Copy from WordPad's Edit menu to store information for copying to other programs.

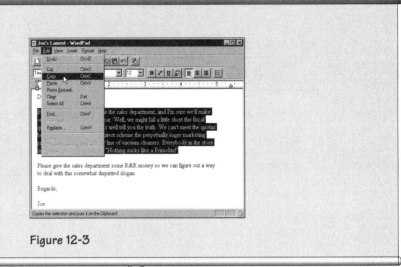

Figure 12-3

heads up

The Clipboard can hold only one chunk of information at a time; each new piece of cut or copied information replaces the previous piece.

extra credit

What, you don't trust me?

How do you know that the information *really* got copied to that special place called the Clipboard? After all, nothing visible happened on-screen. Well, you can peek at the information, just to make sure. Choose the Clipboard Viewer icon from the Start menu's Accessories area, and you should see your information sitting in the Viewer's window.

In fact, if I'm doing a lot of copying, I keep the Clipboard Viewer window open in the bottom corner of my screen so that I can keep a cautious eye on what's going into and out of it.

If you can't find the Clipboard Viewer on your computer, Windows NT may not have installed it in order to save hard disk space. Beg your network administrator to put it on your computer.

Lesson 12-3   Cutting Information

The Cut command isn't much different from the Copy command, actually. Both commands place your selected information on the Clipboard, from which you can paste the information into another program.

But here's the big difference: The Cut command deletes the highlighted information after copying the information to the Clipboard. That lets you move the information to another program.

For example, here's how to cut a word or two from WordPad for later pasting into another program:

1 **Load WordPad.**

2 **Load Fax Cover from the Dummies 101\Windows NT folder.**

3 **Select the word *Comments* from the Fax Cover document.**

Double-clicking on a word is a quick way to highlight it, as you learned from Table 12-1.

4 **Choose Cut from WordPad's Edit menu.**

Poof! The highlighted word, *Comments,* disappears immediately, having been yanked to the Windows NT Clipboard for later action.

Choose the Copy command to *copy* information to another location. Use the Cut command to *move* information to another location. Shortcut-lovers can press Ctrl+X or Shift+Delete to cut the highlighted information as well.

Pasting Information

Lesson 12-4

After you cut or copy information to the Clipboard, you can paste that information into another place. Basically, that process involves two steps: locating a spot to paste it and pushing the Paste button. You'll learn both steps in this lesson.

1 **Load WordPad.**

2 **Load Joe's Lament from the Windows NT folder in your Dummies 101 folder.**

3 **Copy the first paragraph from the Joe's Lament file.**

You did this exact step in Lesson 12-2.

4 **Open Notepad.**

5 **Choose the Paste command from the Edit menu.**

The paragraph you copied from WordPad magically appears in the Notepad file. Notice how the paragraph appears where the cursor happens to be in Notepad — in this case, at the very beginning of the file.

6 **Return to WordPad and select the second paragraph from the Joe's Lament file.**

7 **Cut the paragraph.**

You learned how to complete Step 7 in Lesson 12-3.

Notes:

8 **Return to Notepad and select the Paste command.**

This time, the second paragraph appears in the Notepad file. Don't save this file — you'll need the original for the next lesson.

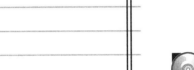

Two shortcut commands for the Paste command are Ctrl+V and Shift+Insert.

Lesson 12-5

Harnessing the Power of Drag and Drop

Notes:

What's the point of using Windows and all the Windows programs that come with it? Is there anything special about Windows? Yes, there is, and it relates directly to what we've talked about in this unit: editing, copying, and pasting. Windows and Windows applications support a special feature called "Drag and Drop" that enables you to make quick copies of information from one place in your file to another, or from one of your files to another — without having to go through the bother of keyboard shortcuts or menu pull-downs. Here's a simple drag-and-drop operation to put this powerful editing tool to work for you:

1 **Load WordPad.**

2 **Load Joe's Lament from the Windows NT folder in your Dummies 101 folder.**

3 **Select the entire paragraph from the Joe's Lament file that begins with the words "Everything's going great."**

Select the paragraph by sliding your mouse pointer over it while holding down your left mouse button, as you learned in Lesson 12-1. The selection should show the same highlighted text as in Figure 12-2.

4 **Click the mouse a second time *and hold the left button down* over the selected text.**

The mouse cursor will "grow" a little box underneath its arrow.

This is the crucial step to drag and drop — the second click *and hold* over the selected material.

5 **Drag the mouse down so that the blinking text cursor in WordPad is located on the line beneath the line that begins, "Please give the sales department" in the document.**

The blinking text cursor is your guide to knowing where your text is going to be placed.

6 **Release the mouse button.**

The results should appear similar to Figure 12-4.

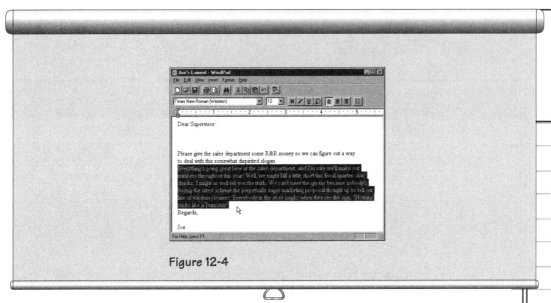

Figure 12-4

Figure 12-4: "Dragging and dropping" highlighted words can be a quick way of moving them within programs or even to some other programs.

on the test

Drag-and-drop editing works just like it sounds: You drag information to another location and drop it. After you master the mechanics of clicking and dragging the mouse through a sea of words, you'll find that this can be much more convenient than copying and pasting. Just drag it and it's done. You don't lose any information in your file, and you can drag a single word, a line of text, a whole paragraph, or whole pages of information to another place in your WordPad document. You may need to do some tweaking — if you drag an entire paragraph, you may need to also select a blank line above or below it and drag that along to make sure the text formatting is correct. In Figure 12-4, for example, you see that you need to press the Enter key between paragraphs to make them nice and neat.

Feel free to practice this and experiment with dragging and dropping.

on the test

Hold the Ctrl key down as you drag and drop your selected text and your information will be copied, not moved, to its new location.

extra credit

Drag and drop copy

Drag-and-drop copying has many implications. With Windows NT, you can drag and drop information not just from inside your document but also between separate documents in the same program, or even between documents in different programs. You can drag and drop information easily between Microsoft Office applications such as Word, Excel, and PowerPoint. (Microsoft Office isn't included with your copy of Windows NT, but it might already be installed in your office system or on the network.) With minor wrinkles, the technique works the same way as you just did here — just drag the information you've selected to another place in your document or, literally, into another program.

☑ Progress Check

If you can do the following, you've mastered this unit:

❑ Select information.

❑ Copy information and paste it into other places.

❑ Cut information and paste it into other places.

Unit 12 Quiz

Notes:

Circle the letter of the correct answer or answers for each question. (Just to keep things lively, some questions have more than one right answer.)

1. **Which action can't be seen on-screen?**

   A. Pasting

   B. Selecting

   C. Copying

   D. Cutting

2. **If you select some text and press the spacebar, what happens?**

   A. The text disappears.

   B. The text is replaced with a space.

   C. A spacebar replaces the text.

   D. The spacebar disappears.

3. **Selected information and highlighted information both mean this:**

   A. Information that's been professionally desktop published.

   B. Information that's been chosen for later action.

   C. Information that's of global importance.

   D. Information that stands out in a textbook.

4. **To retrieve information that you've accidentally cut, you do this:**

   A. Press Ctrl+V.

   B. Press Shift+Insert.

   C. Press Alt+Backspace.

   D. Grab a Band-Aid.

5. **To cut highlighted information and put it on the Clipboard, you do this:**

   A. Choose Cut from the Edit menu.

   B. Press Ctrl+X.

   C. Press Shift+Delete.

   D. Grab scissors.

6. **The Copy and Cut commands do the same thing except for this:**

    A. The Cut command deletes the highlighted information after copying it to the Clipboard.

    B. The Cut command is more sterile.

    C. The Copy command needs a printer ribbon.

    D. The Copy command puts a second copy of the information into your program.

7. **To paste information, you do this:**

    A. Choose Paste from the Edit menu.

    B. Press Ctrl+V.

    C. Press Shift+Insert.

    D. Lick the back of it.

8. **To drag and drop information to a new location, you do this:**

    A. Select the text, click and hold down the mouse button while dragging the text to its new location.

    B. Click the mouse over the text and drag.

    C. Select the text, press Ctrl+C, and then Ctrl+V.

    D. None of the above.

9. **To copy information as you drag and drop it, you do this:**

    A. Click the mouse over the text, hold the Ctrl key, and drag.

    B. Select the text, click and hold the mouse, press the Ctrl key, and drag.

    C. Select the text, press Ctrl+C, and then Ctrl+V.

    D. Yell real loud as you drag.

Unit 12 Exercise

1. Open Paint.

2. Open Eau de Froggie and select a portion of it.

    Click on either of the top two "dotted line" icons at the top of Paint's toolbox. Then, while holding down your mouse button, run the mouse pointer over the portion of the picture you want to select.

3. Select Copy.

4. Open WordPad and select Paste.

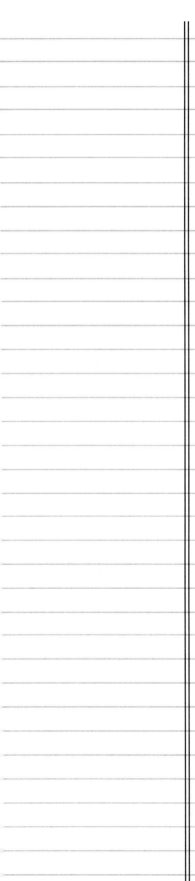

Part III Review

Unit 7 Summary

▶ **Starting a program by double-clicking:** Windows NT lets you start a program in several ways. Double-clicking on the program's icon in the Start menu is the easiest way. Or if you know the program's filename, you can double-click on that name in the My Computer or Explorer program.

▶ **Starting a program from the desktop:** Clicking the right mouse button on a blank part of the desktop brings up a menu that lets you create new documents. Clicking on the New section, for example, brings up programs ready to create new text documents, WordPad documents, sounds, and other types of files.

▶ **Starting a program by using the Run box:** The least common method of starting a program is to type the program's filename in the Start menu's Run box.

▶ **Starting a program by double-clicking on a filename:** Finally, you can start a program by double-clicking on the name of a file that the program has created. Clicking on the name of a file created in WordPad, for example, tells Windows NT to load WordPad and then load the file into WordPad.

Unit 8 Summary

▶ **Opening files from the File menu:** All Windows NT programs let you open files by following the same basic steps: Choose Open from the program's File menu, click on the file's name in the box that appears, and click on the OK button.

▶ **Opening files from My Computer and Explorer:** You can also open a file by double-clicking on its name from within My Computer or Explorer.

▶ **Opening files from shortcuts:** Finally, you can open a file by double-clicking on a shortcut that leads to that file.

Unit 9 Summary

▶ **Save in a location you can find later:** When saving a file, be sure to save it in a location that you'll be able to find later. For example, you may want to create a new folder on your hard drive, as Unit 5 discusses.

▶ **Saving a file: All Windows NT programs let you save a file by following the same basic steps:** Choose Save from the program's File menu. If you're saving the file for the first time, Windows NT asks you to choose a name and location for the file. The program automatically uses that name and location whenever you save the file again.

▶ **Saving a file with a new name or in a new location:** To save the file with a different name or in a different location, use the Save As command from the program's File menu. In some programs, the Save As command also lets you save the file in a different *format* — a way of saving information that lets other types of programs read it.

▶ **Filenames:** A filename can contain up to 255 characters. Windows 3.11 and DOS programs can only use 8-character filenames, so Windows NT sometimes truncates filenames when you swap files with friends using older computers.

Unit 10 Summary

▶ **WYSIWYG:** Most Windows programs use *WYSIWYG*. Pronounced *wizzy-wig*, it stands for *What You See Is What You Get,* meaning that the images you see on-screen are the same as the images you see on the printer.

Part III Review

▶ **Setting up a printer:** Windows NT uses a special Add Printer Wizard to help you set up a printer for use with your personal computer.

▶ **Printing a file:** Almost all Windows programs print the same way: You choose Print from the File menu. The program asks whether you'd like to change any of the settings on your particular brand of printer. Click on the OK button, and the program sends the information to the print queue, a special program that routes information to the printer. (That way, you can keep working while your computer prints in the background.)

Unit 11 Summary

▶ **Setting up a printer:** The Windows NT Add Printer Wizard program can also help you set up a other office printers for use with your computer. One of the Wizard's features is its use of *network printing* and its capability to let you share the printer you're installing with other computer users on your company's *network*.

▶ **Connecting to a shared printer:** Offices often share printers among their workers. To use one of those shared, "networked" printers, just click on that printer's name from the menu that appears when you print a file.

Unit 12 Summary

▶ **Cutting, copying, and pasting:** Cutting, copying, and pasting information are primary ingredients in Windows NT. In Windows NT, all the programs are aware of each other, so you can easily move information from one program to another.

▶ **Selecting information:** The process starts when you *select* information — highlight it by dragging the mouse cursor over it while holding down the mouse button. Some programs also have Select options built into their Edit menus.

▶ **Choosing the Cut or Copy command:** Next, either cut or copy the information to the Windows NT Clipboard, a special holding tank for temporarily holding data. Cutting deletes the data from the program; copying sends a duplicate image to the Clipboard. Both the Cut and Copy commands are on the program's Edit menu.

▶ **Pasting information:** Finally, put the cursor in the program where you'd like the information to appear and choose Paste from the program's Edit menu. The program puts a copy of the information from the Clipboard into the program.

▶ **Dragging and dropping:** You can *drag and drop* selected text to any other location in your document. Select your desired text, click and hold the left mouse button over the highlighted text, and simply drag the mouse to the location where you want the text to be placed. If you want to copy that text to a new location, hold down the Ctrl key as you drag. Though it takes a little getting used to, with a bit of practice you'll probably find yourself using this powerful editing technique quite a bit.

▶ **Undoing accidental cuts:** If you accidentally cut or delete something important from your document, simply paste it back in by using the Paste command. Pressing Alt+Backspace often undoes any past action, too.

Part III Test

The questions on this test cover all the material presented in Part III, Units 7 through 12.

True False

T F 1. Clicking on a program's icon in My Computer starts that program.

T F 2. Although Explorer can copy files and programs, you can't use it to load programs.

T F 3. Copying new information to the Clipboard erases any old information on the Clipboard.

T F 4. The Add New Printer Wizard does not support network printing.

T F 5. Using the Add New Printer Wizard, you can select among literally hundreds of different printers to find the one you need.

T F 6. Many printers let you choose among various options before printing.

T F 7. You should not save files until you've finished working on them.

T F 8. Programs can't always read files that other programs created.

T F 9. You can copy information from one program's window into another program's window fairly easily.

T F 10. Programs can store files in only one particular format.

T F 11. The three letters that a program tacks onto the end of a filename are known as an *extension.*

T F 12. Windows NT uses a file's extension to identify which program created which file.

T F 13. Dragging and dropping only works with moving text; you can't use it to copy.

Multiple Choice

For the following questions, circle the correct answer or answers. Remember, each question may have more than one right answer.

14. **What do the letters DOC, BMP, and TXT have in common?**

    A. They are all extensions used by Windows NT programs.

    B. They all let Windows NT identify the program that created a particular file.

    C. They all have three letters.

    D. They all appear on either WordPad, Paint, or Notepad files.

15. **Windows NT can load programs from within these other programs:**

    A. My Computer

    B. Explorer

    C. The Clipboard

16. **To open a file from within a program, you need this information:**

    A. The file's name

    B. The file's current folder

    C. The disk drive containing the file's current folder

    D. The file's size

Part III Test

17. **This is the proper pronunciation of the term ASCII:**

    A. *ASK-too*

    B. *ask-TOO*

    C. *ASK-ee*

18. **Almost all word processing programs can read files saved in this format:**

    A. WordPad format

    B. ASCII format

    C. Notepad format

    D. Paint format

19. **You usually load programs through this program:**

    A. The Start menu

    B. My Computer

    C. Explorer

20. **After you choose Copy from the Edit menu, how can you be sure that the information has been copied?**

    A. The selected information disappears.

    B. You can look inside the Clipboard Viewer program.

    C. You can paste the information and watch it appear.

21. **To drag and drop copy, what key must you hold down when you perform the drag and drop?**

    A. Alt

    B. Shift+F2

    C. Ctrl

    D. Ctrl+Shift

Matching

22. **Match up the following keystrokes with the corresponding action:**

    A. Alt+F, S   1. Open a file.

    B. Alt+F, P   2. Create a new file.

    C. Alt+F, O   3. Print a file.

    D. Alt+F, N   4. Save a file.

    E. Alt+F, X   5. Exit the program.

23. **Match up the following tasks with the corresponding action:**

    A. To highlight a word   1. Double-click next to it in the left margin.

    B. To highlight a paragraph   2. Hold down Ctrl and click in the left margin.

    C. To highlight an entire document   3. Double-click on it.

    D. To highlight pointer text   4. Hold down the mouse while dragging the cursor over the text.

Part III Lab Assignment

In this lab assignment, pretend that a friend of yours wants a copy of your Eau de Froggie picture for his presentation. Because the company's cheap equipment can't handle color, he needs it stored in Paint's monochrome BMP format. By completing this assignment, you'll open a program, load and save the file, print it, and do a little cutting and pasting on the side.

Step 1: Open a program

Open the Start menu, and then load the Paint program.

Step 2: Load a file

Load the Eau de Froggie file from the Windows NT folder in the Dummies 101 folder.

Step 3: Save a file in another format

Save the frog picture in monochrome BMP format onto one of your floppy disks.

Step 4: Print a file

Print Eau de Froggie, and then close the Paint program.

Step 5: Cut and paste

Load WordPad. Then write this two-paragraph note to your friend:

---

type your address here

type the date here

Jerry Tode
3423 Lagoon Ave.
Riverside, CA 92000

Hey, Jerry, here's that picture of the Frog Perfume that you wanted. Hope it's what you need to make the presentation bubble.

Say hello to the wife and kids for me.

Best,

type your name here

Cut the first paragraph from the letter; then paste the paragraph back into the letter. (It probably looked better that way, anyway.) Finally, print the letter.

The Free Programs

Part IV

In this part . . .

Everybody likes to get something for nothing. The Microsoft marketing mavens certainly know that, judging by the number of "freebie" programs tossed into the Windows NT software box. Sure, Windows NT comes with My Computer and Explorer — programs that can manage files and launch programs. But Windows also comes with a handful of desktop tools: Paint, and Notepad, for example. Some of these little programs work better than others; some barely work at all. And others, like Internet Explorer, let your computer hop onto the Internet and surf the World Wide Web, swapping information with computers around the world.

This part of the book tackles the programs that Microsoft tossed into the Accessories area of the Start menu's Programs section. You discover which of the little programs come in handy at work, and which ones aren't worth the effort.

Finally, because you've completed half of the book, you should be relatively familiar with the Windows NT "feel." You know how to move windows and files around on your computer. You know how to make the mouse's desktop dances turn into productive, "point-and-click" work on-screen.

The other parts of this book teach you how to use Windows NT, sometimes in hypothetical ways. This part of the book, by contrast, teaches you how to create something practical with each program. When you're through, you'll know how to write letters, call the intranet or Internet (if your computer is hooked up to it), and do other computer tasks that you've seen other people do on their computers. This part is probably where you'll have the most fun.

Investigating Internet Explorer

Prerequisites
- A modem
- A phone line
- An Internet Service Provider
- Internet Explorer software
- Navigating windows with a mouse (Lesson 2-1)
- Using the Start menu (Lesson 4-2)
- Using the My Computer and Explorer programs (Unit 5)
- Starting a program (Unit 7)

Objectives for This Unit

✓ Connecting to the Internet or an intranet

✓ Moving from place to place on the Web

✓ Going to a specific Web page

✓ Searching for subjects on the Web

✓ Returning to favorite places on the Web

You've probably seen funny words like `http://www.cocacola.com/` peering at you from a can of Coca-Cola. Coworkers in neighboring cubicles talk about grabbing satellite weather pictures from the Internet before heading to work in the morning. Magazine and television advertisements assault the world with oodles of other strange "http" buzzwords.

Sometimes it seems like you're the only one who's not sitting in front of a computer, logging on to the Internet, and surfing the Web.

Today's world belongs to the *Internet* — that huge string of computers circling the globe. Now, with the slick sounds and groovy graphics of the World Wide Web riding on top of the Internet, millions of people are pointing and clicking their way onto various Web pages and grabbing the goods.

Suddenly, another dimension of the World Wide Web has become the rage in companies: intranets. No, it's not a typo. Intranets are basically a part of the World Wide Web that's built especially for your company and specifically used inside your company for sharing information and special applications. The odds are good that you'll be using an intranet at your place of work within the next year or two — if you aren't already.

This chapter explains just what the Internet and its World Wide Web are supposed to do, how to use the Windows NT Internet Explorer *Web browser* to connect to them, and most important, how to turn everything into valuable tools for finding the information you need. Whether you surf through your company's Intranet or anywhere else on the Web, you'll be using a Web browser such as Internet Explorer.

on the test

Intranets are a company's way of harnessing the World Wide Web in a safer and more secure way, for sharing information and applications.

Lesson 13-1   Connecting to the Internet

You need three basic things to connect to the Internet:

> ▶ **An Internet Service Provider (or ISP):** A service, much like your electric company, that lets you connect your computer to the Internet's network of computers. (And just like the electric company, Internet Service Providers charge for their services: The going rate seems to be about $20 a month for unlimited usage, but it often varies.) Ask your friendly computer store owner for the names of some Internet Service Providers; somebody at the store can probably give you a company name and local phone number.
>
> If you're hooked up at the office, they're picking up the tab. (That's why so many people play on the Internet at work — it's free there.)
>
> ▶ **A computer, phone line, and a modem:** A *modem* is the gadget that lets your computer connect to the telephone lines. Your office's Information Systems (IS) technician can tell you whether you already have one, or whether you can even have one in your office.

Web browser lets you surf the Web

> ▶ **A Web browser:** Software that lets you move to different areas on the Internet's World Wide Web. The latest versions of Windows NT come with a free version of the Microsoft *Internet Explorer* Web browser. The Microsoft Plus package of add-ons for Windows NT also came with a version of Internet Explorer.

Several other companies market Web browsers; in fact, the Netscape Navigator Web browser currently has about 70 percent of the market. In an effort to catch up, Microsoft is giving away Internet Explorer with the current version of Windows NT.

Setting up your computer to use the Internet's World Wide Web can be a little tricky, so you might want to bring over a computer-savvy friend or Web-head IS technician. Luckily, you only have to set everything up once. Some Internet Service Providers — called *ISPs* by hip computer folk — offer tech support over the phone lines, as well. (Don't throw away all the papers with the fine print, because that's usually where the phone number hides.)

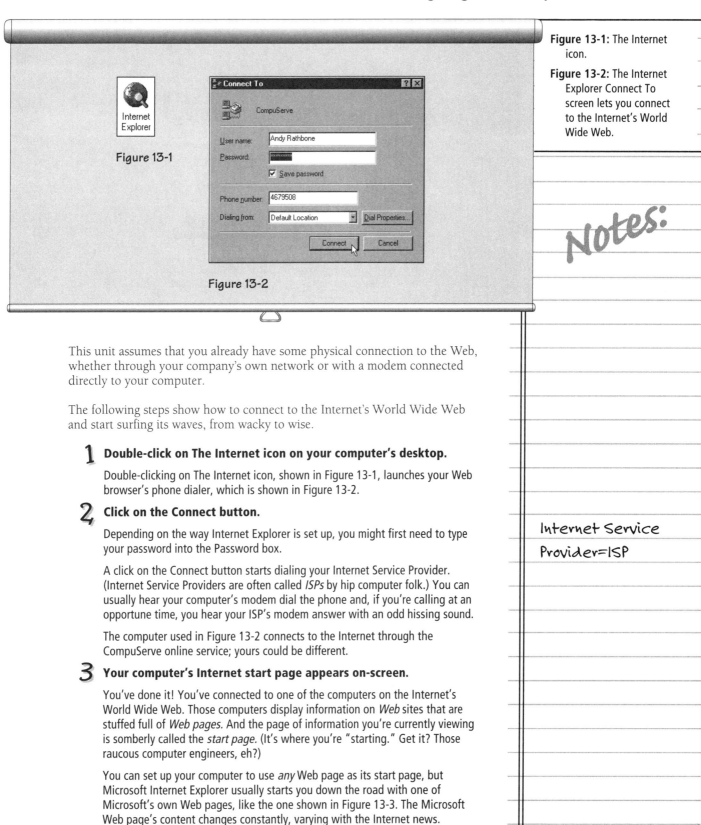

Figure 13-1

Figure 13-2

Figure 13-1: The Internet icon.

Figure 13-2: The Internet Explorer Connect To screen lets you connect to the Internet's World Wide Web.

Notes:

This unit assumes that you already have some physical connection to the Web, whether through your company's own network or with a modem connected directly to your computer.

The following steps show how to connect to the Internet's World Wide Web and start surfing its waves, from wacky to wise.

1 Double-click on The Internet icon on your computer's desktop.

Double-clicking on The Internet icon, shown in Figure 13-1, launches your Web browser's phone dialer, which is shown in Figure 13-2.

2 Click on the Connect button.

Depending on the way Internet Explorer is set up, you might first need to type your password into the Password box.

A click on the Connect button starts dialing your Internet Service Provider. (Internet Service Providers are often called *ISPs* by hip computer folk.) You can usually hear your computer's modem dial the phone and, if you're calling at an opportune time, you hear your ISP's modem answer with an odd hissing sound.

The computer used in Figure 13-2 connects to the Internet through the CompuServe online service; yours could be different.

Internet Service Provider=ISP

3 Your computer's Internet start page appears on-screen.

You've done it! You've connected to one of the computers on the Internet's World Wide Web. Those computers display information on *Web* sites that are stuffed full of *Web pages.* And the page of information you're currently viewing is somberly called the *start page.* (It's where you're "starting." Get it? Those raucous computer engineers, eh?)

You can set up your computer to use *any* Web page as its start page, but Microsoft Internet Explorer usually starts you down the road with one of Microsoft's own Web pages, like the one shown in Figure 13-3. The Microsoft Web page's content changes constantly, varying with the Internet news.

Figure 13-3: By pointing and clicking on various areas of a Web page, you move to different Web pages to see different things.

Figure 13-3

From here, you're ready to start traveling around on the Internet's World Wide Web — and the very next lesson shows you how to start moving from place to place.

on the test

A *start page* is the page your computer automatically displays when your Web browser connects to the World Wide Web. Sure, Web browsers let you change your start page to any Web page you want, but you have to start somewhere — so that page is called your start page. Then when you click on a button and move to a different Web site full of information, you start at that Web site's home page. The *home page* is simply a menu that lets you begin moving around within that Web site. A start page and home page don't really differ much, and they can even be the same thing. But Web hippies expect you to know the difference.

Q/A session

Question: Just what are the Internet and the World Wide Web?

Answer: The U.S. Government, worried in the 1960s that a single bomb could wipe out its favorite computers, moved them far apart. It hooked up some powerful computers over some fast phone lines for a speedy way of moving information around. If a computer blows up — or simply crashes — other computers quickly take over, and the messages still get through. Academic institutions hopped aboard to push the technology forward.

Known as the Internet, this vast network of computers still runs today. In fact, it's going commercial: The World Wide Web is a subset of the Internet's computers that's letting just about anybody join in the fun.

The World Wide Web looks sort of like a convention center kiosk, where you push buttons to find out which booth is serving a quick hamburger. On your computer, by contrast, special Web browser software connects to the Internet's vast network of computers, where you can point and click your way from location to location. A World Wide Web page is a graphics-based, interactive page of visual information that can contain text, sounds, pictures, and even videos to give information and entertainment to the viewer. Older methods of computer communicating, such as bulletin board systems, were text-based, non-interactive, and often hard to work with. The Internet is a whole new ball game.

By pointing and clicking on various places on your screen, you move to different Web sites, visiting things like real estate ads, newspapers, the FBI's Most Wanted list, fan clubs, restaurant menus, and thousands of other subjects, from serious to somber, from weird to wildly wacky.

Many people simply click from page to page, "Surfing the Web" like television's "Channel Surfers." Others use the Web's fast indexes to research specific subjects.

Either way, it's a fast-growing field with a promising future.

Question: What's an intranet, and how is it different than the Internet?

Answer: An intranet is basically a tiny World Wide Web that is built especially for your company and used exclusively by the computer users in your company. Intranets use Web pages just like the normal World Wide Web — they even look the same — but only people in your company can access and use them. When a company builds its own intranet, the company usually isolates their intranet from the rest of the Internet by using special Firewalls that block outside access to your company's internal network. Why? Because your company usually has sensitive information in its network and on its intranet. Do you want competitors, hackers, and Internet crooks snooping thorough your personnel file? Companies also use intranets for creating and distributing special training courses to employees, for large-scale communications (such as e-mail), and high-end groupware productivity applications. That's where I'll leave it, but be assured that intranets are becoming a huge market.

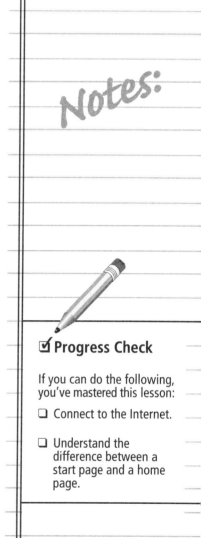

Notes:

☑ **Progress Check**

If you can do the following, you've mastered this lesson:

❑ Connect to the Internet.

❑ Understand the difference between a start page and a home page.

on the test

A *Web address*, also known as a URL, begins with the letters `http://` and describes the location of a Web site of information within the World Wide Web. When you arrive at the Web site, you'll be greeted by that Web site's *home page* — a "Welcome" menu that describes your location and its features. Finally, when you move around within that Web site, you will see that Web site's *Web pages*.

Moving from Place to Place on the Internet or an Intranet

Lesson 13-2

Thankfully, the Internet and intranets are much easier to navigate than most worldwide journeys. No lost luggage, hour-long delays in fogged-in airports, or lost cash in cruise ship casinos. In fact, it's almost too easy to navigate: You can easily find yourself lost at first. (Don't worry; it's easy to get back home, as you'll find out later in this lesson.)

Figure 13-4: A Web-
button-revealing hand.

Figure 13-4

Notes:

buttons take a
variety of
different shapes

Like most things in Windows, the mouse provides the easiest way to control
events. When you point and click on a Web page's various buttons, the Web
takes you to the place represented by that button. The strange part is that the
buttons can take such a variety of different shapes. Sure, some buttons look
like buttons; but others look like underlined words, pictures, spinning balls,
or other oddities.

The following steps will teach you how to recognize a button when you see
one and to know what will happen *before* you click on it.

1 Complete Lesson 13-1 and connect to a Web page.

Any page will do; you can use the Start page your computer dumps you at.

**2 Without clicking a mouse button, slide the mouse slowly over the
screen at random.**

Keep an eye on the mouse pointer — it might surprise you.

**3 When the mouse pointer changes shape, it's hovering over a
button.**

When the mouse pointer transforms into a little hand like the one shown in
Figure 13-4, it's found a button and it's straining to "push" it.

**4 Click the mouse button while pointing at the button you've found
on-screen.**

The Web browser goes to work, fetching the Web page assigned to the button
that you clicked on. You've done it — you've moved to a new page on the
World Wide Web! That's all there is to navigating the World Wide Web; just a
lot of aiming at weird things on-screen and clicking the mouse.

**5 Click the mouse button on the button marked Back in Internet
Explorer's upper-left corner. (It has a left-pointing arrow above it.)**

The Web browser goes to work again, but this time it simply takes you back to
the page you just departed from. If you point and click on the Web page's
buttons — and use the Back arrow button to cycle back to familiar territory
when you get lost — you needn't worry about getting stuck in foreign caverns.

There's more: If you decide you *liked* that Web site you just visited, click on the
Forward arrow button right next to the Back arrow button. That takes you
forward along the path of Web sites you've been walking, while the other
button takes you backward.

Finally, if you stumble across a Web page you want to revisit easily the next
time you fire up your computer, be sure to check out Lesson 13-5.

The arrow buttons have a long memory. By clicking on the Back arrow button repetitively, you can cycle back through many of the Web pages you departed from. Likewise, repetitive clicks on the Forward arrow button take you forward, returning you to where you've been, if you so desire. The buttons lose their memories when you stop your Web session and exit your software.

heads up

Microsoft and the rest of the World Wide Web refer to buttons on a Web page as *hyperlinks*. To tell if something on a page is a hyperlink, slide your mouse pointer over it. If the pointer changes to a hand, you've found a hyperlink.

Some friendly Web pages fill their pages with an abundance of hyperlinks to make sure that you don't miss anything. Microsoft's Web page (refer to Figure 14-2), for example, lets you read about Brad Silverberg by clicking on his face, as the little hand testifies. But you can also read about Brad Silverberg by clicking on the adjacent words "Internet Explorer Security — An Open Letter," the underlined words "open letter," or the word "Vision" above his head. Your pointer turns into a hand over each of those areas, and a click on any of them takes you to the same Web page.

☑ **Progress Check**

If you can do the following you've mastered this lesson:

❑ Recognize a button before you click on it.

❑ Use the Forward and Back arrow buttons.

How Do I Move to a Specific Web Page?

Lesson 13-3

Somebody passed you a business card with their Web page listed on it? Or do you just want to check out Coca-Cola's Web page? Well, if you can type that weird `http://` stuff with your computer's keyboard, you can move to that specific Web page. This lesson shows you how.

1 **Complete Lesson 13-1 to connect to the World Wide Web.**

You'll be deposited at your Start page. Now, look at the top of the Internet Explorer for a long box marked Address. Inside, you'll see the Web address for your Start page. If you're starting at the Microsoft Web site, for example, you might see something like `http://home.microsoft.com/`.

2 **Click anywhere on the words in the Address box.**

The strip of letters becomes highlighted.

3 **Type the new address into the Address box.**

The first letter of the new address knocks the old address out of the Address box. Be very careful not to make any typographical errors while typing your new address, however. Nothing will explode, but your Web browser will just tell you it can't find that particular address. The Internet can be a cranky, exact science.

☑ Progress Check

If you can do the following, you've mastered this lesson:

❑ Move to a specific Web page.

4 Press Enter.

The Internet will do its best to connect with the computer that runs your desired Web page. Usually, it gets there. Sometimes it doesn't. (Better make sure that you typed that name right.) Also, don't be surprised if a much-desired Web page just vanishes: Sometimes Web Pages' caretakers stop taking care of them, and they pull them off the computers. Or maybe they switched to a different Internet Service Provider, changed their Web address, and didn't tell anybody.

But there's still a way to find specific Web pages, as Lesson 13-4 demonstrates.

Tip: Looking for a place to get a little practice in? Then choose Web Tutorial from the Internet Explorer's Help menu. It answers some questions and takes you on a gentle path through the networks.

Lesson 13-4

Searching for Specific Subjects on the Web

browsing=pointing and clicking across the network without a destination in mind

Browsing can be the most fun on the World Wide Web. Pop yourself in front of a computer and start wandering through the world's computer networks, looking at people's pets, shopping at trendy stores, and reading magazines and newspapers. *Browsing* means spending your time pointing and clicking your way across the network with no destination in mind.

Most Web sites contain hyperlinks to other Web sites; some of those hyperlinks carry related information, and others are listed just for fun.

But if you're searching for specific information, quick and speedy, these steps show how to find it.

1 As shown in Lesson 13-1, connect to the World Wide Web.

That should be a breeze by now; if not, it's time to bring a friend over to get set up.

2 Click on the Internet Explorer Search button along the center of its top bar.

The Web browser takes you to the Microsoft Internet Search area. An electronic librarians' catalog for performing detailed searches.

3 Type a few words describing your subject and press Enter.

For example, if you're looking for information on stocks and bonds, you'd start by typing **stocks and bonds** and press Enter. In a few moments, the Index program reveals the results of its search, as shown in Figure 13-5. (Feel free to experiment with the different types of searches; AltaVista often works well.)

Internet Search area=librarians' electronic catalog for performing detailed searches

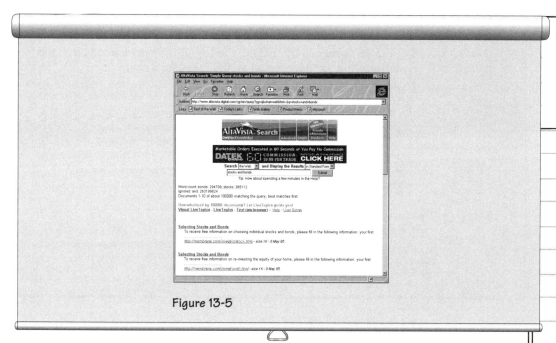

Figure 13-5

Figure 13-5: By typing a few words into Internet Explorer's Search area, you perform detailed searches of the vast Internet.

Notes:

As shown in Figure 13-5, Internet Explorer features several different Internet indexes, all run by different companies that use slightly different methods of indexing. If you're having trouble finding what you want with one index, switch to another: Click on the Yahoo! button, for example, or search on the AltaVista index. Although both indexes usually carry many of the same sites, you'll also usually find a few different Web sites pertaining to your quest.

Tip: Searching for specific things can be as difficult as a college statistics course. If you're having trouble remembering your AND but NOTs, click on the index's Help or Tips area for a quick refresher.

☑ Progress Check

If you can do the following, you've mastered this lesson:

❑ Access the Microsoft Internet Search area.

❑ Search the Internet for specific information.

Returning to Favorite Places on the Web

Lesson 13-5

Finally found a favorite place on the Web? Want to make sure that you can find it again? No problem. Thankfully, you don't have to write down Web addresses on scraps of paper by your computer. Here's how to add your favorite Web sites to a quick-and-easy Internet Explorer pull-down menu.

1 **Connect to the Internet, as shown in Lesson 13-1.**

2 **Move to a site that you know you'll want to revisit.**

Either stumble across a winner by browsing or locate a specific chunk of information in an index. When you locate a Web site that you'll want to revisit before the next department head meeting, head for Step 3.

☑ Progress Check

If you can do the following, you've mastered this lesson:

❑ Add Web sites to the Internet Explorer Favorites menu.

❑ Access Web sites by clicking on the Internet Explorer Favorites button.

3 **Click on Favorites from along the top of the Internet Explorer and choose Add to Favorites when the menu falls down.**

4 **Click on the OK button.**

Now, whenever you click on the Internet Explorer Favorites button, that Web page will be listed on the pull-down menu. Click on the Web page's description, and the Internet Explorer will whisk you to the page.

on the test

To keep things tidy, Internet Explorer lets you organize your favorite Web sites into different folders within its pull-down menu.

Tip: Spot a favorite graphic or wallpaper on a Web site? Click on it with your right mouse button, and a menu appears, letting you copy it to your own computer for turning into wallpaper. You can also copy text from a Web page just as you would copy it from a word processor: Highlight the text with the mouse and choose Copy from the Edit menu.

Unit 13 Quiz

Circle the letter of the correct answer or answers to each question.

1. **A start page is what I see when I turn on my computer.**

   A. True

   B. False

   C. No, it's what I see when I load the Internet Explorer.

   D. No, it's what I see when I first connect to the World Wide Web for a Web session.

2. **A Home page is the first page you see when you connect to a Web site.**

   A. True

   B. False

3. **Which of the following looks the most like a Web address.**

   A. `osopretty:`

   B. `(teepee)`

   C. `4936 Arachnid Ave.`

   D. `http://www.gibson.com`

4. **This button is a "safety" for returning you to the Web page you just left:**

   A. Back

   B. Home

   C. Search

   D. Stop

5. **Internet Explorer comes with an index for looking up subjects.**

   A. No, it comes with two indexes.

   B. No, it can connect to more than five indexes.

   C. Actually, it can connect to several different indexes that should all be tried.

   D. The Internet can only be browsed aimlessly.

6. **When your Internet Explorer's pull-down menu becomes crowded with favorite Web site addresses, you can do the following:**

   A. Delete the ones you're not visiting anymore.

   B. Organize the sites into pop-out folders, much like the Start menu.

7. **How is a company's intranet different from the normal Internet?**

   A. There's no difference.

   B. A company's intranet is mainly internal and separated from the normal World Wide Web by firewalls.

   C. A company's intranet is used for special applications such as in-company training and internal e-mail.

   D. Intranets are boring and business-like.

Unit 13 Exercise

1. Connect to the Internet or office intranet.

2. Spend an hour simply pointing and clicking on pages, clicking when your mouse pointer turns into a hand.

3. Right-click on various on-screen graphics, and turn them into wallpaper on your own computer.

4. Add favorite Web pages to your Favorites menu.

5. Search for your favorite subjects by using the Search feature.

Unit 14
• • • • • • • • • • •

Using Microsoft Exchange for Your E-Mail

Objectives for this Unit

✓ Add and edit entries in your e-mail Address Book

✓ Send and receive e-mail from your computer

Prerequisites

▶ Pointing and clicking the mouse (Unit 2)

▶ Moving and sizing windows (Unit 3)

▶ Loading a Program (Unit 6)

▶ Opening a File (Unit 7)

E lectronic mail is quickly becoming one of the most widely used communications tools in business. At your desk, you can maintain contact with coworkers and outside business contacts by using the e-mail features on your computer. Windows NT Workstation provides a useful set of features for creating, managing, sending, and receiving electronic mail. The package is called *Microsoft Exchange,* and this chapter shows how to put it to work on your Windows NT computer.

With Microsoft Exchange, you can send e-mail to other users on the network and to computer users anywhere in the world (if your company lets you, that is). Actually, e-mail is less sensitive and time-intensive than browsing the Web (covered in Unit 13), and e-mail provides a way to maintain your outside working contacts without taking too many resources from the network. Because Windows 95 also uses a version of Microsoft Exchange, you can easily communicate with Windows 95 users on your network as well as Windows NT users.

Figure 14-1: The Windows NT Address Book lets you store e-mail addresses to your coworkers and friends.

Figure 14-2: The Address Book can keep track of Internet Addresses, company network addresses, and addresses from other services.

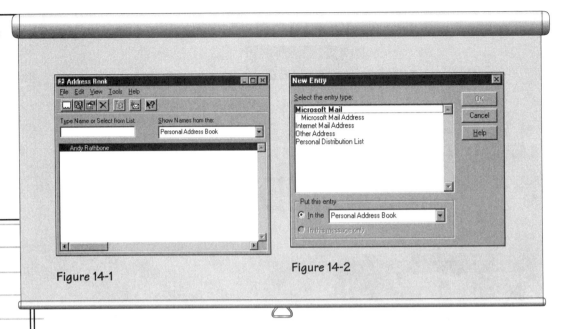

Figure 14-1

Figure 14-2

Lesson 14-1

Add and Edit Entries to your E-Mail Address Book

Without an address, an envelope stays put. So this lesson shows how to use Exchange's Address Book for keeping track of everybody's e-mail addresses. You'll learn how to add new addresses, and use those as the base for creating e-mail messages in the next lesson.

You can find the Address Book in several places; this lesson opens it from the Inbox application.

1. **Double-click the Inbox icon on your desktop.**

2. **From the Inbox's Tools menu, choose Address Book, or click the Address book button on the toolbar.**

   The Address Book application appears similar to that shown in Figure 14-1. (If you're starting the Address Book for the first time, no names will be listed in the window.)

3. **From the Address Book's File menu, choose New Entry.**

   The New Entry dialog box appears, as shown in Figure 14-2.

   In this dialog box, you must choose the type of mail system the other party uses: Microsoft Mail, the Internet, or other options. For this example, we'll use an Internet Mail Address.

4. **Choose Internet Mail Address from the Select the entry type: box.**

heads up

   E-mail addresses can be added to the Personal Address Book, and to the Postoffice Address List, depending on where you click in the New Entry form. Most of the time, you should place new addresses in the Personal Address Book. The Postoffice Address List is usually managed by the Network Administrator, and any new addresses you place in it can cause unexpected problems.

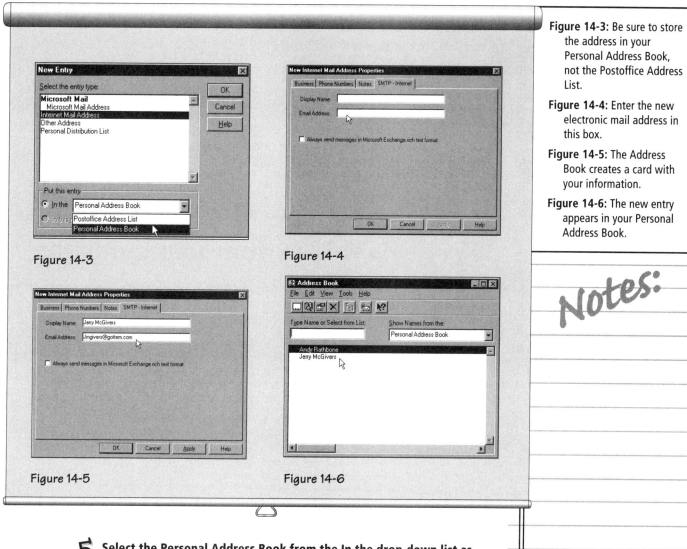

Figure 14-3

Figure 14-4

Figure 14-5

Figure 14-6

Figure 14-3: Be sure to store the address in your Personal Address Book, not the Postoffice Address List.

Figure 14-4: Enter the new electronic mail address in this box.

Figure 14-5: The Address Book creates a card with your information.

Figure 14-6: The new entry appears in your Personal Address Book.

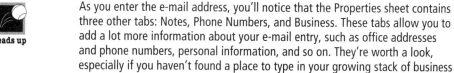

5 Select the Personal Address Book from the In the drop-down list as shown in Figure 14-3, if it isn't already displayed.

6 Click on OK.

The New Internet Mail Address Properties sheet pops up, as shown in Figure 14-4. This is where you enter your new electronic mail address.

7 In the Display Name box, enter the name of the person whose address you're creating.

8 In the Email address box, enter the person's e-mail address. A typical result is shown in Figure 14-5.

As you enter the e-mail address, you'll notice that the Properties sheet contains three other tabs: Notes, Phone Numbers, and Business. These tabs allow you to add a lot more information about your e-mail entry, such as office addresses and phone numbers, personal information, and so on. They're worth a look, especially if you haven't found a place to type in your growing stack of business cards.

heads up

9 To add the entry to the address book, click on OK.

A new entry is placed in the Address book, as shown in Figure 14-6.

To check the contents of any address book listing, double-click on it. Its Properties sheet appears.

When you use Address entries in new messages, the name is displayed, but its electronic mail address will be hidden. This is nothing to be concerned about; it is just how Exchange works.

Why have we used the Address book before creating e-mail? Exchange is not the easiest or best-organized e-mail package you'll ever see; becoming accustomed to the address book actually helps keep you organized and reduces confusion.

Lesson 14-2   Receiving E-Mail from Your Computer

Even with its complicated setup and structuring, the Inbox isn't anything like a full-featured e-mail package such as Qualcomm Eudora Pro or Lotus cc:Mail. But it can still toss around a flurry of electronic mail when it's really needed.

Note: Most Internet e-mail is plain text and can't use fancy formatting.

The Address Book can be easily edited; replying, sending and forwarding mail are fairly easy operations. If you're sending information throughout your company, you can quickly add text formatting features such as fonts to your e-mail to make it more readable. Sending formatted e-mail over the Internet is a different matter, because most Internet e-mail is delivered as plain text and can't use fancy typefaces and other things.

Receiving your e-mail is usually a simple process.

1 Double-click on the Inbox icon on your desktop.

This time, instead of stepping through the Messaging Setup Wizard, your e-mail Inbox will be displayed similar to that shown in Figure 14-7.

2 If you didn't have any mail waiting, choose the Deliver Now Using option from the Tools menu.

Inbox will automatically grab your new mail and send off any outgoing mail.

The Inbox's Toolbar, shown along the window's top in Figure 14-7, is where you'll be able to locate most of the program's key features. Table 14-1 shows the function of each of the Inbox Toolbar's buttons, from left to right.

Table 14-1	The Inbox Toolbar's Buttons
This Button...	*...Does This*
Up One Level	Allows you to navigate through different levels of e-mail folders
Show/Hide Folder List	Displays or hides list of mail-related folders
New Message	Enables you to create a new e-mail message

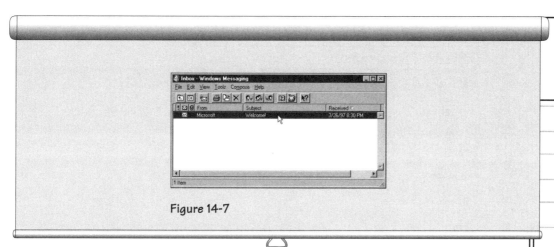

Figure 14-7

Notes:

This Button...	...Does This
Print	Prints the selected e-mail message without having to open it
Move Item	Moves the selected message to another folder
Delete	Deletes the currently selected e-mail or e-mails from the Inbox
Reply to Sender	Respond to the message's sender using their return address
Reply to All	Replies to all of the senders using their return addresses
Forward	Sends a copy of the currently selected message
Address Book	Displays the address book
Inbox	Opens the Inbox
Help	Opens the Exchange on-line Help system

Although there are no gridlines, Exchange lists your messages into a table with rows and columns. The column along the top, shown beneath the Toolbar in Figure 14-7, shows an exclamation mark, a small envelope, a paper clip, and some labels (From; Subject; Received; and Size). Those show characteristics of your e-mails, as listed in Table 14-2.

Table 14-2	Exchange E-Mail Symbols
This Button...	*...Does This*
Exclamation Mark	Importance. A checkmark here means signifies an urgent message
Envelope	Item type. Shows type of entry in list: e-mail or folder

(continued)

Table 14-2 (continued)

This Button...	...Does This
Paper Clip	Attachment. Indicates if a data file has been attached to the e-mail
From:	Shows the sender
Subject:	The subject at the head of the e-mail
Received:	Shows the date and time the e-mail was received
Size	The size of the message, including any attachments

heads up

To reduce items you don't need, you can add or remove columns from the Inbox by choosing the View menu, and then choosing Columns.

Lesson 14-3

Sending E-Mail from Your Computer

Notes:

To create and send a new e-mail message using Inbox, follow these steps.

1 From the Compose menu, choose New Message.

Figure 14-8 shows the New Message composition window. It also contains a pair of toolbars. The top one provides a selection of basic e-mail functions, including Send, Save, Print, as listed from left to right in Table 14-3. A formatting toolbar is also provided but isn't available when the window first appears, as shown in Figure 14-8.

heads up

Press Ctrl+N for a keyboard shortcut to create a new message.

Note: Don't be intimidated by all the confusing buttons in any of Windows NT's Toolbars. Just holding the mouse pointer over the button usually brings a little message explaining the button's mission in life.

Table 14-3   E-Mail Button Functions in the New Message Window

This Button...	...Does This
Send	Sends the e-mail message in the current window
Save	Saves the message to disk without sending it
Print	Prints the message
Cut	Deletes selected text
Copy	Copies selected e-mail text to memory
Paste	Pastes any copied text into the document
Address Book	Displays the Address Book window

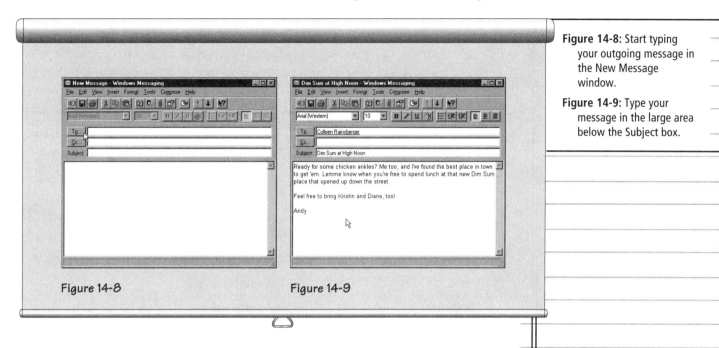

Figure 14-8

Figure 14-9

Figure 14-8: Start typing your outgoing message in the New Message window.

Figure 14-9: Type your message in the large area below the Subject box.

This Button...	...Does This
Check Names	Spell Checks Recipient names against the Address Book
Insert File	Allows you to search for and attach (or insert as plain text) a file in your system to the message
Properties	Displays the Properties sheet for the current e-mail message. Here, for example, you can attach a receipt for delivery or for reading, so you know that the recipient both got the message and read it
Read Receipt	Attaches a Read Receipt to the message
Importance: High	Places a High Importance alert on the e-mail
Importance: Low	Places a Low Importance alert on the e-mail
Help	Displays on-line help for the Messaging application

2 **To select an e-mail address, click on the To button.**

The Address Book appears.

3 **Double-click on a name in the address book, and click on OK.**

If you want more than one person to receive the same message, you can add their e-mail addresses by selecting them in the Address Book and clicking on the Cc button, which copies them over to the proper box.

4 **Type a topic line in the Subject: box.**

5 **Type the message.**

The message goes in the large box below the Subject line. Figure 14-9 shows an example of an e-mail message after you've followed these steps.

Notes:

As you can see, after you enter some text in the message, the formatting toolbar comes to life in the Message window. Table 14-4 describes its tool buttons, from left to right.

Table 14-4	Message Window Tool Button Functions
This Button...	**...Does This**
Font	Displays a pull-down list from which you can select any font that's installed in your system
Font Size	Change the size of the font for your selected text with this setting
Bold	Applies boldface to selected text
Italic	Italicizes selected text
Underline	Underlines selected text
Color	Applies a color from a drop-down list to selected text
Bullets	Adds bullets to text to create a bulleted list
Decrease Indent	Decreases the indent of a paragraph by one tab stop (if paragraph is indented)
Increase Indent	Indents a paragraph by one tab stop to the right
Align Left	Aligns text to left margin
Align Center	Centers text on the page
Align Right	Aligns text to the right margin

6 **Type in your message text and format it if desired.**

Note: Press Ctrl+S to save a message.

7 **From the Message window's File menu, choose Save.**

8 **Close the Message window.**

Note: Press Ctrl+M to send all unsent messages from the Inbox.

9 **To send the message, from the Inbox's Tools menu, select Deliver Now Using, and then Internet Mail.**

For an easy way to send all your mail, simply press Ctrl+M.

Adding text formatting to an e-mail message

Here's a quick exercise to apply some formatting to an e-mail message:

1. **Create a message with your name and address at the top, a "Dear so-and-so" salutation and some message text.**

2. **Select the name and address at the top and format it by clicking on the Center tool button.**

3. **With the centered lines still selected, apply a Bold effect to them.**

4. **Select the main body text of the message, and apply a different font.**

5. **Change the font size of the body text.**

This formatting won't work through the Internet, but it will work if you're sending it to somebody else through your company's own e-mail system.

Microsoft has now released a new version of Exchange. Called Exchange 5.0, it boasts significant improvements, especially with enhanced support for Internet-related technicalities. What does this mean for you? Probably very little to start with, but the Network Administrator will probably be very excited about it.

Unit 14 Quiz

1. **What is Exchange's main function for end-users?**

    A. Internet e-mail

    B. Internal company e-mail

    C. A personal valet

    D. None of the above

2. **What is the Personal Address Book used for?**

    A. To build e-mail address lists

    B. To create databases for mailing lists

    C. To collect URL bookmarks for Web browsing

    D. None of the above

3. **What kinds of text formatting can you add to a Microsoft Mail message?**

   A. Boldface and Italics

   B. Centering

   C. Different Fonts and Font Sizes

   D. Multiple columns of text

4. **Can you send one message to multiple recipients?**

   A. Yes

   B. No

   C. Sometimes

   D. Only on Internet connections

Unit 14 Exercise

1. Open your address book.

2. Enter a coworker's email address into the address book.

3. Write a greeting message to that coworker.

4. Spell-check your message

5. Send your message to the coworker.

Part IV Review

Unit 13 Summary

▶ **The Internet:** The *Internet* is a huge network of computers around the world. Your computer becomes part of this network when it joins the *World Wide Web* — a portion of the Internet set aside for sending information through words and graphics.

▶ **Company Intranets:** A fancy term for a mini-Internet that works only inside your company, an intranet is used for things like company e-mail, training, and other applications. Intranets are becoming very popular in business, so it's likely you'll run into one sooner or later.

▶ **Internet Explorer:** Microsoft Internet Explorer is one of many *Web browsers* — software for navigating the World Wide Web and exploring its many pages of information. Internet Explorer currently comes free with Windows NT.

▶ **How to navigate Web pages:** Web pages contain *hyperlinks* — special buttons that lead the Web browser on to even more pages of information. By pointing and clicking on these hyperlinks, Web users can browse their way across computer networks, much like television's channel surfers flip through various television stations.

Unit 14 Summary

▶ **Exchange/Microsoft Mail:** Windows NT now comes free with an e-mail program called *Exchange* that can coordinate your e-mail.

▶ **Inbox:** Exchange's Inbox lets you send and receive e-mail to people in your company's network, as well as through outside services like the Internet.

▶ **Setting up Exchange:** Exchange can be very difficult to set up. Don't try to do it yourself unless you have the office network administrator within yelling distance.

Part IV Test

The questions on this test cover all the material presented in Part IV, Units 13 and 14.

True False

T   F   1. You don't need anything else except the Internet Explorer software to begin browsing the Web.

T   F   2. Internet services always charge by the minute.

T   F   3. Double-clicking on the Internet icon on your Windows NT browser lets you start setting up your system to use the Internet.

T   F   4. A Web address is the street location of your office.

T   F   5. After you display a Web page, you can't go back to the previous page you looked at.

T   F   6. Internet Explorer lets you call other computers and send faxes to them.

T   F   7. You can copy information from the World Wide Web onto your own computer.

T   F   8. The World Wide Web looks like a newspaper without pictures.

Multiple Choice

For each of the following questions, circle the correct answer or answers. Remember, each question may have more than one right answer.

9. **What is a Web page?**

    A. An electronic mail program

    B. A text-based Bulletin Board System for sharing software

    C. A graphical page of information displayed over the Internet

    D. A spider's mural in his living room

10. **A Web page can display this type of information:**

    A. Text

    B. Pictures

    C. Sounds

    D. Videos

11. **What's the term for browsing aimlessly across Internet web pages?**

    A. Web Slurping

    B. Web Surfing

    C. Web Waving

12. **You connect to the Internet with the following things:**

    A. A computer and modem

    B. A telephone line

    C. An Internet Service Provider

    D. Internet browser software

Matching

13. **Match up the following tasks with the programs that accomplish them:**

    A. Browsing the Web   1. Internet Explorer

    B. Simple text editing   2. Notepad

    C. Browsing intranets

Part IV Lab Assignment

In this part, you learned how to put the Microsoft main accessory programs to work in a project, creating a useful item by the end of each unit.

Because this lab assignment spans two units, it's a little different. Instead of telling you to create more projects, it encourages you to go back over the units you've mastered, changing them subtly to meet your needs more fully.

Step 1: Find out about your company's intranet

Talk to your boss or your co-workers about any possible intranets that may be available for your use. Ask if you can have your system set up to access them and request a couple of pages on the intranet that you might be able to look at. (Training is a common application on intranets.)

Step 2: Spend some time Web browsing

Drop a little television time at the door and spend some time moving about on the libraries of the World Wide Web, visiting zoos, museums, crafts fairs, and educational institutions. Check out the Web sites for your company's competitors, too! (You can bet that they'll probably have them.)

Fixing Problems

In this part . . .

They were picked last at dodge ball during elementary school, but now they're the trendiest people on the block. Today's computer nerds are not only trendy, they're overworked, and they're never there when you need them.

This part of the book teaches you how to perform some basic Windows NT fixes yourself. Plus, you'll learn how to install new programs.

Finally, this part teaches you how to use the next best thing to a personal computer guru: the help system built into Windows NT.

Organizing Your Desktop

Prerequisites
- Loading a file (Unit 8)
- Navigating windows with a mouse (Lesson 2-1)
- Dragging and dropping (Unit 12)
- Using Explorer and My Computer (Units 5 and 6)

Objectives for This Unit

- ✓ Moving things around on your desktop
- ✓ Arranging strategic shortcuts
- ✓ Doing tasks quickly
- ✓ Starting programs automatically with Windows

Even after learning how to drive a car, you need to look at a map once in a while. Sure, you can just point in a certain direction and put the pedal to the metal — but that's rarely the fastest or most fuel-efficient way to arrive at the destination.

Because Windows NT offers so many different ways to do things, setting it up efficiently is difficult. Which desktop setup works best? No one real answer exists, of course. Just as everybody's desktop differs at least slightly in real life, all Windows NT users will want their own assemblage of shortcuts, icons, and folders.

This unit shows you a few setups to sample; perhaps by picking and choosing from the different lessons, you'll come up with the desktop you've always wanted. Don't feel that you have to use any of these ideas; if you think that some of them are trash, feel free to drag them to the Recycle Bin. (That's what it's there for.)

Lesson 15-1   Creating Desktop Shortcuts

Notes:

Although Windows NT makes a decent effort, it doesn't leave much in the way of a desktop, as shown in Figure 15-1.

First, everything's hidden — you need to start clicking to find most of the buttons. And because Windows NT doesn't know what sort of tasks you'll be doing most often, it doesn't know which buttons to move to the forefront. This lesson shows you how to customize Windows NT to meet your own special needs.

1 **Read the Welcome screen tip.**

When Windows NT first starts up, it persistently flashes a "helpful tip" onto the screen, as shown in Figure 15-1. Give the tips a chance to soak in — some of them can be useful down the road. In fact, clicking on the box's Next Tip button lets you flip through all the tips as fast as you can read and click.

2 **Click in the Show this Welcome screen next time you start Windows box (the checkmark should disappear), and then click on the window's Close button.**

Following Step 2 turns those little tip windows off so that they won't pop to the front of the screen each time you reload Windows.

3 **Double-click on the My Computer icon.**

The My Computer window opens up.

4 **With your right mouse button, drag and drop your floppy disk drive icon to the top-right corner of your desktop.**

A menu appears, as shown in Figure 15-2, asking whether you want to Create Shortcut(s) Here or Cancel.

5 **Choose the Create Shortcut(s) Here option.**

Putting a shortcut to your floppy disk drive on your desktop gives you easy access, as shown in Figure 15-3. To move or copy to a floppy, just drag and drop it to your new shortcut. Do the same for your B drive, if you have one.

Shortcuts can be valuable time-savers if you take the time to set them up. Feel free to put shortcuts to your most commonly used programs and directories on your desktop by dragging and dropping them with the right mouse button.

create desktop
shortcuts to floppy
drives

deleting shortcuts
doesn't hurt the
original files

on the test

Deleting a shortcut deletes only the button that starts the program, not the program itself. The program stays in the same location.

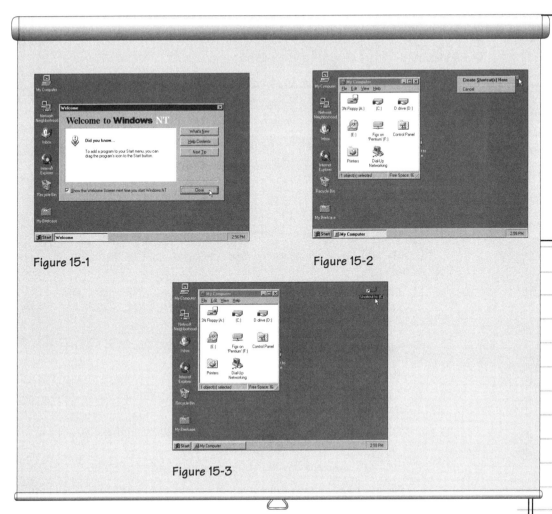

Figure 15-1

Figure 15-2

Figure 15-3

Figure 15-1: Most desktops in Windows NT start out looking somewhat like this.

Figure 15-2: Dragging and dropping with the right mouse button always brings up a menu that gives you more control over your actions.

Figure 15-3: Drag and drop files to your floppy drive's shortcut to save time.

extra credit

Q/A session

Question: I turned off my Welcome Tip screens! How can I turn them back on?

Answer: To turn those daily tips back on, click on your desktop's background, press F1 to bring up the Help menu, and click on the Help window's Index tab.

Next, click in the first box and type **Tip of the Day**, and then click on the Display button. Another box appears. Huff, puff.

Double-click on the Tips: Viewing the Welcome screen again listing, and yet *another* box appears. Click on the little arrow in that box, and the Tip of the Day returns.

Now, click in the Show this Welcome Screen next time you start Windows box; a check mark appears. That check mark ensures that the tip stays there, and you won't have to repeat this nonsense until you get tired of the tips again.

Lesson 15-2   *Organizing Folders*

Notes:

Like it or not, just about everybody uses their computer for work. That's why having a work directory is so important. By creating a folder on your hard drive called Work — and then storing all your work files inside it — you'll always know where to find them.

The next few steps show you how to make your own, easily accessible, Work Folder:

1 **Open My Computer and double-click on your C drive icon.**

The My Computer program shows you the folders currently stored on your C drive.

2 **Choose New from the newly opened window's File menu, and choose Folder.**

A blank folder appears in the window.

3 **Type Work.**

Windows NT assigns the word *Work* to the folder.

4 **Open your new Work folder, and create two folders inside it for your two current work projects.**

Make one of those folders for **John's Harebrained Marketing Plan** and the other for **Alice's Crossword Puzzle Scores.**

5 **Create a shortcut on your desktop that leads to the folder.**

You can create this shortcut just as you did in the preceding lesson — with the ol' drag and drop with the right mouse button.

Now, whenever you're ready to work, just double-click on your desktop icon. That puts you right at your Work folder, with no hemming or hawing. You'll immediately have your two important work projects in front of you.

As your projects change, change your folders. Create an Old Projects folder in your Work folder, for example, and move the completed projects into it as you finish them.

on the test

Shortcuts can summon folders just as they can launch programs.

to remove shortcuts, drag them to the Recycle Bin

Starting Programs Automatically with Windows NT

Lesson 15-3

on the test

Ever find yourself using just one program over and over? In fact, the first thing you do when you start Windows NT is to load that single program and get to work?

The eager-to-please Windows NT is happy to load that program for you automatically when it loads itself — if you adhere to the following steps:

1 **Click on the Start button with your right mouse button, and then choose <u>O</u>pen from the menu.**

The My Computer program hops to the screen, showing you the folders and programs currently stored on your Start menu.

2 **Double-click on the Programs folder.**

A new box pops open.

3 **Double-click on the StartUp folder.**

A window pops open, listing the programs currently listed in the StartUp folder. Those programs, if any are listed, currently load themselves and run automatically whenever you load Windows NT.

4 **Drag and drop your program's icon into the StartUp folder.**

You can drag and drop that program's icon from Explorer or My Computer — the program automatically turns into a proper shortcut when you let go of the mouse button.

Close down all the open windows, and you're through. The next time you restart Windows NT, your favorite program will be on-screen waiting for you.

☑ Progress Check

If you can do the following, you've mastered this unit:

❑ Create a shortcut.

❑ Organize a folder.

❑ Add a program to the Windows NT StartUp folder.

Unit 15 Quiz

For each question, circle the letter of the correct answer or answers. Remember, a question may have more than one right answer.

1. **Deleting a shortcut does this:**

   A. Deletes a push-button that starts a program or opens a folder

   B. Deletes the push-button and the program or folder

   C. Deletes the push-button, but only moves the program or folder to the Recycle Bin

   D. Moves the shortcut to the Recycle Bin

2. **Windows NT can do these things when you first load it:**

   A. Load a program

   B. Crash

   C. Open folders

   D. Open doors

3. **Shortcuts can bring the following things to the screen:**

   A. Programs

   B. Folders

   C. Files

   D. Accusations of cheating

Unit 15 Exercise

Because this unit was more a series of tips than a sequential lesson plan, the exercise follows suit. Try out the following tips and circle the ones you want to remember:

1. To reopen a recently opened file, click on the Start button and choose Documents. Chances are, your file's name will be sitting there, waiting to be clicked into action.

2. To keep incoming material from spreading all over your desktop or hard drive, create a Junk folder on your hard drive. When new files come in, just store them there until you decide on a more organized place to put them.

3. Icons looking a little spread out across the desktop? Click on the desktop with your right mouse button and choose Line up Icons from the menu. Windows NT immediately scoots the icons into straight, evenly spaced lines.

4. Want to peek inside a file really quickly? Click on the file's name in Explorer or My Computer (or the Open File box of just about any Windows NT program) and choose Quick View from the menu. Windows NT immediately gives you a look-see without actually opening the file.

5. Some part of Windows NT has you baffled? Click on the desktop's background, press F1, and click on the Help window's Contents tab. Double-click on the book icon marked Troubleshooting, and Windows NT lists the problems that it's ready to help with. If you're lucky and your problem is on the list, then Windows NT can unleash a software troubleshooter program that will help to solve the problem.

Using the Windows NT Help Program

Objectives for This Unit

✓ Finding help in Windows NT

✓ Finding help for Windows NT programs

✓ Customizing the Help program

✓ Finding help for specific problems

Prerequisites

◗ Navigating windows with a mouse (Lesson 2-1)

◗ Using the Start menu (Lesson 4-2)

◗ Loading and running programs (Unit 7)

Computers can do just about everything, according to the sales guy on TV. But then how come computers can't help you change the margins in your funky new word processor?

Well, at least Windows NT makes an effort. Microsoft built a Help system into Windows NT that's supposed to be as welcome to baffled users as the Auto Club is to stranded motorists.

Unfortunately, the system's advice rarely rates full-fledged computer geek status; on the contrary, the hints often sound like an electrical engineer's bare-bones notes.

Although the Windows NT Help system is overly complicated, it's much better than the underpowered versions that came with earlier versions of Windows. This unit shows you how to drag the most help from it as possible.

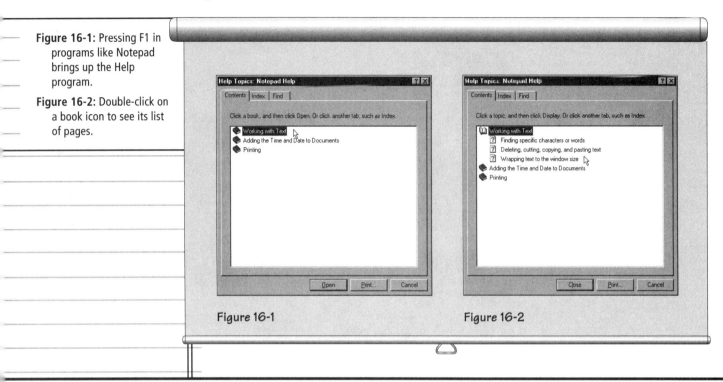

Figure 16-1

Figure 16-2

Lesson 16-1 — Using the Windows NT Help Program

Just as some neighborhoods don't get all the good cable TV channels, not all Windows NT programs come with a built-in Help system. But follow these steps to see if your current program offers Help — and how helpful it will be.

1 Load a program — Notepad, in this case — and press F1.

Sometimes just pressing F1 instantly summons a helpful bit of advice, as shown in Figure 16-1. The little book icons work like folders; double-click on the book icon that sounds the most helpful to see its contents.

2 Double-click on the Help program's Working with Text book for information about that subject.

The book opens up, spilling its list of more specific subjects, as shown in Figure 16-2.

3 Click on Wrapping text to the window size.

The Help program brings a window explaining how to perform that task to the screen, as shown in Figure 16-3.

By double-clicking on the various book icons and reading bits and pieces of different helpful explanations, you should eventually solve the problem that's bugging you.

Unfortunately, not all programs come with a built-in Help system. If your program is one of those unlucky few, pressing F1 won't summon a helpful bit of advice. Pressing F1 twice won't do anything, either; we tried. Also, some

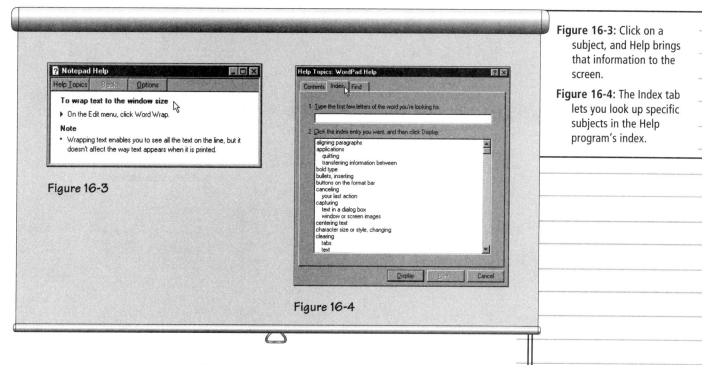

Figure 16-3

Figure 16-4

Figure 16-3: Click on a subject, and Help brings that information to the screen.

Figure 16-4: The Index tab lets you look up specific subjects in the Help program's index.

programs have better Help systems than others. Some programs even set up their Help system to be the main documentation for the software and skimp on the printed documentation.

Tip: Hand resting on the mouse? Choosing Help Topics from the program's Help menu does the same thing that pressing F1 does.

If you don't see your subject listed in the contents page, chances are that the Help program doesn't have anything to say about it. The Help system is pretty basic.

on the test

Pressing F1 brings up Help in most programs, but not all of them.

Finding Help for General Problems

Lesson 16-2

Probably the fastest way to find help for a nagging problem is to simply jump around, clicking on the words that you see in the Help program shown in Figure 16-1. But if you want to be *sure* that the Help program doesn't have an answer for your problem, the following steps teach you how to make more precise searches for certain subjects.

For example, here's how to forage for help on setting margins in WordPad:

1 **Load WordPad and press F1.**

The Help program box, similar to the one in Figure 16-1, appears.

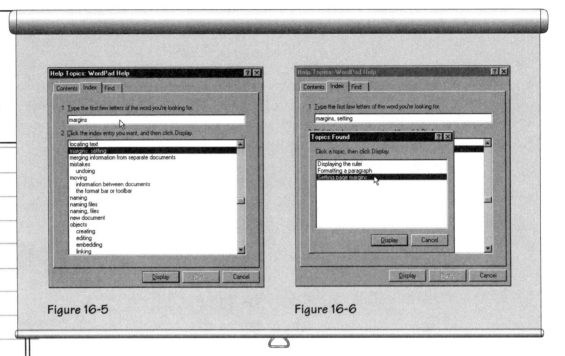

Figure 16-5: Type the first few letters of the subject, and the Index section looks it up.

Figure 16-6: Double-click on the margins topic for even more information.

Figure 16-5   Figure 16-6

2 **Click on the Index tab.**

An indexed list of the Help program's contents appears, as shown in Figure 16-4.

3 **Type the first few letters of the word** margins **in the box.**

The Help program starts showing you the indexed entries beginning with the word *margins,* as shown in Figure 16-5. See how it found an index entry for *margins, setting*?

4 **Double-click on the margins entry.**

A box that brings up more specific margin-related tasks appears, as shown in Figure 16-6.

5 **Double-click on the Setting page margins topic for even more information.**

A box appears, giving you explicit instructions for setting page margins in WordPad.

on the test

Tip: If you stumble across some helpful Help information, place an electronic note on the spot so that you can find it later. Just choose Annotate from the Options menu and type your note. Click on the note's Save button, and a little paper clip is attached to that Help page. Clicking on the paper clip brings up the note for future reference.

on the test

Remember: Windows NT searches alphabetically by subject, so search by generalities. For example, search for *margins* instead of *changing margins.*

click on blank part of desktop and press FI for help with Windows NT itself

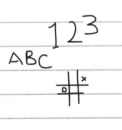

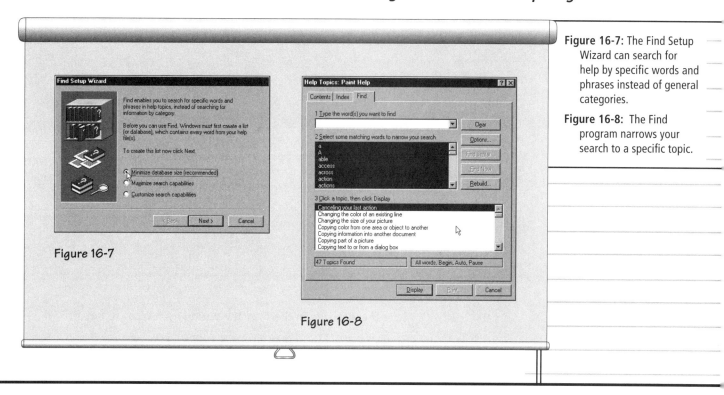

Figure 16-7

Figure 16-8

Figure 16-7: The Find Setup Wizard can search for help by specific words and phrases instead of general categories.

Figure 16-8: The Find program narrows your search to a specific topic.

Finding Help for Specific Problems
Lesson 16-3

Sometimes you want help for a specific problem now, and you don't want to mess around with general, subject-oriented menus. The solution? Tell Windows NT to make an index of *every* word in its help system, no matter how insignificant it may appear. Then search through that complete index.

The advantage, of course, is that you'll know whether Windows NT mentions your problem. After all, you've told it to update its index to include every word, not just generalities like *margins*. The disadvantage is that these complete indexes take some time to create and can consume a lot of space on your hard drive.

But if you want to make sure that help is available if you want it, follow these steps (we'll use WordPad as an example):

1 **Load WordPad, press F1, and click on the Find tab.**

The Find Setup Wizard program appears, as shown in Figure 16-7, ready to create your index.

2 **Click on the Next button to choose** **Minimize database size.**

3 **Click on the Finish button.**

Your hard drive makes whirling noises as Windows NT rummages through the WordPad Help file, sorting through all its contents. After it's through, the Find window comes to the screen, as Figure 16-8 shows.

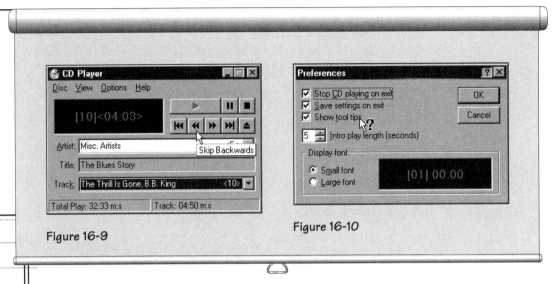

Figure 16-9

Figure 16-10

4 **Type the word** line **in the Type the word(s) you want to find box.**

As you type the letters, the Find program narrows down your search until it comes up with entries that contain the word *line*.

Double-click on any topic that the Find program came up with to see whether it solves your questions. If it does, great. If it doesn't, head back to the Find program — you only have to make the index once, and it's always there for your use.

Lesson 16-4 — Finding Help in a Dialog Box

☑ Progress Check

If you can do the following, you've mastered this unit:

❏ Find help about Windows NT.

❏ Find help for Windows NT programs.

❏ Customize the Help program.

❏ Find help for specific problems.

Dialog boxes can be confusing with their buttons, forms, and unlabelled icons. What does what? Here's a quick way to figure them out:

1 **Load the WordPad program.**

2 **Rest your mouse pointer over a button on the WordPad program.**

After a few seconds, a box appears and explains the button's function, as shown in Figure 16-9. (Microsoft calls these little balloons *ToolTips,* but we won't test you on that.)

3 **Choose Print from the File menu.**

The Print dialog box appears, listing various settings that you can make for the program.

4 **Click on the little question mark icon in the Preference box's top-right corner, and click on any item, as shown in Figure 16-10.**

Unit 16 Quiz

Circle the letter of the correct answer or answers to each of the following questions. Remember that some questions have more than one answer to keep you from coasting. (After all, you're almost done with the book.)

1. **Pressing F1 always brings up the Help program.**

    A. True

    B. False

2. **Does Windows NT let you mark helpful pages with electronic annotations?**

    A. Yes

    B. No, that's ridiculous.

3. **How does the Windows NT Help system display topics across the screen?**

    A. It sorts them alphabetically by first word.

    B. It sorts them alphabetically by category.

    C. It sorts them numerically by creation date.

    D. It doesn't sort them.

4. **To search for help in WordPad about typing italic text, which phrase would work best?**

    A. Typing italic text

    B. Italic text

    C. Italic

    D. Typing slanted text

Notes:

Unit 16 Exercise

With 16 units under your belt, you've probably punched the F1 key a few times. Therefore, these exercises are tips more than they are mandatory study aids. Nevertheless, give them a run-through before moving on to the next unit.

1. Click on a blank part of your desktop, press F1, and double-click on the Troubleshooting book icon. If you see any topics that are giving you problems, double-click on them. Windows NT leads you through steps that may improve the situation.

2. Load Help and experiment with it *before* you have a problem.

3. For either a good way to practice or create supreme confusion, load Help and try out Help's Help program, which shows you how to use Help.

4. Keep an eye out for the little question mark icon in the corner of some dialog boxes. That icon can be handy for finding help when you're filling out confusing Windows NT forms.

5. Finally, look for underlined words in the Help program. Clicking on them often brings up their definition or more helpful material.

Part V Review

Part V Test

Unit 15 Summary

▶ **Organizing your desktop:** Just as everybody's real desk differs a little in organization, so should Windows NT. Feel free to create folders for your current work projects and create shortcuts to those folders on your desktop. Use a program constantly? Put a shortcut for it in your StartUp folder so that it loads itself automatically whenever you load Windows NT.

Unit 16 Summary

▶ **The Windows NT Help program:** Windows NT comes with a built-in help program designed to offer assistance when you're in a jam. Sometimes it's helpful, but it's often filled with jargon that's difficult to understand. Luckily, the Help program includes a built-in glossary, letting you click on a word to see its definition.

▶ **Helpful Wizards:** Also, the Help program comes with built-in Wizards and Trouble-shooters — pieces of software that ask you questions and use your answers to try to solve the problem.

▶ **Press the F1 key:** When you're confused, try pressing F1 for advice. If you see a question mark icon within a program, click on it, and then click on the part of the program that confuses you. Sometimes that action brings helpful hints as well.

The questions on this test cover all the material presented in Part V, Units 15 and 16.

True False

T   F   1. Shortcuts are used to make your programs run faster.

T   F   2. Clicking on an underlined word or phrase in the Windows NT Help program brings up more helpful information pertaining to that word.

T   F   3. The Find Setup Wizard is used to set up Help reference lists for various Windows NT programs.

T   F   4. Windows NT comes with several built-in files that you can use for wallpaper.

Multiple Choice

For each of the following questions, circle the correct answer or answers. Remember, each question may have more than one right answer.

5. **Which of these keys usually brings up the Windows NT Help program?**

   A. F2

   B. F?

   C. F1

   D. F7

6. **Which of the following is easiest to install?**

   A. Drivers

   B. Programs

   C. The one that comes with an installation program and network administrator

Part V Test

Matching

7. **Match up these types of Windows NT files with their probable uses:**

   A. Troubleshooter   1. An icon that loads a Windows NT program, folder, or file

   B. Wizard   2. A symbolic button

   C. Icon   3. A program that helps install something

   D. Shortcut   4. A Help program that fixes problems

   E. Folder   5. A storage area for files

Part V Lab Assignment

Congratulations! But don't tell your friends or coworkers that you've finished the course, or they'll be calling *you* when they're struggling to install a new piece of software. Then again, isn't it nice to be on the other end of the struggle for a change?

Step 1 Practice using the Help program

Budget 15 minutes of practice time for using the Help program. You'll get the most use out of Help if you practice with it *before* you need to use it.

Answers

Unit 1 Quiz Answers

Question	Answer	If You Missed It, Try This
1.	A, B, C	Review Lesson 1-1.
2.	A	Review Lesson 1-1.
3.	C, D	Review Lesson 1-3.
4.	B	Review Lesson 1-3.
5.	B	Review Lesson 1-2.

Unit 2 Quiz Answers

Question	Answer	If You Missed It, Try This
1.	B	Review Lesson 2-1.
2.	B, C, D	Review Lesson 2-1.
3.	B	Review Lesson 2-1.
4.	B, C	Review Lesson 2-1.
5.	D	Review Lesson 2-2.
6.	D	Review Lesson 2-2.

Unit 3 Quiz Answers

Question	Answer	If You Missed It, Try This
1.	C	Review Lesson 3-1.
2.	A, B	Review Lesson 3-1.

3.	A, B, C	Review Lesson 3-1.
4.	A	Review Lesson 3-5.
5.	B	Review Lesson 3-1.
6.	B	Review Lesson 3-3.
7.	B	Review Lesson 3-4.

Part I Test Answers

Question	Answer	If You Missed It, Try This
1.	True (although you need to press Ctrl+Alt+Del to start using it)	Review Lesson 1-1.
2.	False	Review Lesson 1-2.
3.	False	Review Lesson 1-3.
4.	False, although a mouse is much handier	Review Lesson 2-1.
5.	False	Review Lesson 3-1.
6.	False	Review Lesson 3-3.
7.	False	Review Lesson 3-3.
8.	True	Review Lesson 2-1.
9.	False	Review Lesson 3-3.
10.	True	Review Unit 3.
11.	False	Review Lesson 3-5.
12.	False	Review Lesson 2-2.
13.	True	Review Lesson 2-2.
14.	False	Review Lesson 2-2.
15.	A, B, D	Review Lesson 2-1.
16.	A, D	Review Lesson 3-1.
17.	A, B, C, D	Review Lesson 1-2.
18.	A, B, C, D	Review Lesson 2-1 and Table 2-1.
19.	B	Review Lesson 3-5.
20.	C	Review Lesson 3-4.
21.	A, B, C	Review Lesson 3-3.
22.	A, B, C, D	Review Lesson 2-1.

23.	A, 4	Review Lesson 2-2.
	B, 1	
	C, 2	
	D, 3	
	E, 5	
24.	A, 5	Review Lesson 3-4.
	B, 4	
	C, 3	
	D, 2	
	E, 1	
25.	A, 3	Review Lesson 3-1.
	B, 1	
	C, 4	
	D, 2	
	E, 5	

Unit 4 Quiz Answers

Question	Answer	If You Missed It, Try This
1.	A, D	Review Lesson 4-1.
2.	A, B, C	Review Lesson 4-1.
3.	A	Review Lesson 4-2.
4.	A	Review Lesson 4-2.
5.	A	Review Lesson 4-3.
6.	D	Review Lesson 4-3.
7.	A, B, C	Review Lesson 4-3.
8.	B	Review Lesson 4-3.
9.	A	Review Lesson 4-3.
10.	B	Review Lesson 4-3.

Unit 5 Quiz Answers

Question	Answer	If You Missed It, Try This
1.	C	Review Lesson 5-1.
2.	A, B	Review Lesson 5-1.
3.	C	Review Lesson 5-1.
4.	A, B, C	Review Lesson 5-1.

5.	A	Review Lesson 5-1.
6.	A	Review Lesson 5-1.
7.	A	Review Lesson 5-2.
8.	D	Review Lesson 5-2.
9.	D	Review Lesson 5-2.
10.	D	Review Lesson 5-2.
11.	A, B, C, D	Review Lesson 5-3.
12.	A	Review Lesson 5-3.
13.	B	Review Lesson 5-3.
14.	A, but only if the files are all next to each other	Review Lesson 5-4.
15.	A	Review Lesson 5-5.

Unit 6 Quiz Answers

Question	Answer	If You Missed It, Try This
1.	A, B C	Review Lesson 6-1.
2.	A, B, C	Review Lesson 6-3.
3.	A, B	Review Lesson 6-4.
4.	C	Review Lesson 6-6.
5.	A, C, D	Review Lesson 6-6.

Part II Test Answers

Question	Answer	If You Missed It, Try This
1.	False; very few CD-ROM drives can write to compact discs	Review Lesson 5-1.
2.	False	Review Lesson 4-3.
3.	True	Review Lesson 4-1.
4.	True	Review Lesson 4-1.
5.	True	Review Lesson 4-3.

6.	True, but a mouse is much handier	Review Lesson 4-3.
7.	False	Review Lesson 4-3.
8.	True	Review Lesson 5-3.
9.	True	Review Lesson 5-5.
10.	True	Review Lesson 5-6.
11.	True	Review Lesson 6-6.
12.	True	Review Lesson 6-1.
13.	C	Review Lesson 4-1.
14.	A, B, C	Review Lessons 4-1 and 5-4.
15.	A, B, C, D	Review Lesson 5-1.
16.	A, B, D	Review Lessons 4-3, 5-3, and 5-4.
17.	B	Review Lesson 5-1.
18.	A, B, D	Review Lesson 5-1.
19.	A, B, C	Review Lesson 5-6.
20.	B	Review Table 5-1.
21.	A, 3 B, 4 C, 1 D, 2 E, 5	Review Lessons 4-1 and 5-1.
22.	A, 3 B, 2 C, 1 D,4	Review Lesson 5-2.

Unit 7 Quiz Answers

Question	Answer	If You Missed It, Try This
1.	A, B	Review Lesson 7-2.
2.	A	Review Lesson 7-1.
3.	A, B, C	Review Lesson 7-2.
4.	B	Review Lesson 7-2.
5.	B, C, D	Review Lesson 7-3.

Unit 8 Quiz Answers

Question	Answer	If You Missed It, Try This
1.	C	Review Lesson 8-1.
2.	A, B	Review Lesson 8-1.
3.	D	Review Lesson 8-1.

Unit 9 Quiz Answers

Question	Answer	If You Missed It, Try This
1.	A, B, C, D	Review the Unit 9 introductory text.
2.	A	Review Lesson 9-1.
3.	D	Review Lesson 9-2.
4.	A, B, C	Review Lesson 9-2.
5.	C	Review Lesson 9-3.

Unit 10 Quiz Answers

Question	Answer	If You Missed It, Try This
1.	A, B, C	Review Lesson 10-1.
2.	A	Review Lesson 10-1.
3.	A	Review Lesson 10-4.
4.	A, B	Review Lesson 10-4

Unit 11 Quiz Answers

Question	Answer	If You Missed It, Try This
1.	B	Review Lesson 11-1.
2.	A	Review Lesson 11-1.
3.	A	Review Lesson 11-1 and 11-2.
4.	A, B, C	Review Lesson 11-3.

Unit 12 Quiz Answers

Question	Answer	If You Missed It, Try This
1.	C	Review Lesson 12-2.
2.	A	Review Lesson 12-1.
3.	B	Review Lesson 12-1.
4.	A, B, C	Review Lesson 12-1.
5.	A, B, C	Review Lesson 12-3.
6.	A	Review Lesson 12-3.
7.	A, B, C	Review Lesson 12-4.
8.	A	Review Lesson 12-5.
9.	B	Review Lesson 12-5.

Part III Test Answers

Question	Answer	If You Missed It, Try This
1.	False; *double*-click on the icon	Review Lesson 7-1.
2.	False	Review Lesson 7-2.
3.	True	Review Lesson 12-2.
4.	False	Review Lesson 11-1.
5.	True	Review Lesson 10-1.
6.	True	Review Lesson 9-3.
7.	False	Review Lesson 9-2.
8.	True	Review Lesson 9-3.
9.	True	Review Lesson 12-1.
10.	False	Review Lesson 9-3.
11.	True	Review Lesson 9-3.
12.	True	Review Lesson 9-3.
13.	False	Review Lesson 12-5.
14.	A, B, C, D	Review Lesson 8-1.
15.	A, B	Review Lessons 7-1 and 7-2.

16.	A, B, C	Review Lesson 8-1.
17.	C	Review Lesson 9-3.
18.	B, C (Notepad saves in ASCII format)	Review Lesson 9-3.
19.	A	Review Lesson 7-1.
20.	B, C	Review Lesson 7-1.
21.	C	Review Lesson 12-5.
22.	A, 4	Review Lesson 8-1.
	B, 3	Review Lesson 8-1.
	C, 1	Review Lesson 9-4.
	D, 2	Review Lesson 9-2.
	E, 5	Review Lesson 1-2.
23.	A, 3	Review Lesson 8-1.
	B,1	Review Lesson 8-1.
	C, 2	Review Lesson 8-1.
	D, 4	Review Lesson 8-1.

Unit 13 Quiz Answers

Question	Answer	If You Missed It, Try This
1.	B, D	Review Lesson 13-1.
2.	A	Review Lesson 13-1.
3.	D	Review Lesson 13-1.
4.	A	Review Lesson 13-2.
5.	C	Review Lesson 13-4.
6.	A, B	Review Lesson 13-1.
7.	B, C	Review Lesson 13-1.

Unit 14 Quiz Answers

Question	Answer	If You Missed It, Try This
1.	A, B	Review Lessons 14-2 and 14-3.
2.	A	Review Lesson 14-1.
3.	A, B, C	Review Lesson 14-3.
4.	A	Review Lesson 14-3.

Part IV Test Answers

Question	Answer	If You Missed It, Try This
1.	False	Review Lesson 13-1.
2.	False	Review Lesson 13-1.
3.	True	Review Lesson 13-1.
4.	False	Review Lesson 13-1.
5.	False	Review Lesson 13-2.
6.	False	Review Lesson 13-1.
7.	True	Review Lesson 13-5.
8.	False	Review Lesson 13-1.
9.	C	Review Lesson 13-1.
10.	A, B, C, D	Review Lesson 13-1.
11.	B	Review Lesson 13-1.
12.	A, B, C, D	Review Lesson 13-1.
13.	A, 1	Review Unit 13.
	B, 2	Review Unit 12.
	C, 1	Review Unit 13.

Unit 15 Quiz Answers

Question	Answer	If You Missed It, Try This
1.	D	Review Lesson 15-1.
2.	A	Review Lesson 15-3.
3.	A, B, C	Review Lesson 15-1.

Unit 16 Quiz Answers

Question	Answer	If You Missed It, Try This
1.	A	Review Lesson 16-1.
2.	A	Review Lesson 16-2.

3.	B	Review Lesson 16-2.
4.	C	Review Lesson 16-2.

Part V Test Answers

Question	Answer	If You Missed It, Try This
1.	False	Review Lesson 15-1.
2.	True	Review Unit 16's Exercises.
3.	True	Review Lesson 16-3.
4.	True	Review Lesson 16-1.
5.	C	Review Lesson 16-1.
6.	C	Review Unit 15.
7.	A, 4	Review Unit 16.
	B, 3	Review Unit 1.
	C, 2	Review Lesson 2-2.
	D, 1	Review Lesson 15-1.
	E, 5	Review Unit 5.

About the CD

The *Dummies 101: Windows NT* companion CD contains files for the book's lesson plans and exercises, but I've also thrown in some other files and programs that I don't have the space to cover in this book. It's all stuff you might want to fiddle with when using Windows NT.

Before you can use any of the CD files, you need to install them on your computer. But don't worry: The installation process is easy, fairly quick, and installed in detail a few sections ahead.

heads up

After you install the *Dummies 101: Windows NT* exercise files, please don't open them and look around just yet. One wrong click, and you can mess up a file, which would prevent you from following along with the book lesson that uses the file. (You'd have to go through the installation process again to get a fresh copy.) Your best bet is to follow the installation instructions given in this appendix, jump right into Unit 1, and wait until I tell you to use a particular file before opening it up. Besides, the exercise files don't mean much except in the context of the lessons.

In fact, I suggest not playing around with *any* of the CD files and programs until you've been through the book. You open and use most of the files and programs in the course of the book, and the ones that you don't probably won't be of much use to you until you're more comfortable with Windows anyway.

System Requirements

Before installing the CD, make sure that your computer has the following installed:

- Microsoft Windows NT Workstation 4.0

- At least 25MB of free hard-disk space available if you want to install all the items from this CD (you need less space if you don't install every item)

- CD-ROM drive — double-speed (2x) or faster

- Monitor set to display 256 colors (Please do not run your monitor with a setting higher than 256 colors, or the CD may not function properly.)

If you need more information on PC or Windows NT basics, check out *PCs For Dummies,* 4th Edition, by Dan Gookin or *Windows NT For Dummies* by Andy Rathbone and Sharon Crawford (both published by IDG Books Worldwide, Inc.).

What's on the CD

Here's a list of everything that you install from the CD, along with the lesson in which the file or program is first used (if applicable) — see the lesson for more information about the file.

Exercise Files:

Joe's Lament	Lesson 5-4
Eau de Froggie	Lesson 7-4
Fax Cover	Lesson 12-3

Extra Programs:

Internet Explorer	None
WinZip	None
CleanSweep Demo	None

Putting the CD Files on Your Hard Drive

The exercise files are sample documents and artwork that you use while following along with the lessons in the book. You need to put these files on your hard drive. After you're done with the book, you can remove the files easily.

Some of the extra programs are integrated with the lessons in the book; the CleanSweep demo and the WinZip program are just some cool stuff that you'll find useful with Windows NT. Finally, the CD contains a version of Internet Explorer Version 3.02, which is probably more recent than the copy that came with your copy of Windows NT 4.0.

heads up

If you have problems with the installation process, you can call the IDG Books Worldwide, Inc., Customer Support number: 800-762-2974 (outside the U.S.: 317-596-5261).

Using the CD

With Windows NT up and running, follow these steps:

1 Insert the Dummies 101 CD (label side up) into your computer's CD drive and wait about 30 seconds to see whether AutoPlay starts the CD for you.

Be careful to touch only the edges of the CD. The CD drive is the one that pops out with a circular drawer.

If your computer has the Windows CD AutoPlay feature, the CD installer should begin automatically, so just click the OK button that appears. If you see the CD installer window (it looks like a piece of notebook paper with the book's title), go to the section, "Installing the exercise files."

If nothing seems to happen after a minute or so, continue to Step 2.

2 If the installation program doesn't start automatically, click the Start button and click Run.

3 In the dialog box that appears, type d:\seticon.exe **(if your CD drive is not drive D, substitute the appropriate letter for D) and click OK.**

A message informs you that the program is about to install the icons.

4 Click OK in the message window.

After a moment, a program group called Dummies 101 appears on the Start menu, with a set of icons. Then another message appears, asking whether you want to use the CD now.

5 Click Yes to use the CD now or click No if you want to use the CD later.

If you click No, you can start the CD later simply by clicking the Dummies 101 - Windows NT CD icon in the Dummies 101 program group (on the Start button).

(Re)Starting the CD

If you closed the CD installer after you installed the icons, restart it by double-clicking the My Computer icon and then double-clicking the CD-ROM icon. This works only if your CD-ROM drive automatically starts the CD installer when you pop it in your CD-ROM drive.

If you had to follow Step 2 in "Using the CD," you can restart the CD by clicking the Start button, clicking Dummies 101, and clicking Dummies 101 - Windows NT CD. When the installer starts to run, click the OK button that appears on-screen.

Installing the exercise files

Click the Install Exercise Files button in the CD's window and follow the instructions that appear on-screen to install the exercise (sometimes known as *practice*) files on your computer.

To make the installation and the exercises in this book as simple as possible, let the installer place the exercise files in the recommended location. If you really want to put the files somewhere else, you can change the location by following the on-screen instructions (make sure that you remember where you put them if you customize the location).

Unless you change the location, the exercise files are installed to C:\Dummies101\Windows NT.

You don't have to do anything with the files yet — we tell you when you need to open the first file. The files are meant to accompany the book's lessons. If you open a file prematurely, you may accidentally make changes to the file, which may prevent you from following along with the steps in the lessons. So please don't try to open or view a file until you've reached the point in the lessons where we explain how to open the file.

If at some point you accidentally modify an exercise file and want to reinstall the original version, just run the CD again and click on Install Exercise Files once more. If you want to save your modified versions of files, either move the files to another folder before reinstalling the originals or tell the exercise file installer to place the new replacement file in a different folder.

Accessing the exercise files

You'll find detailed instructions on how to access files when you first need to open a file in Unit 5 of the book.

Removing the exercise files and icons

Once you're done with the lessons in the book, you might want to delete the exercise files. If you installed an icon to run the CD installer as shown in Step 2 in the section, "Using the CD," you may want to get rid of the icon for the CD as well.

Deleting the exercise files is easy.

1 **Double-click the My Computer icon.**

2 **Double-click the Drive C icon.**

3 **Click once on the Windows NT folder.**

I assume that you let the CD installer copy the files to the folder it recommended. If you decided to change the recommended location for the exercise files, you may need to open additional folders to find where you saved the exercise file folder.

4 **Choose File⇨Delete.**

Depending on your Windows NT settings, you might see a message asking if you really want to delete these items. Click the appropriate button to indicate Yes.

heads up

As soon as you delete the exercise files, they are as good as gone, and the only way to get them back is to run the CD and choose Install Exercise Files again. (This won't bring back your changes to the files; they disappeared with the modified file.) If you want to keep any of the installed files, move them to a different folder *before* you delete the exercise file's folder.

If you installed an icon to your Start button to run the CD installer, here's how to remove it.

1 Click the Start button, choose Settings, and then choose Taskbar, .

2 Click the Start Menu Programs tab at the top of the window.

3 Click the Remove button.

A window appears that shows all the items on your Start menu.

4 In the window, click the tiny plus sign next to the Dummies 101 folder.

If this is the only Dummies 101 CD you've used, you'll find only the Dummies 101 - Windows NT CD icon. If you've used other Dummies 101 CDs, you'll see a few more icons here for those CDs. Your goal here is to remove only the Dummies 101 - Windows NT icon.

5 Click once on the Dummies 101 - Windows NT CD icon.

6 Click the Remove button and then click the Close button.

If the Dummies 101 program group doesn't have any other icons in it, you can delete that as well by repeating the steps and selecting the Dummies 101 folder for removal.

Removing programs installed from the CD

You might decide to uninstall the programs available from the Choose Software section of the CD. Most software designed for Windows NT has some sort of uninstall feature that you can use to remove the program. The key word is "most." Not all Windows programs make it easy to remove a program.

To remove a program, look in these locations for the selections you need.

▶ Click the Start button, choose Programs. Here you might find the name of the program or the name of the company that made it. Open that program group, and choose the icon named Uninstall or Remove.

▶ Click the Start button, choose Settings⇨Control Panel, and double-click the icon Add/Remove Programs. Listed on the Install/Uninstall tab of the window are any programs that Windows NT can remove for you.

If these two options don't work, you have two more options.

▶ Drop by your computer store and pick up a program designed to uninstall programs from your computer, like CleanSweep, Uninstaller, and RemoveIt. (*Remember:* The CD contains a demo version of CleanSweep.) These programs are also great for cleaning up the old files that build up on your computer over time.

▶ Locate the folder in Windows that contains the software for the program and delete it, and then delete the program's icons from the Start menu.

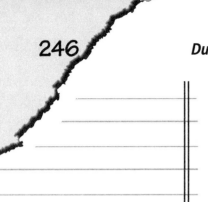

heads up

Deleting the program's folder is usually OK to do for some programs, but sometimes your computer may still have other information about the program that can't be removed in this way. Also, there is a chance that you could delete files that are shared by other programs you still use. **Never delete anything from the Windows folder** unless you know *exactly* what you are doing. Be careful!

Extra Stuff

In addition to the exercise files, the CD contains a few extra programs you may find useful.

heads up

Remember that you must already have Microsoft Windows NT 4.0 installed on your computer in order to use this Dummies 101 CD. Windows NT 4.0 is sold separately at computer stores and is not included on this CD. This CD cannot be used with Microsoft Windows 3.1 or 3.11. Please see "System Requirements" earlier in this appendix for more requirement information.

WinZip

Sooner or later you'll encounter a file ending in the strange letters ZIP. Why? Because that file has been *zipped* — a popular method for compacting a bunch of files into a single small file. Zipping files makes them easier to e-mail and fit onto floppy disks. Plus, zipped files are often easier to store on a floppy disk.

heads up

WinZip isn't the same as a Zip drive. WinZip is a program that takes a bunch of files and squishes them into a single file on your hard drive or floppy disk. A Zip drive is a piece of hardware that squishes bunches of files onto special-sized disks.

CleanSweep demo

Programs are often easier to install than to remove. Programs tend to come on several files, which scatter themselves around on your hard drive. CleanSweep can scour your hard drive to find remnants of a program you want to remove. This demonstration version of CleanSweep gives you a glimpse of the full program in action.

This demo expires in 30 days. If you want to order the complete program, visit `www.quarterdeck.com` or drop by your local computer store.

Internet Explorer

Windows NT comes with a freebie copy of Internet Explorer. But because the bustling world of the Internet changes so quickly, it's probably already out-of-date. Here's a copy of Internet Explorer 3.02, which was the latest copy out when I wrote this book. Unit 14 explains how to put Internet Explorer to work.

If You've Got Problems
(Of the CD Kind)

I tried my best to compile programs that work on most computers with the minimum system requirements. Alas, your computer may differ, and some programs may not work properly for some reason.

The two likeliest problems are that you don't have enough memory (RAM) for the programs you want to use, or you have other programs running that are affecting the installation or running of the program. If you get error messages like Not enough memory or Setup cannot continue, try one or more of these methods and then try using the software again:

- Turn off any anti-virus software that you have on your computer. Installers sometimes mimic virus activity and may make your computer incorrectly believe that it is being infected by a virus.

- Close all running programs. The more programs you're running, the less memory is available to other programs. Installers also typically update files and programs. So if you keep other programs running, installation may not work properly.

- Have your local computer store add more RAM to your computer. Adding more memory can really help the speed of your computer and allow more programs to run at the same time.

If you still have trouble with installing the items from the CD, please call the IDG Books Worldwide Customer Service phone number: 800-762-2974 (outside the U.S.: 317-596-5261).

Index

(continued)

Notes

(c) This limited warranty gives you specific legal rights, and you may have other rights which vary from jurisdiction to jurisdiction.

6. **Remedies.**

   (a) IDGB's entire liability and your exclusive remedy for defects in materials and workmanship shall be limited to replacement of the Software, which may be returned to IDGB with a copy of your receipt at the following address: Disk Fulfillment Department, Attn: *Dummies 101: Windows NT,* IDG Books Worldwide, Inc., 7260 Shadeland Station, Ste. 100, Indianapolis, IN 46256, or call 1-800-762-2974. Please allow 3–4 weeks for delivery. This Limited Warranty is void if failure of the Software has resulted from accident, abuse, or misapplication. Any replacement Software will be warranted for the remainder of the original warranty period or thirty (30) days, whichever is longer.

   (b) In no event shall IDGB or the author be liable for any damages whatsoever (including without limitation damages for loss of business profits, business interruption, loss of business information, or any other pecuniary loss) arising from the use of or inability to use the Book or the Software, even if IDGB has been advised of the possibility of such damages.

   (c) Because some jurisdictions do not allow the exclusion or limitation of liability for consequential or incidental damages, the above limitation or exclusion may not apply to you.

7. **U.S. Government Restricted Rights.** Use, duplication, or disclosure of the Software by the U.S. Government is subject to restrictions stated in paragraph (c) (1) (ii) of the Rights in Technical Data and Computer Software clause of DFARS 252.227-7013, and in subparagraphs (a) through (d) of the Commercial Computer—Restricted Rights clause at FAR 52.227-19, and in similar clauses in the NASA FAR supplement, when applicable.

8. **General.** This Agreement constitutes the entire understanding of the parties and revokes and supersedes all prior agreements, oral or written, between them and may not be modified or amended except in a writing signed by both parties hereto which specifically refers to this Agreement. This Agreement shall take precedence over any other documents that may be in conflict herewith. If any one or more provisions contained in this Agreement are held by any court or tribunal to be invalid, illegal, or otherwise unenforceable, each and every other provision shall remain in full force and effect.

Dummies 101 Disk Installation Instructions

With Windows NT up and running, follow these steps:

1 Insert the Dummies 101 CD (label side up) into your computer's CD drive and wait about 30 seconds to see whether AutoPlay starts the CD for you.

Be careful to touch only the edges of the CD. The CD drive is the one that pops out with a circular drawer.

If your computer has the Windows CD AutoPlay feature, the CD installer should begin automatically, so just click the OK button that appears. If you see the CD installer window (it looks like a piece of notebook paper with the book's title), go to Appendix B.

If nothing seems to happen after a minute or so, continue to Step 2.

2 If the installation program doesn't start automatically, click on the Start button and click on Run.

3 In the dialog box that appears, type d:\seticon.exe **(if your CD drive is not drive D, substitute the appropriate letter for D) and click on OK.**

A message informs you that the program is about to install the icons.

4 Click on OK in the message window.

After a moment, a program group called Dummies 101 appears on the Start menu, with a set of icons. Then another message appears, asking whether you want to use the CD now.

5 Click on Yes to use the CD now or click on No if you want to use the CD later.

If you click on No, you can start the CD later simply by clicking on the Dummies 101 - Windows NT CD icon in the Dummies 101 program group (on the Start button).

IDG BOOKS WORLDWIDE REGISTRATION CARD

RETURN THIS REGISTRATION CARD FOR FREE CATALOG

Title of this book: Dummies 101®: Windows NT®

My overall rating of this book: ❏ Very good [1] ❏ Good [2] ❏ Satisfactory [3] ❏ Fair [4] ❏ Poor [5]

How I first heard about this book:

❏ Found in bookstore; name: [6] _____

❏ Advertisement: [8] _____

❏ Word of mouth; heard about book from friend, co-worker, etc.: [10] _____

❏ Book review: [7] _____

❏ Catalog: [9] _____

❏ Other: [11] _____

What I liked most about this book:

_____

_____

What I would change, add, delete, etc., in future editions of this book:

_____

_____

Other comments:

_____

_____

Number of computer books I purchase in a year: ❏ 1 [12] ❏ 2-5 [13] ❏ 6-10 [14] ❏ More than 10 [15]

I would characterize my computer skills as: ❏ Beginner [16] ❏ Intermediate [17] ❏ Advanced [18] ❏ Professional [19]

I use ❏ DOS [20] ❏ Windows [21] ❏ OS/2 [22] ❏ Unix [23] ❏ Macintosh [24] ❏ Other: [25]_____

(please specify)

I would be interested in new books on the following subjects:

(please check all that apply, and use the spaces provided to identify specific software)

❏ Word processing: [26] _____

❏ Data bases: [28] _____

❏ File Utilities: [30] _____

❏ Networking: [32] _____

❏ Other: [34] _____

❏ Spreadsheets: [27] _____

❏ Desktop publishing: [29] _____

❏ Money management: [31] _____

❏ Programming languages: [33] _____

I use a PC at (please check all that apply): ❏ home [35] ❏ work [36] ❏ school [37] ❏ other: [38] _____

The disks I prefer to use are ❏ 5.25 [39] ❏ 3.5 [40] ❏ other: [41]_____

I have a CD ROM: ❏ yes [42] ❏ no [43]

I plan to buy or upgrade computer hardware this year: ❏ yes [44] ❏ no [45]

I plan to buy or upgrade computer software this year: ❏ yes [46] ❏ no [47]

Name: _____ Business title: [48] _____ Type of Business: [49] _____

Address (❏ home [50] ❏ work [51]/Company name: _____)

Street/Suite# _____

City [52]/State [53]/Zipcode [54]: _____ Country [55] _____

❏ **I liked this book!** You may quote me by name in future IDG Books Worldwide promotional materials.

My daytime phone number is _____

IDG BOOKS

®

THE WORLD OF COMPUTER KNOWLEDGE

❏ YES!

Please keep me informed about IDG's World of Computer Knowledge.
Send me the latest IDG Books catalog.